The United States Supreme Court

Lawmaking in the Third Branch of Government

William C. Louthan
Ohio Wesleyan University

Prentice Hall
Englewood Cliffs, NJ 07632

Library of Congress Cataloging-in-Publication Data

LOUTHAN, WILLIAM C.
   The United States Supreme Court : lawmaking in the third branch of
government

   Includes bibliographical references and index.
   ISBN 0-13-933623-0
   1. United States. Supreme Court. 2. Judicial review—United
States. 3. Judicial process—United States. 4. United States—
Constitutional law. I. Title.
KF8742.L68 1991
347.73′26—dc20   90-36228
[347.30735]   CIP

Editorial/production supervision and
  interior design: Marianne Peters
Cover design: Patricia Kelly
Prepress buyer: Debra Kesar
Manufacturing buyer: Mary Ann Gloriande

 © 1991 by Prentice-Hall, Inc.
A Division of Simon & Schuster
Englewood Cliffs, New Jersey 07632

Printed in the United States of America
10 9 8 7 6 5 4 3 2 1

ISBN 0-13-933623-0

Prentice-Hall International (UK) Limited, *London*
Prentice-Hall of Australia Pty. Limited, *Sydney*
Prentice-Hall Canada Inc., *Toronto*
Prentice-Hall Hispanoamericana, S.A., *Mexico*
Prentice-Hall of India Private Limited, *New Delhi*
Prentice-Hall of Japan, Inc., *Tokyo*
Simon & Schuster Asia Pte. Ltd., *Singapore*
Editora Prentice-Hall do Brasil, Ltda., *Rio de Janeiro*

For
FRANCIS R. AUMANN
my mentor while in graduate school
at Ohio State University
and
EARL E. WARNER
my mentor while teaching public law at
Ohio Wesleyan University

Contents

Preface

This book presents a short but comprehensive examination of the United States Supreme Court, emphasizing the Court's centrality to policy making, proximity to power politics, and visibility to the public. It is set within a context of relevant constitutional law and designed to stimulate consideration of the provocative practical questions of policy which the Court's decisions and opinions generate.

The book's organizational scheme reflects the author's conclusion, based on two decades of experience teaching courses on the Supreme Court and American constitutional law, that readers are more nearly intrigued by the politics of Supreme Court appointments and their policy consequences than they are by arcane and dry descriptions of the Court's power and jurisdiction. The dynamics of Supreme Court appointment politics, simply put, are more exciting and less difficult to comprehend than are discussions of the Court's structure and its decision-making processes. Hence, Chapter One examines the tensions between continuity and discontinuity associated with the appointment politics of the 1970s and 1980s, the Burger-Rehnquist-O'Connor alliance, the new federalism, and the new conservative activism. The first chapter ends with a preliminary assessment of the Burger years. Chapter Two examines the political factors shaping the place and posture of the Supreme Court in the structure of the judicial system. Chapter Three examines the evolution of the Court and of the Constitution in American history, ending with a more detailed account of the policy controversies dominating Burger's last years as Chief Justice than is presented in Chapter One. Chapters Four and Five give careful treatment to the Court's processes and participants, respectively. Chapter Six presents a typology of theories attempting to explain how and why Supreme Court justices decide cases as they do. Above all else, however, the Supreme Court is a policy maker. Thus, Chapters Seven and Eight analyze the Court's work as it acts to allocate and limit governmental powers. Chapter Nine is, at once, a conclusion and a prolegomenon, a summary of where the Court stands in the 1990s with a new Chief Justice (Rehnquist) and two new Associate Justices (Scalia and Kennedy), and a preliminary prediction of the Court's direction as we approach a new century. Thus, the book ends where it began with an examination of appointment politics (including the ill-fated Bork nomination), the impact of the new appointees on the Court's internal politics, and the role of the Court as a policy maker. Thus, although apparently disjointed when compared with the topical or chronological organization of most casebooks and some other textbooks, this book maintains its organizational clarity by keeping *the Court's role as a lawmaker amidst policy controversies* at the center of its attention throughout, and especially in Chapters One, Three, Seven, Eight, and Nine.

Throughout, this book treats the United States Supreme Court as an *institution,* its law as *constitutional development,* its justices as *political philosophers* and *policymakers,* and its opinions as the closest thing we have to an original *American political theory* since the *Federalist Papers.* It is not intended as an exposé, although some Supreme Court myths are exposed; nor is it intended as a flattering apologia, although the law is properly revered. Most of the available Supreme Court literature tends to portray the Court as remote and impersonal. This is because its justices are not elected, rarely give public speeches, and are generally thought to be inaccessible. Hence, a recent journalistic account of power politics in Washington, D.C., characterizes the Court as "an aloof and anonymous body." Yet the Court is much less a bureaucracy than are our other national political institutions, and the Court is commonly the subject of complaint and denunciation. Thus, in this book, the Supreme Court is portrayed as the least abstract and, at least potentially, the most visible of our national institutions.

As in most texts, this book's sources are largely secondary, but its methods are clearly eclectic. While necessarily legalistic in its primary approach, this book does not underplay the role of politics in the Court's processes nor does it underutilize behavioral science data that help explain those processes. At the same time, this book adopts a value-critical approach to the study of the Court. The book rests on the assumption that the contest of values inherent in and flowing from the Court's decisions and opinions cannot be adequately described or understood with an approach pretending to a scholarly but all too illusory objectivity. The Supreme Court is the "Schoolmaster of the Republic" but its lessons are not always well received by its pupils. Thus, Supreme Court controversies appear at the core of nearly every chapter. The United States Constitution is an "unfinished" document, always in a state of "becoming." As a "living" document, a set of practices and discourses, the Constitution is the product of a wide variety of forces in conflict over the resolutions to the conflicting values embodied in the document's very language and structure.

Supreme Court justices, then, cannot escape politics because, in part, politics involves discourse about contested values—the very stuff of many of the disputes that come to the Court each year. Thus, as Justice William Brennan once observed, Supreme Court justices are not mere umpires but *lawmakers in the third branch of government.*

In short, this is a book on the Supreme Court that is up-to-date and that involves the reader in a value-critical manner and at a level of sophistication currently not widely available.

ACKNOWLEDGMENTS

I wish to thank the Ohio Wesleyan University for a Regular Faculty Leave (Fall Semester 1984) and a Special Faculty Leave (Fall Semester 1988) during which the bulk of the writing was completed. I also wish to thank the Word Processing Center at Ohio Wesleyan for its excellent work in the preparation of the manuscript. A special word of appreciation is due to my colleague, Professor Craig Ramsay, who kept me in ready supply of literally thousands of newspaper clippings related to my research. Linda Greenhouse and Stuart Taylor, Jr., who have reported for so long and so well on the Supreme Court for the *New York Times* are also to be thanked up front, beyond the many times their names appear in endnotes. While I know neither of them, their careful and timely reporting and analyses were very helpful to me as I thought about, and then executed, this project.

I would also like to mention the following reviewers who provided helpful comments: Thomas A. Chambers, Golden West College; William Merril Downer, Thiel College; and Richard L. Pacelle, Jr., Indiana University.

Finally, a warm expression of thanks to Mrs. Janice Schroeder for the benefit of her superb secretarial services. She is truly the departmental secretary *par excellence.*

$\boxed{I}$

From Warren to Burger

Supreme Court Appointment Politics and Their Policy Impact

THE SUPREME COURT: DECISIONS, VALUES, AND POLICIES

The United States Supreme Court decides concrete cases and controversies (about 400 each year, less than half of which are accompanied by lengthy written opinions). The Court's written opinions, which attempt to justify its decisions, however, often proceed in a general way to survey subjects and proclaim policies that transcend the outcome of the particular cases it decides. Many of the Court's written opinions are searching examinations and assessments of values associated with the American political system. The Court is thus involved in the evolution of the fundamental and frequently contradictory ideals of American constitutional government. In other words, the United States Supreme Court, like other institutions of government, authoritatively allocates values. In turn the Court's opinions provide crucial if not comprehensive insights into the nation's ideals. Hence, the Court has been referred to as the "Schoolmaster of the Republic."[1] Its lessons, however, are not always received with enthusiasm or regarded with esteem by its pupils.

In this century the Supreme Court has invalidated state laws prohibiting the marriage of a man and a woman of different races, upheld some and rejected other laws requiring the sterilization of persons with low IQs or who have committed specified felonies, rejected attempts by local governments to use zoning laws in a manner that would have the practical effect of breaking up families, and protected the right of women to choose an abortion.[2] In so doing the Court has commented in a general way on such crucial matters as whom to marry, whether and when to have children, what constitutes a family, and whether to terminate a pregnancy.

In recent years alone the Court has attempted to teach us a variety of other lessons. Why we may not engage in a public protest by burning our draft cards, but why it may be permissible in some circumstances to burn the American flag. Why there is a constitutional right to sexual privacy for heterosexuals, but why the Constitution does not bar criminal prosecutions for homosexual relations between consenting adults even in the privacy of their own homes. Why some types of preference may be given to minorities when admitting applicants to law and medical schools, but why other types of preferential admissions are illegal. Why, in criminal cases, prosecutors may not exclude blacks from juries based on the mere possibility that they would favor black defendants, but why death penalty laws may be perfectly permissible despite statistical evidence that killers of whites, especially black killers, are far more likely to be condemned to death than are killers of blacks. Why, in death penalty cases, emotionally charged evidence about the impact of a murder on a victim's family may be barred at a death-sentencing hearing (because it might inflame the jury against the defendant), but why, in some circumstances, it may be perfectly permissible to use the death penalty against an accomplice in a crime even if the accomplice did not personally kill or intend to kill anyone. Why the Congress may impose limits on the amount of money that may be contributed to candidates in an election campaign, but why Congress may not place a similar ceiling on total campaign expenditures. Why the government may not require a moment of silent prayer in the public schools or require that the creationist theory of humankind's origins be given equal time in public schools that teach the theory of evolution, but why it may be perfectly permissible for a city to erect a nativity scene as part of an official Christmas display. Why the government may not prefer males to females when two persons are otherwise equally qualified to be the administrator of an estate. Why the government may not permit males in the armed services an automatic dependency allowance for their wives but require female members to prove their husbands are in fact dependent, but why it is perfectly permissible for the government to require draft registration for males and not females.

It is true, of course, that the Supreme Court makes many concrete decisions that do not require an interpretation of the United States Constitution. It is also true that in many instances even those decisions that do require constitutional interpretation are narrowly drawn and the outcome affects only the persons directly involved in the case—the "parties" to the dispute—and thus hold little importance for the rest of us. However, more often than most Americans realize, the Supreme Court does render decisions of great, often enduring public policy significance. In many such instances the Court's decisions are based on its reading of a Constitution that is neither exacting nor confining. As the American statesman and abolitionist Thaddeus Stevens said long ago, the text of the Constitution was intended to adapt to the "advancing progress of a higher morality."[3] It is perhaps the case that no other period in American history better illustrates Stevens's point than the period from 1953 to 1986. During these years, the Court was led first by Chief Justice Earl Warren (1953–69) and then by Chief Justice Warren Burger (1969–86). All the decisions described in the preceding paragraph (and many more decisions) were made during this period. It was a period of national political turmoil—the civil rights movement, the Vietnam War and student protests, Watergate and other highly publicized political scandals, assassinations, urban race riots, racial and sexual injustice in education and the job market feeding fears of prejudice and political polarization, the women's movement, and declining public trust in the government's ability to handle the problems of governance. And, on the Supreme Court, it was a period of rapidly changing personnel. Only three of the eight justices serving with Earl Warren when he retired in 1969 remained on the Court when Warren Burger retired in 1986. As the Court responded to the problems of this era, Earl Warren sounded much like Thaddeus Stevens a century earlier when he said that the Court's job in constitutional cases is to construe the provisions of a document which draw their meaning from the "evolving standards of decency that mark the progress of a maturing society."[4]

In this chapter, in order to give the work of the Supreme Court a contemporary flavor within the context of the relevant constitutional law and politics, we will examine the Warren and Burger years as an introduction to our study of the Court as a political institution. We will observe that while the values of American society have their origins in the past, those values must be continually produced, pronounced, and protected.[5] The Court may not be perfectly suited to perform such tasks, but it is undoubtedly better prepared to do so than are the other branches of American government because it is composed of justices who have the time and the training for what one of its justices once called "the sober second thought."[6] In addition, although not entirely insulated from politics, when compared with the Congress and the presidency the Court is far more removed from the current clash of interests, and hence far better placed to play the role of the scholar in sorting out the enduring values of society.[7] As Dean E.V. Rostow observed in 1952 just before the commencement of the Warren era, our Supreme Court justices "are inevitably teachers in a vital national seminar."[8]

THE POLITICAL ROLE OF THE WARREN COURT

On May 22, 1944, Private Trop of the United States Army escaped from an army stockade in French Morocco, where he had been confined for a breach of discipline. The next day while walking along a road toward Rabat, Trop climbed aboard a passing army truck and surrendered to authorities. A general court martial convicted Trop of desertion during wartime and sentenced him to three years at hard labor, forfeiture of all pay, and a dishonorable discharge. Eight years later Trop applied for a passport, which was denied on the ground that under the Nationality Act of 1940 anyone convicted of wartime desertion automatically thereby lost citizenship. Trop then brought suit in the federal courts seeking a declaratory judgment that he was a citizen. In 1958 the United States Supreme Court ruled in Trop's favor. For the Court's majority, Chief Justice Earl Warren reasoned that while the Congress may prescribe regulations governing military obligations (such as prohibiting wartime desertion), any congressional act that prescribes the consequences of a failure to abide by such regulations (such as the consequences of expatriation) is a penal measure, a law designed and intended to punish. The question, then, Warren proceeded, is whether expatriation is a form of punishment that the Constitution allows. The answer, he concluded, is no. The Eight Amendment to the Constitution prohibits "cruel and unusual punishment." Warren granted that the authors of the Constitution probably intended this clause to forbid physical mistreatment, torture, or abuse. But, he argued, expatriation is even more cruel and primitive than torture because it strikes at the very core of the individual's status in society. Thus, this expatriation provision of the Nationality Act of 1940 must be declared unconstitutional as a violation of the Eighth Amendment.[9] In dissent Justice Felix Frankfurter argued strongly that the Court, by invalidating the expatriation provision, was exercising the policy-making power entrusted, not to the Court, but to the Congress. He confessed that he, too, thought the measure in question to be overly harsh. There was the hint that had he been a member of Congress when the bill was passed, he would have voted against it. But as a United States Supreme Court justice, Frankfurter asserted his role to exclude the making of policy choices and the substitution of his view of wise public policy for that of the Congress. Warren, on the other hand, asserted his belief that Supreme Court justices are "oath-bound" to protect the Constitution, and he at least appeared to endorse the notion, as the saying goes, that part of the Court's job is to "keep the Constitution current." The provisions of the Constitution, he asserted in *Trop*, "draw [their] meaning from the *evolving* standards of decency that mark the progress of a maturing society" (italics added). Eleven years later, on the day Warren stepped down from the chief justiceship, he made his meaning clear in his last words from the bench: "[T]he Court *develops* the eternal principles of our Constitution in accordance with the problems of the day. . . . The Court serves only 'the public interest' as guided by the '*conscience*' of the individual Justices" (italics added).[10] The record of the Warren Court (1953–69), whatever the motivations of its justices, illustrates this theme.

The Warren Court rejected the doctrine of "separate but equal" in the public schools and required their desegregation.[11] The Warren Court entered the "political thicket" of legislative malapportionment to require that federal and state legislative districts be apportioned according to the formula of "one man, one vote."[12] The Warren Court outlawed "school prayer"[13] and made it more difficult to regulate what many would consider pornography.[14] Against strong resistance by many of the states, the Warren Court made most of the provisions of the Bill of Rights, most controversially the rights of the accused, applicable to the states. Also, the Warren Court required that those arrested must be informed of their rights[15] and those accused must be guaranteed a fair trial.[16] All the issues raised by these cases had been on the nation's political agenda for at least a generation prior to the commencement of the Warren era, and many had been on the Court's docket in other cases for decades. The willingness of the Warren Court to take on these issues and the directions in which the Court took its conclusions earned for Earl Warren the label of leader of the most "liberal," "civil libertarian," and "activist" Supreme Court in history.

During the Warren era the Court was both highly controversial and highly revered. It was controversial, in part, because specific decisions produced opposition (for example, a 1966 public opinion poll revealed a 65 percent negative response to the *Miranda* decision requiring that those arrested be informed of their rights).[17] It was controversial also because some of its decisions in internal security cases were viewed by the political right as being "soft on communism" (for example, in the late 1950s the nation's landscape blossomed with "Impeach Earl Warren" billboards sponsored by the John Birch Society).[18] Even from presumably more moderate groups such as the American Bar Association (ABA) and the Conference of State Chief Justices there came criticism of the Warren Court's "political activism" and its exercise of "essentially legislative powers."[19] But the Warren Court was also revered because, like Courts of other eras, it was viewed as part of the political system and given added respect because of the American devotion to "the law of the Constitution." Thus, public opinion polls exhibited a broad reservoir of *general* support and high le4els of *general* confidence in the Warren Court decisions, and opposition to specific decisions only rarely stirred opponents to political activity directed against the Court.[20]

WARREN'S RETIREMENT AND THE
APPOINTMENT OF BURGER

Earl Warren once told his law clerks that there ought to be a mandatory retirement age for Supreme Court justices. He told them that it should be 70, until he reached that age, and then he thought it should be 75. When he finally announced his intention to retire in June 1968, Warren was 77. Yet it was not his age but his conclusion that Republican Richard Nixon would be elected president in November and his concern that Nixon, given the opportunity, would appoint justices distant from the Warren Court philosophy that was the crucial factor framing Warren's decision to step down. He wanted the incumbent Democratic president, Lyndon Johnson, to name his successor. He wanted there to be continuity between his Court and the next one. His letter to Johnson indicated only his "intention to retire." He gave no specific date when he would step down, stating that his intention to retire would be "effective at [Johnson's] pleasure." Johnson accepted the retirement "effective at such time as a successor is qualified." As things turned out, Warren was to stay on as chief justice for another year.[21]

On June 27, 1968, the day after President Johnson announced Warren's intention to retire, Johnson nominated Associate Justice Abe Fortas to replace Warren and become the nation's sixteenth chief justice. Though not unexpected, this was an unusual move. Of the fifteen previous chief justices only two had been elevated to the position while sitting on the Court as associate justices (Edward Douglas White in 1910 and Harlan Fiske Stone in 1941). Historically, it had been thought there are inherent problems in elevating a sitting justice, notably the disruption of finely tuned interpersonal relationships among the justices and, given the inevitable jealousies, the impairment of the chief's ability to play the role of leader of the Court. But the Fortas nomination was to encounter far more serious obstacles. In his Senate confirmation hearings and the debates that followed, Fortas was accused of a variety of improprieties, including "cronyism" with Johnson administration officials, participation in White House strategy meetings on the Vietnam War, and the acceptance of a $15,000 lecture fee raised by interests with business before the Supreme Court. Much of the criticism was directed more nearly at the Warren Court than at Fortas, criticism in some instances of Warren Court decisions made long before Fortas had become one of the Court's justices. The opposition, led by Republican senator Robert Griffin, staged a six-day filibuster. When a cloture motion to end the filibuster failed, Fortas withdrew his name from nomination.

It was October 1968. Johnson was a lame duck. It was increasingly clear that Nixon would become the next president in January 1969. Nixon had made the Warren Court a political target in his campaign for the presidency. He had pledged to "strengthen the peace forces against the criminal forces" in American society and had promised to appoint justices who would be "strict constitutionists," "caretakers of the Constitution not superlegislators."[22] Indeed, the timing of Warren's indication that he intended to retire had been based largely on his desire to enable Johnson, not Nixon, to name his successor. Clearly Warren had hoped for a successor who would try to preserve the policy impact of the Warren Court's work. Nevertheless, Johnson, angry over the rejection of his friend Fortas, refused to make another nomination. Johnson knew this would enable Nixon to appoint the new chief justice—the very thing Warren had hoped to avoid. But Johnson asserted that since he could find no person better qualified than Fortas to succeed Warren, he would not "send another name to the Senate for this high office."[23] On January 20, 1969, Warren, still the chief justice, swore in Richard Nixon as president, the person who would now name his successor. Once in office, Nixon obtained Warren's consent to remain as chief justice until the end of the 1968–69 term in order to guarantee continuity in the work of the Court. By then, however, the Court's new era had already begun. The Senate had confirmed Nixon's nomination of a new chief justice. It would be Warren E. Burger.

Nixon and Burger first met at the 1948 Republican National Convention, where Burger was the floor manager for his home-state candidate, Minnesota governor Harold Stassen. Four years later, at the 1952 Republican National Convention, Burger played a crucial role in Eisenhower's nomination. With Eisenhower's election to the presidency, Burger was brought to Washington in 1953 as assistant attorney general in charge of the Claims Division of the Justice Department. In 1956 Eisenhower appointed Burger to the prestigious U.S. Court of Appeals for the D.C. Circuit. As a federal appeals court judge, Burger established a reputation as a conservative, particularly in criminal cases. He wanted to put an end, he said, to the "barbed wire of legalism which the Supreme Court has erected, protecting hundreds of criminals from punishment." And for *U.S. News and World Report* he wrote an article titled "What to Do about Crime in the U.S." from which, Nixon told him later, Nixon had taken ideas for his 1968 campaign speeches.[24]

For chief justice, Nixon wanted a person with judicial experience, "a professional judge." He wanted a person with fully predictable views as a "solid conservative," not a "bleeding heart" liberal or "social activist." He also wanted a person sufficiently young to serve long enough to lead the Court in a conservative direction for at least ten years. Burger seemed to fit the bill. Nixon announced his nomination on May 19, 1969. The U.S. Senate was quite receptive, taking only eighteen days to complete the confirmation process. At the Judiciary Committee's hearings the senators praised Burger and criticized the Warren Court. The committee voted unanimously to recommend Burger's confirmation to the whole Senate, which voted its confirmation, 74-3, just six days later.[25] Would Burger do the job? Turn the Court around and move it in a conservative direction? Earl Warren, who had not been consulted by Nixon on the appointment of his successor, knew that the president wanted to remold the Court in his own image, but he predicted that the work of the Warren Court would not be undermined or undone.[26] As we will learn later in this chapter, Warren's optimism has proven largely unwarranted. Would Burger possess the political skills necessary to mold and hold together the Court's voting blocs to achieve a lasting change in the Court's posture? At least one of Burger's former colleagues on the court of appeals thought he would not: "He's a very emotional guy who somehow tends to make you take the opposition position on issues. To suggest that he can bring the Court together . . . is simply a dream."[27] That observation has proved prophetic.

FORTAS'S RESIGNATION AND THE APPOINTMENT OF BLACKMUN

On May 5, 1969, *Life Magazine* reported that Justice Abe Fortas was receiving an annual consulting fee of $20,000 from the family foundation of financier Louis E. Wolfson, who was then serving a prison term for selling unregistered stocks. Granting that Wolfson had tendered a fee for certain research services, Fortas explained that he had refused the assignment and paid back the money he had received. For a time, at the urging of his friend Justice William O. Douglas, Fortas fought back, declaring his innocence. However, under pressure from Chief Justice Warren, whose strict sense of morality led him to label Fortas's behavior a "blot" on the Court, Fortas suddenly resigned on May 16. He was guilty of no wrongdoing, he said, but was resigning so that the prestige of the Court would be unimpaired.[28] Fortas was now the first Supreme Court justice in American history to resign under pressure of public criticism. Thus Nixon was given his second opportunity (within just four months of assuming the presidency) to appoint a new justice.

Nixon had received support from key southern senators in the 1968 campaign, and he now hoped to pay off his political debt by appointing to the Court a conservative from the South. He nominated South Carolinian Clement F. Haynsworth, chief judge of the Fourth Circuit Court of Appeals. Almost immediately the nomination ran into difficulties. The Justice Department's own report on Haynsworth's record on the appeals court granted that he had written a number of restrictive civil rights and anti-union opinions that had been overturned in previous years by the very Supreme Court to which he was now a nominee. Additional research done by the mounting opposition showed that Haynsworth was also guilty of minor conflicts of interest (for example, his participation in deciding a case involving a company in which he held stock)[29] and possibly other financial improprieties. Weeks of heated debate followed, but most expert Court-watchers expected Haynsworth to be confirmed. After all, only one Supreme Court nominee had been rejected by a Senate vote in the twentieth century, and that was the rejection of Judge John Parker, a Hoover nominee way back in 1930. It was to the surprise of most, then, that the Senate voted 55-45 to reject the Haynsworth nomination. Undaunted, Nixon nominated another southerner to fill the Fortas seat, Judge G. Harrold Carswell of the Fifth Circuit Court of Appeals. An investigative reporter soon thereafter discovered a campaign speech Carswell had given earlier in his career while running for local public office in which he declared: "Segregation of the races is proper and the only practical and correct way of life in our states. I have always so believed and I shall always so act."[30] He would yield to no man, he went on to say, in his vigorous belief in the principle of white supremacy. Naturally, there followed an outcry from opponents of the nomination and a retraction from Carswell. The opposition then attacked Carswell's slender credentials and intellectual mediocrity. Conservative Republican senator Roman Hruska attempted to defend Carswell by arguing that "there are a lot of mediocre judges and people and lawyers in the world and they are entitled to a little representation."[31] With supporters such as that, Carswell hardly needed opponents. Furthermore, moderate and liberal members of the Senate were provoked by Republican House leader Gerald Ford's threat that if the Senate rejected Carswell, the House would attempt to impeach liberal justice William O. Douglas. Douglas writes in his autobiography that that threat cost Carswell at least five votes in the Senate.[32] Carswell was rejected 51-45. Not only had the rejection of Haynsworth been the first since 1930, but now the double rejection (for the same seat) was the first since 1894 (the double rejection of President Cleveland's nominations of William Hornblower and Wheeler Peckman).

Nixon was bitterly angry but decided to back off temporarily from what was now being labeled his "Southern strategy." He still wanted a justice with predictable conservative views but would now turn to the Middle West in search of a "safe" nominee. He found his man in Eighth Circuit Court of Appeals judge Harry A. Blackmun. Blackmun was a long-time Minnesota friend of Chief Justice Burger. They had gone to grade school together and Blackmun had been the best man at Burger's wedding. As an appeals court judge Blackmun was known for his scholarly opinions. He was always engrossed in his work. He was independent yet fundamentally conservative. It was expected that Blackmun and Burger would vote together most of the time. The press quickly dubbed them the "Minnesota Twins."

There were some minor problems with the nomination. Blackmun held some stocks that might cause conflicts of interest, and perhaps had already done so on the appeals court. To avoid a comparison with Haynsworth, Blackmun made his records public before announcement of the nomination. There was also a newspaper story suggesting that Blackmun had improperly received from Burger (or had at least been offered) assistance in sorting out recent Supreme Court decisions. Blackmun was angered by the account, since his association with Burger was the thing he was most sensitive about. But that problem blew over. In his interview with Nixon, Blackmun was asked by the president whether any of his three daughters were "hippie types." Blackmun said they were not.[33] The announcement of Blackmun's nomination finally came in April 1970. On June 22 he was easily confirmed by the Senate. However, the confirmation came too late to enable Blackmun to participate in any of the year's decisions. The prolonged fight to fill the Fortas seat had taken a full year. This was the first time since the Civil War that the Supreme Court had met short handed for an entire term.

Though Blackmun participated in none of the decisions of the 1969–70 term, he did arrive in time to vote on nearly 200 petitions for review and thus helped to decide what cases the Court would hear the next year. In many of these cases Blackmun's vote was crucial because there were already three of the four votes required to hear cases. Burger was opposed to granting the hearings. Blackmun voted to hear only four. Burger was pleased. The Court's liberals were disappointed and concluded that Burger had finally received the additional conservative vote he needed to help him shift the Court's direction.[34] Indeed, for two years Blackmun did vote regularly with Burger and appear to join the Court's conservative bloc. But as we will learn later in this chapter, by the mid-1980s Blackmun had migrated to the moderately liberal side.

FURTHER DEPARTURES AND THE ARRIVAL OF POWELL AND REHNQUIST

If Nixon had hoped to remold the Supreme Court with conservative appointees, he could not have hoped to have so many opportunities so quickly. In September 1971 Justices Black and Harlan, both suffering from serious illnesses, resigned. Not only did this give Nixon the opportunity to fill two vacancies simultaneously (an opportunity last enjoyed by Roosevelt in 1940), but it also meant that Nixon would have a total of four vacancies to fill in less than three years in office. Over the Court's long history vacancies have occurred on the average about once every two years. A president with average luck can thus expect to make two appointments in one four-year term. Rarely would this be enough to alter significantly the Court's policy-making direction. It would not have been enough for Nixon, who inherited a Court consisting of at least six generally liberal justices. Four appointments might do it, but it was not to be accomplished without another political furor.

Hesitant and attempting to be more careful this time, Nixon created a "leak" to the effect that Black's seat would go to Virginia congressman Richard Poff. But Poff had been a consistent opponent of civil rights legislation in the House and had signed the controversial "Southern Manifesto" in 1956. The ABA's Committee on the Federal Judiciary, not always known for its high standards (it had given rubber-stamp approval to both Haynsworth and Carswell), indicated its disapproval of Poff. Opposition mounted rapidly. To spare his family the controversy Poff withdrew his name from consideration. Next, Nixon sent a list of six names to the ABA committee for its evaluation. The committee, concluding the list was mediocre, asked the president to send over the names of "some people of stature." Angered again, Nixon scrapped his list, discontinued the practice of submitting the names of possible nominees to the ABA for study, and went on television to announce his nominations. To replace Black he would nominate Lewis F. Powell, a respected lawyer from Richmond, Virginia, and former president of the ABA. To replace Harlan he would nominate William H. Rehnquist, then an assistant attorney general in the Justice Department and former Supreme Court law clerk. The potential moderate-to-liberal opposition in the Senate, which knew little of either man, first regarded the nominees as "fallback" candidates but then, with some relief, concluded they were better than Nixon's initial choices. Both were confirmed, although Rehnquist only with some difficulty.[35]

Lewis F. Powell was regarded at the time of his nomination as a moderate. He had articulated some conservative views denouncing civil disobedience and criticizing Supreme Court decisions that asserted the criminal suspect's right to remain silent. These views were balanced by his advocacy of expanded legal services for the poor and his leadership in school desegregation while president of the Richmond school board. A minor flap occurred at his Senate confirmation hearings over an article he had written advocating the wiretapping of domestic radicals, but that apparently mattered little to the Senate, which voted 89 to 1 to confirm. Rehnquist's background presented greater problems. An outspoken conservative since his law school days at Stanford, he had been a Goldwater ally in the 1964 presidential election. In more recent years he was on record as favoring unlimited presidential war powers, the mass arrest of demonstrators, "no knock" entry by the police, and preventive detention. However, in his Senate confirmation hearings Rehnquist promised that as a member of the Supreme Court he would disregard his personal beliefs and be guided only by the law of the Constitution. In the end he was confirmed by a vote of 68 to 26.[36]

THE DEPARTURE OF DOUGLAS AND THE APPOINTMENT OF STEVENS

With the appointment of four new justices in less than three years, it was now possible to talk about the "Burger Court." By the mid-1970s, changes in the Court's direction and overall philosophy were increasingly apparent. The dilution of major Warren Court precedents was well underway. Perhaps for this reason, if no other, liberal justice William O. Douglas hoped desperately to remain on the Court until after the 1976 presidential election when, if a Democrat were elected, he could retire in the hope that his successor would more nearly reflect his views than Burger's. But a series of strokes made that impossible. Effectively incapacitated, Douglas retired in 1975. President Ford now had an opportunity to appoint a replacement for the man he had once attempted to impeach. He had to be careful however, for a direct slap at Douglas with an ultraconservative appointment would not go over well in the Democrat-controlled Senate. Also, being a moderate himself, Ford preferred a middle-of-the-roader. He thus settled on John Paul Stevens. Stevens seemed safe enough. Though a registered Republican, Stevens had never involved himself in partisan politics. A respected Chicago lawyer with a firm specializing in antitrust cases, Stevens had taught part time at Northwestern Law School, from which he had graduated in 1947. He had clerked for liberal Supreme Court justice Wiley Rutledge in 1947–48 and had spent the last five years in the Seventh Circuit Court of Appeals, to which he had been appointed by Nixon in 1970. He was confirmed 98 to 0 by a Senate convinced he would be a "centrist" on the court. He was warmly welcomed to the Court by another centrist, Justice Potter Stewart. In the mid-1970s Stewart was the self-styled leader of the Court's moderate center for whose support the conservative Burger wing and the liberal Brennan wing competed. Stewart began to call Stevens the "wild card." When competing for Stevens's vote, the prevailing proverb among the justices became "It's four to four, and we're down to the 'wild card.'"[37]

The moderate center was to shrink six years later, however, with the retirement of Justice Stewart. If Richard Nixon had been uncommonly lucky in having four Supreme Court vacancies to fill, President Jimmy Carter followed with uncommonly bad luck. His administration (1977–81) passed without a single vacancy. Stewart's retirement in 1981, then, was to benefit the newly elected conservative president Ronald Reagan. Reagan's choice made history.

A WOMAN ON THE COURT:
THE APPOINTMENT OF O'CONNOR

In the 1978 Broadway play *First Monday in October,* * the premise of which is the appointment of the first woman to the Supreme Court, a surly incumbent justice insists on calling the new appointee "Madame Justess." It is quite doubtful that any of the eight incumbents of 1981 were so disrespectful to Sandra Day O'Connor. "A person for all seasons," Reagan described her when he made the historic nomination. And so it seemed at the time. Born on a ranch in Arizona, O'Connor graduated from high school at age 16. She then compiled a distinguished academic record while earning economics and law degrees at Stanford, where she was a law school classmate of Rehnquist. Although O'Connor served as editor of the *Stanford Law Review* and was elected to the Order of the Coif (the national law school honorary), she had difficulty finding a job upon graduation. She applied for a job with a California law firm in which William French Smith (later Reagan's attorney general) was a partner and was offered a position as a secretary. Later she worked briefly as a deputy county attorney in California and then as an assistant state attorney general in Arizona. In 1969 she was appointed to a vacancy in the Arizona state senate, ran successfully for the seat in 1970, and was elected Senate president in 1972—the first woman to hold such a position. Always active in Republican party politics, O'Connor chaired the Arizona Committee to Re-Elect Nixon in 1972. In 1974 she was appointed to the Arizona Court of Appeals, where she sat when elevated to the U.S. Supreme Court by Reagan.[38] As both politician and judge, O'Connor had compiled a generally conservative record. Nonetheless there was concern among those in the "New Right" that she was too liberal (mostly because of confusion about her stance on abortion). Thus when O'Connor joined the Court, some conservatives felt betrayed by Reagan and predicted that O'Connor would be a liberal. Because of the conservative opposition, liberals breathed a sigh of relief assuming that O'Connor was a mainstream Republican. As we will learn later in this chapter, both sides have turned out to be wrong. O'Connor's conservatism on the Court has been second only to that of Rehnquist. That duo, along with the chief justice, now forms the Burger Court's conservative bloc.

THE EARLY BURGER COURT:
CONTINUITY AND DISCONTINUITY

Supreme Court eras are commonly named for the chief justice whose leadership shapes them, and they are measured by the extent to which their impact

---

* The title of the play is derived from the tradition of beginning a new term of the Supreme Court on the first Monday in October.

endures beyond the presidential administration that named the Court's members (see Figure 1–1). Whereas there have been 41 American presidents, there have been only 17 American chief justices. The Marshall Court (1801–35) endured over six presidential administrations; the Taney Court (1836–64) endured over nine; the Warren Court (1953–69) endured over four; and the Burger Court lasted 17 years over four presidential administrations. While its enduring impact must be left to the analysis of future scholars, the Burger Court's departure from the Warren era is clear.

There were indications early on that Burger meant to alter the Court's direction. Predictably, the initial indication of change was in the handling of criminal cases. In fact, in August 1969, even before Burger's first term began, the new chief justice made a discovery that angered him. It had to do with *in forma pauperis* petitions ("IFPs"), which are applications for Supreme Court review by poor persons who cannot afford attorneys or filing fees. These IFPs are commonly handwritten notes, often illegible and incomprehensible, from prisoners who allege that their constitutional rights have been violated. Traditionally, the chief justice's law clerks read the petitions and make recommendations for or against a full review. Most such petitions are both frivolous and groundless. Few, even during the Warren era, received a full hearing, though Warren had believed that some would have merit and that the Supreme Court, being the last bastion of hope for persons who know no law and have no political clout, should consider IFPs carefully. Now, in August 1969, the new chief discovered how the old chief had accomplished that objective. Warren had instructed his clerks not only to summarize the points raised in an IFP but also to raise any point and make any argument that the petitioner could have raised in his or her own behalf. In short, since the petitioner had no lawyer and knew no law, the clerk should act as the petitioner's attorney. Burger was enraged. He told his clerks that the Supreme Court is not a public defender's office. Warren's practice of giving assistance to indigent petitioners would stop.[39]

Although only a minor matter in the broad scheme of things, this incident was a predictor of things to come in criminal cases. The differences between the Warren Court and the Burger Court were clear after

FIGURE 1–1   The Court: From Warren to Burger

THE WARREN COURT 1969	Warren Fortas Black Harlan Douglas Stewart Brennan Marshall White
THE BURGER COURT 1986	Burger Blackmun Powell Rehnquist Stevens O'Connor Brennan Marshall White

only one year. In 1968–69, Warren's last full year as chief justice, the prosecution won only 31 percent of the criminal cases decided by the Court. In 1969–70, Burger's first full year as chief justice, the prosecution won 62 percent of the criminal cases decided. And between 1971 and 1975 the first major departures from Warren Court doctrine occurred when the famous "*Miranda* rules" were diluted. As mentioned earlier, the Warren Court had ruled in *Miranda v. Arizona* (1966) that a criminal suspect must be informed of his or her right to remain silent and right to counsel. Any confession or incriminating statement made by a suspect in the absence of such warnings would be illegally obtained and inadmissible at trial. This was, of course, one of the most controversial of the Warren Court decisions, widely criticized by conservatives and law enforcement personnel. Many Court-watchers predicted it would be overturned by the Burger Court. However, sudden and complete changes in direction are rarely wrought by the Supreme Court. As legal theorist and once Supreme Court justice Oliver Wendell Holmes observed, "Continuity with the past is not a duty; it is merely a necessity."[40] Accordingly, the Burger Court's approach was not to completely overturn but to significantly dilute the *Miranda* decision. In *Harris v. New York*[41] the court held that illegally obtained confessions *could* be admitted against a defendant, if he took the stand in his own defense, in order to impeach his credibility as a witness. Four years later the Court applied this same principle to a case in which the suspect *was* told of his rights and asked for a lawyer but police questioning continued before the lawyer arrived.[42] Clearly, from then on when suspects requested counsel, the police would be tempted to press their interrogation vigorously to obtain incriminating statements before that counsel arrived. Also in 1975 the Court ruled that after a suspect has exercised the right to remain silent (under *Miranda*) about one crime, the police may still question the suspect about another.[43] As Justice Brennan pointed out in dissent, this decision virtually empties *Miranda* of principle because it "encourages police asked to cease interrogation to continue the suspect's detention until the police station's coercive atmosphere does its work and the suspect responds to resumed questioning." The *Miranda* decision was still good law, but its meaning had been diluted and its application weakened.

The early Burger Court also worked to dilute other major and controversial Warren Court precedents in the area of legislative apportionment. The Warren Court had held in a series of decisions in the early 1960s that congressional and state legislative districts must be, as nearly as possible, equal in size. One person's vote must be, as nearly as possible, equal to every other person's vote. These were the famous "one man, one vote" decisions.[44] Of course, in practical terms it is not possible for every legislative district in a system to be perfectly equal in size. Thus, the crucial question became, What is the maximum possible deviation from perfect equality that the Court will allow? The Warren Court would rarely permit more than a 3 to 5 percent deviation; the early Burger Court allowed deviations as high as 11 percent.[45] Although the principle of "one man, one vote" remained, and continuity with the past was preserved, the principle had been diluted. In practical terms, greater inequality was possible, and another discontinuity with the Warren era was achieved.

In the equally controversial areas of racial equality and alleged pornography, the early Burger Court's break with the past was more decisive and dramatic. In the area of racial equality, it was a clearly settled principle of the Warren Court that racial impact is a sufficient basis for demonstrating racial discrimination in the allocation of municipal services, employment, public accommodations and public housing, zoning, and school desegregation. The early Burger Court changed all that. In 1976 the Burger Court held that adverse racial impact in the use of an employment test by the District of Columbia did not constitute a case of discrimination in the absence of proof of discriminatory intent.[46] Further, the Court referred to nonemployment cases in the process and implied that the same proof of discriminatory intent would now be required in housing, services, accommodations, and zoning cases as well. Since only public officials know what their intent is (and are not likely to admit to discriminatory intent), what all this meant as a practical matter was "that public officials could now discriminate on the basis of race as long as they didn't admit it."[47] In the area of alleged pornography, no Court, including the Warren Court, has held that hard-core obscenity is protected by the First Amendment's freedom of expression. But the Warren Court had held since the mid-1950s that alleged pornography could be regulated by government censorship or confiscation only if the material in question was "*utterly without* redeeming social value."[48] That rule made it difficult for government censors to win obscenity cases. However, in a case decided in 1973[49] the Burger Court altered the rule. Now the government censor would have to prove only that the material was "*lacking* in serious literary, artistic, political or scientific value." In addition, in making decisions about alleged pornography, no single national standard but local community standards could be applied. It should be noted here that the decision, like many others of the 1972–75 period, was reached by a 5-4 vote of the justices, with all four Nixon appointees in the majority. There could be little doubt, then, that changes in the Court's personnel were producing changes in the Court's policies.

THE LATER BURGER COURT: "NEW RESTRAINT" OR "CONSERVATIVE ACTIVISM"?

With the appointments of Justices Stevens and O'Connor, the Burger Court of the 1980s received mixed reviews. It was hailed as "cautious and restrained," charged with "conservative activism," and criticized for its "confused jurisprudence." Part of the explanation for such widely varied assessments lies in the strained interpersonal relations among some of the justices and their consequent shifting alliances. (These are described at the end of this chapter.) The explanation also lies in the fact that the Burger Court of the 1980s did not move consistently in any one direction. At times the Court appeared careful and restrained, almost humble, while deferring to the other branches of the national government and to the states. Such restraint was evident, for example, in the Court's deference to Congress in upholding Congress' new all-male draft registration law[50] and in its deference to the presidency in upholding the Carter-Reagan Iran Settlement Agreement.[51] The Court was also increasingly deferential to the states by limiting federal court jurisdiction to review state court decisions.[52] The Court did reach a number of decisions generally regarded as liberal. These included its ruling that illegal alien children are entitled to a free public education,[53] its holding that male students may not be barred from a state-operated nursing school,[54] and its decision that racially discriminating schools are ineligible for federal tax exempt status.[55] But the Court also reached a number of decisions generally regarded as conservative. These included the Court's ruling that the president is absolutely immune from civil suit for illegal acts taken in his term,[56] its holding that a city may sponsor a nativity scene as part of an official Christmas display without violating the constitutionally required separation between church and state,[57] and its decision to allow the admission of evidence obtained by police in "objectively reasonable" reliance on a search warrant that later proves to be defective.[58]

In the Court's last few terms under Burger, as the conservative bloc gained dominance, the Court came in for criticism made in public by one of its own members. Although it is highly unusual for a Supreme Court justice to use a public speech to raise disagreements with colleagues, Justice Stevens did just that in a 1984 address to the ABA. Appearing to charge the Court's majority with "conservative activism," Stevens asserted that the Court had cast restraint aside and gone out of its way in order to move the law to the right.[59] Meanwhile, a variety of Court-watchers charged that the Court, while reaching both conservative and liberal decisions, had increasingly produced a "confused jurisprudence." This is the charge that although the Court had reached its decisions by a majority vote (commonly 5-4 or 6-3 in the controversial cases), it had been unable to produce written opinions justifying its decisions to which a majority of the justices subscribe. As a result, the American public may know what the Court has decided in important cases because the votes of the justices are a matter of public record, but they have difficulty understanding the reasons for those decisions because the justices in the majority have voted the same way for different reasons. The Court's decisions are clear, but its doctrine is confused. To a large extent this confusion was a product of the fragile and shifting voting coalitions among the justices on the Burger Court in the 1980s.

VOTING PATTERNS AND BLOCS IN THE BURGER COURT OF THE 1980S

The leading characteristics of the Burger Court of the 1980s were (1) an increasing polarization of the liberal and conservative wings, with Justice Blackmun migrating to the liberal bloc; (2) an increasing number of cases decided by a single vote; and (3) a decreasing influence of the chief justice, especially in the highly contested cases.

The most indissoluble voting bloc became that of Justices Brennan and Marshall, the two liberal holdovers from the Warren era. In 1981–82, for example, Brennan and Marshall voted together in 92.3 percent of the cases decided. The conservative bloc came to consist of the chief justice, Justice Rehnquist, and Justice O'Connor. In 1981–82, for example, the three voted together 85.4 percent of the cases. These two blocs tended to compete, in the contested (nonunanimous) cases, for the "swing votes" of Justices Blackmun, Stevens, Powell, and White. The typical 5-4 decision going in the conservative direction, for example, consisted of a Burger-Rehnquist-O'Connor-Powell-White majority. In the contested cases Blackmun, once Burger's "Minnesota Twin," migrated to the liberal side. In 1981–82, for example, Blackmun voted with the Court's most liberal justice, Mr. Brennan, 48 times and with the Court's most conservative justice, Mr. Rehnquist, only 21 times. Justice Stevens, the "wild card," remained the Court's greatest centrist, writing, by far, more dissenting opinions than any other justice. In the contested cases, however, he was more likely to end up on the liberal than the conservative side.

Increased polarization and competition for the votes of the centrists led to an increase in cases decided by a single vote. Many of these were extremely important cases, including the presidential immunity, the all-female nursing school, and the alien children education rights cases mentioned earlier. Frequently, the written opinions in these cases were marked by wrangling and personal animosity.

All this occurred with little moderating influence exercised by the chief justice, who seemed to be playing a less and less important role and writing fewer and fewer important opinions. In part this was because he was sometimes on the losing side. Even when he was with the majority and was entitled as the chief justice to assign the writing of the majority opinion, however, he frequently did not do so unless substantial agreement existed among the justices. In 1981–82, for example, Burger wrote the opinion in nine of the fifteen cases decided unanimously but only one of the opinions in the thirty-three cases decided by a single vote. Every other justice wrote at least two such opinions. This was probably because the authorship of opinions in highly contested cases requires the skill of building and holding together uneasy coalitions, something Burger did not do well. In 1982 he did write a few opinions in important cases such as the Bob Jones University discrimination case mentioned earlier, but that case was decided by an 8-1 vote. Generally, Burger's profile was high only when there was little disagreement among the justices.[60]

During Burger's last two years on the Court (the 1984–85 and 1985–86 terms), competition between the Court's conservative and liberal wings for the votes of the centrists, particularly for the vote of Justice Powell, who was emerging as the key "swing" vote, continued. The Court's increased polarization and Powell's increased importance became more evident than ever before. (See Figure 1–2.)

The 1984–85 term began under the spotlight of a presidential election year with both candidates and commentators assuming that the person elected to the presidency might be able to make several appointments to the Court.[61] As things turned out, although Ronald Reagan did win reelection, he did not get a vacancy to fill on the Court until 1986; and the 1984–85 term was one in which his administration's position was rejected by the Court in most of the major cases decided. In one case, the Court invalidated an Alabama state law that provided for a moment of silent prayer in public schools.[62] In another, the Court invalidated (as an "impermissible symbolic union of government and religion") government programs in which public school teachers were provided to parochial schools for remedial and enrichment instruction.[63] In both cases the Reagan administration had loudly argued for the losing side that religion deserves a "special status" in our governmental scheme. In another very important case involving the constitutional principle of federalism, the Court swept away the theoretical underpinnings of the doctrine of "states' rights" when it held that state and

FIGURE 1–2   Decisions by One Vote Margins, 1981–1986

COURT TERM	NUMBER OF DECISIONS WITH FULL OPINION MADE DURING THE TERM	NUMBER OF DECISIONS MADE BY ONE VOTE MARGIN
1981–82	143	33
1982–83	152	32
1983–84	150	29
1984–85	139	19*
1985–86	147	34

*Justice Powell was absent for two months for cancer surgery during the 1984–85 term. The result was that eight cases ended with a 4–4 tie vote.

local governments must pay their employees according to federal minimum wage and hour laws.[64] The Court's polarization and Powell's centrist role are clearly indicated by the 1984–85 term's voting patterns. Of the Court's 139 decisions, 80 were made by less than a unanimous vote. In these 80 contested cases Chief Justice Burger and Justice Brennan were on opposite sides in 56 (70 percent). These included the silent prayer case, the aid to parochial schools case, and the major states' rights case. As for Justice Powell, not only did his extended absence cause eight 4-4 tie votes but, when he was present to vote, he dissented from the Court's decision only six times (as compared with Brennan's forty-one dissents, Marshall's forty dissents, and Stevens's thirty-six dissents). This very low number of dissents from Justice Powell indicated his increasingly important role as a "swing" voter because it meant that the side on which he voted invariably won.[65]

In 1985–86, Warren Burger's last year as chief justice, the Supreme Court was confronted with what one commentator called "an unusual number of politically charged issues."[66] As we have seen, reversing the direction taken by the Supreme Court had been a priority of the Reagan administration ever since Reagan's first election in 1980. But in 1985–86, with Edwin Meese III now the U.S. attorney general and with Charles Fried now the U.S. solicitor general (the federal government's chief advocate before the Supreme Court), the administration became particularly bold in urging the Court to depart from its own precedents to adopt the Reagan agenda. The Court responded by sometimes accepting and by sometimes rejecting the administration's advice. The most publicized administration victory came in *Bowsher v. Synar*,[67] in which the Court protected the president's primacy in executing the laws by invalidating the automatic mechanism for spending cuts that was at the core of the Gramm-Rudman budget-balancing act. In what Solicitor General Fried considered his first major victory in a criminal case, the Court ruled that the police may use deception if necessary to keep a defense attorney away while questioning a suspect.[68] And in *Bowers v. Hardwick*[69] the Supreme Court held that nothing in the Constitution prevents the prosecution of homosexual relations between consenting adults, even in the privacy of their own homes. Mr. Fried praised this decision as an example of the kind of "constitutional methodology" that refuses to "invent rights," a methodology he said he had espoused unsuccessfully in the cases involving rights to sexual privacy.[70] Fried was referring in these comments to such key administration losses before the Court as the one in *Thornburgh v. American College of Obstetricians and Gynecologists*,[71] in which the Court reaffirmed its commitment to abortion rights, which the administration had exhorted it to forsake. Another loss came in a major reapportionment case involving the 1982 Amendments to the Voting Rights Act. Here, the Court spurned the administration's constrictive concept of minority voting rights when it invalidated election districts in North Carolina on the grounds that the drawing of district lines made it too difficult for black voters to elect their choice of candidates to the state legislature.[72] In the area of affirmative action, contrary to Administration urgings the Court reasserted its support for certain circumscribed uses of racial preferences, including the sparing reliance on numerical hiring goals, to reduce job discrimination against minorities.[73]

Analysis of the justices' voting patterns in 1985–86 shows a continuation of the trends evident in the previous term. Brennan and Marshall remained the "liberal duo," joined frequently by Blackmun and Stevens. Burger, in his last year, and Rehnquist, who would become chief justice in 1986–87, constituted the "conservative duo." They were joined most often by O'Connor, White, and Powell. Blackmun's migration to the left and White's migration to the right continued. Powell was even more visible as the "swing" vote in the "center" (voting with the Burger-Rehnquist right in the homosexual rights case decided 5-4, but with the Brennan-Marshall left in the abortion rights case also decided 5-4). Justice O'Connor moved somewhat closer to the center. Normally conservative, she nevertheless voted against the Reagan administration in some key cases. Indeed, in every major case the winning side was supported by either Powell or O'Connor or both.[74]

Chief Justice Burger retired in 1986. Justice Rehnquist was elevated to the chief justiceship, and a conservative court of appeals judge, Antonin Scalia, was appointed by President Reagan to fill Rehnquist's vacant seat as associate justice. Other changes in the Court's composition were to follow. The teachings of the Rehnquist Court and projections of the Court's future role as the nation's schoolmaster will be examined in the last chapter, where we wonder aloud about the Republic's third century. For now, a brief assessment of the Burger years is in order. A more detailed account of the Supreme Court as the country's "council of elders" in the 1980s is presented at the end of Chapter Three.

SCHOOLMASTER OF THE REPUBLIC: ASSESSING THE BURGER YEARS

At first glance the Burger Court's teachings appear to be ambiguous in content and its methods appear to be confused in approach. Burger's Court did exhibit some liberal leanings. It was, after all, the Burger Court that created the right to abortion, first allowed bussing, placed severe limits on the death penalty, and brought sex discrimination under the protection of the Constitution. At the same time, however, the Burger Court was far less inclined than was the Warren Court to provide protection for most classes of civil rights and liberties. In the criminal justice area particularly, the Burger Court tended to narrow the range of protections for the accused and generally favored the prosecution. A shift in both policy preferences and doctrine was clear in such areas as the regulation of obscenity and the protection of press freedoms. In "judicial temperament," that is, the Court's methods and approach, Burger's Court would have to be regarded as extremely activist by some measures. It struck down more federal laws, more state laws, and more of its own precedents than did the Warren Court, and in about the same number of years.[75] Yet at the same time Burger's Court could be considered careful and restrained if the emphasis in analysis were placed on its deference to the president and to state courts. The Court's mixed methods elicited some of the most angry replies of its critics, especially criticisms of the Court's conservatives, who were viewed as restrained when asked to protect civil liberties but as activist when asked to restrict civil liberties or to promote economic interests.

It should not be particularly surprising, then, that the overall performance of the Burger Court has received mixed reviews. Some commentators regard the Burger Court as "sensitive" and "balanced," a Court that "caught the national mood," a Court that "admired Ronald Reagan but by no means all his policies," a Court "distrustful of racial quotas but unwilling to countenance discrimination," a Court that all in all was "an affirmative actor in the American system."[76] Others regard the Burger Court as one regularly producing decisions and opinions lacking in clarity, a Court determined to weaken basic constitutional rights, a Court that with only "disguised duplicity" sought to revitalize long-discarded doctrines of entreprenurial liberty, a Court that at best "produced a pattern of middling, meandering conservatism."[77] Combining these conflicting accounts, one commentator concludes that the Burger Court was a "troubled" and "fragmented" Court in a period of "transition"; it engaged in some "minor remodeling" and "interior redecorating" but left most of the major Warren Court precedents intact.[78] This latter view, observing that the Burger Court did not move in the consistently and clearly conservative direction many had predicted at its beginning, led one commentator to subtitle his book about the Burger Court "The Counter-Revolution That Wasn't."[79] First glances, however, are often superficial, if not overly simplistic or just plain wrong. In this case, the conclusions of those who assert that the Burger Court was surprisingly and strikingly like the Warren Court run directly counter to the position taken in this book, to wit, that the Burger Court as the Republic's schoolmaster moved the teachings of American constitutional law sharply to the ideological right.

Obviously, we must grant to Burger's Court some concessions to continuity. To the extent that the Burger Court did not move as far to the right as some had predicted, there are a number of explanations. First, the Court was governed in its deliberations, as all courts are, by the principle of *stare decisis* ("let the decision stand"), a rule of precedent according to which judges are bound by what has been decided before. Prior decisions are to be applied to similar cases, thus giving the law stability. The Warren Court had left a large legacy of liberal legal precedent, and judges—even policy-oriented Supreme Court justices with a conservative ideological commitment—are not always comfortable overturning an existing law.[80] But the principle of *stare decisis* is not absolute. Judges may find compelling reasons calling for new precedents. Indeed, that most Supreme Court decisions are not unanimous (in fact many, as we have seen, are 6-3 or even 5-4) is proof that the justices can look at the same set of facts and take cognizance of the same governing precedent yet come to different conclusions. In other words, justices have discretion, or leeway, to read their own values or beliefs into the law. Thus, we must find some explanations, in addition to the force of precedent, for the Burger Court's failure to move the law more completely in a conservative direction. A second explanation, then, may be that those persons and institutions that apply the law (for example, the police and prosecutors in criminal cases) had come to regard Warren Court rulings as the status quo and had become accustomed, gradually, to applying them. They had slowly adjusted to a social and cultural consensus. Supreme Court decisions directly reversing Warren Court rulings may well have seemed to the Burger Court justices as undesirable disruptions of widely accepted public policies. Such considerations help explain why Burger's Court tended to limit, circumscribe, and revise Warren Court decisions but not to eviscerate them. Third, the work of the Warren Court had culminated a protracted process of transformation in the Supreme Court's accepted role, a transition from economic activism, when the Court invalidated various regulations of industry and business interests from the turn of the century to about 1937, to civil liberties activism, when the Court expanded the protection of civil rights and liberties, especially in the 1960s. It may well be the case that, with the exception of Rehnquist, the Burger Court justices came to see their job at least in part as that of protector of civil liberties.[81] Finally, some commentators are beginning to find an explanation in the doctrinal arguments and intellectual leadership of Justice Brennan. As the Court's leading liberal theoretician and most effective politician, Brennan was able to shape and cement majorities by formulating principles acceptable to the Court's centrists, something at which Chief Justice Burger was far less successful.[82]

These concessions to continuity fairly noted, we must hasten to emphasize that the overall record of the Burger Court created at most only an illusion of continuity with the Warren years. We can begin a catalog of clearly conservative trends with a consideration of the Burger Court's treatment of access to the Supreme Court's doors, and through access possible assistance. Traditionally, access to the Court to bring a suit has been limited by technical rules of "justiciability" and "standing." The Burger Court's rightward shift is perhaps most explicit in this area. Indeed, Chief Justice Burger early in his tenure warned prospective lawyers against going to law school if their purpose was to seek social change through the judicial process. "That is not the route by which basic changes in a country like ours should be made," he said.[83] If they tried to achieve basic changes through the court system, Burger promised them "some disappointments."[84] Looking back now on the Burger years, we observe a Court with a mind to manipulate rules of access in such a way as to grant a hearing to powerful interests but deny a day in court to those whose interests were ones with which the Court had only slim sympathy.[85] The Warren Court had developed the practice of taking large numbers of cases involving the rights of the accused, especially when access to a Court ruling was sought by the accused. The Burger Court took far fewer cases involving rights of the accused, and when it did, the hearing was frequently sought by the government. The Warren Court had developed the practice of taking large numbers of cases brought by indigents. The Burger Court was far less sympathetic to cases brought by indigents, even in its first few years, and it became nearly hostile to their claims at the end. This may have been a blessing in disguise, however, because gaining access to the Burger Court may not have been very helpful to individuals seeking to protect individual rights against the government. While the Warren Court had supported the individual against the government 66 percent of the time, the Burger Court did so in only 44 percent of the cases it decided.[86]

Indeed, conservative trends abound when the Burger years are given close scrutiny. The Court was indifferent to the rights of prisoners, unenthusiastic about the rights of the poor and powerless to freedom of expression, dissatisfied with politically disfavored modes of school desegregation, unsympathetic to the protection of First Amendment rights in national security cases, insensitive to the rights of criminal defendants, and overly eager to embrace a "cost-benefit" technique to arrive at its decisions when relatively firm philosophical principles would have been a far more reliable and appropriate guide.[87] A brief elaboration on this last point may help catch the tone of the Burger Court's approach to things. We noted earlier that in 1984 the Court created a "good faith" exception to the rule excluding illegally obtained evidence at a criminal trial when it allowed the use of evidence obtained on the basis of a legally deficient search warrant so long as the police had, in good faith, a reasonable belief that the warrant was valid.[88] In an explicit application of cost-benefit comparisons, the Court concluded that the "benefit" of deterring police misconduct by excluding illegally obtained evidence was clearly outweighed by the "cost" of freeing a "clearly guilty" defendant; that is, effective crime fighting by the police is a higher interest than is deterring police misconduct, especially so when the "benefits" of the exclusionary rule are "nebulous" or "speculative" as a deterrent to police misconduct and the "costs" include the politically unpopular right of a criminal suspect going free. The Court's decision in this case placed significant new limits on the constitutional rights of criminal defendants; and as one commentator has observed, the Court's use of cost-benefit comparisons "suggests a troublesome indifference to the fact that basic personal liberties are neither rooted in the law of averages nor assigned on the basis of efficiency."[89]

Still, those who argue that the Burger Court was surprisingly liberal cite in support of their position cases like *Batson v. Kentucky.*[90] In this 1986 ruling the Court held that prosecutors may not exclude blacks from juries based on the mere possibility that they would favor defendants of their own race. Since this decision in part overturned a 1965 ruling of the Warren Court, it has been argued that the *Batson* case provides an instance in which the Burger Court went further than the Warren Court to protect defendants in criminal cases. However, a number of Court commentators subsequently pointed out that this case is better understood, not as a criminal justice case (an area in which the Burger Court was notably more conservative than the Warren Court), but as a race relations case (an area in which the Burger Court was relatively moderate). Even if understood as a criminal justice ruling, however, the decision in *Batson* simply draws attention to the generally conservative trend of the Burger Court against which it was a clear exception.

Although the Burger Court did break new ground in areas such as abortion, gender discrimination, and the rights of aliens and the handicapped, just as it did in such race relations cases as those dealing with affirmative action, the mere citation of its rulings in these areas falls far short of demonstrating that Burger's was a liberal Court. The simple fact is that the problems confronting the Burger Court were different from those confronting the Warren Court. The Burger Court was forced to deal with issues the Warren Court hardly touched.[91] They simply were not on the Warren Court's agenda. In any event, a demonstration that the Burger Court was discernibly more conservative than was the Warren Court does not require a showing that every Burger Court decision was of a conservative sort. It requires only the easy conclusion that the Burger Court was clearly more conservative than the Warren Court would have been had its personnel remained intact for 17 years after 1969. Certainly in such a scenario a Warren Court, had it continued, would have reached similar results to those of the Burger Court in the few instances in which the latter was liberal, but quite different results in the many instances in which the latter was conservative.

A closer examination of the Burger years appears at the end of Chapter Three. The Rehnquist years, and those that still lie ahead, are examined in Chapter Nine.

NOTES

[1] Laurence Tribe, *God Save This Honorable Court* (New York: Random House, 1985), pp. 27, 29.

[2] Ibid., pp. 12–16.

[3] Quoted in Herman Schwartz, ed., *The Burger Years: Rights and Wrongs in the Supreme Court, 1969–1986* (New York: Viking/Elisabeth Sifton Books, 1987), p. xxii.

[4] *Trop v. Dulles*, 356 U.S. 86 (1958).

[5] Alexander Bickel, *The Least Dangerous Branch* (New York: Bobbs-Merrill, 1962), p. 24.

[6] H.F. Stone, "The Common Law in the United States," 50 *Harvard Law Review* 4 (1936) p. 25. Quoted in Bickel, *The Least Dangerous Branch*, p. 26.

[7] Bickel, *The Least Dangerous Branch*, p. 25.

[8] E.V. Rostow, "The Democratic Character of Judicial Review," 66 *Harvard Law Review* 208n15 (1952). Quoted in Bickel, *The Least Dangerous Branch*, p. 26.

[9] *Trop v. Dulles*, 356 U.S. 86 (1958).

[10] Bob Woodward and Scott Armstrong, *The Brethren: Inside the Supreme Court* (New York: Simon & Schuster, 1979), p. 26. This book, written by investigative journalists and regarded by some as just another muckraking expose, contains some errors of fact and legal misinterpretations; however, it paints a vivid behind-the-scenes picture of the Supreme Court at work that a number of respected legal scholars have said they regard to be generally accurate.

[11] *Brown v. Board of Education*, 347 U.S. 483 (1954), 349 U.S. 294 (1955).

[12] *Baker v. Carr*, 369 U.S. 186 (1962); *Wesberry v. Sanders*, 376 U.S. 1 (1964); *Reynolds v. Sims*, 377 U.S. 533 (1964).

[13] *Abington Township v. Schempp*, 374 U.S. 203 (1963).

[14] *Roth v. U.S.*, 354 U.S. 476 (1957).

[15] *Miranda v. Arizona*, 384 U.S. 436 (1966).

[16] *Douglas v. California*, 372 U.S. 353 (1963).

[17] Stephen L. Wasby, *Continuity and Change: From the Warren Court to the Burger Court* (Pacific Palisades, Calif.: Goodyear, 1976), pp. 1, 3, 75–77.

[18] Bernard Schwartz, *Super Chief: Earl Warren and His Supreme Court* (New York: New York University Press, 1983), pp. 280–81.

[19] Ibid., pp. 282–83.

[20] Wasby, *Continuity and Change*, p. 75.

[21] B. Schwartz, *Super Chief*, pp. 681–82.

[22] Jack Harrison Pollack, *Earl Warren: The Judge Who Changed America* (Englewood Cliffs, N.J.: Prentice Hall, 1979), p. 283.

[23] B. Schwartz, *Super Chief*, pp. 722, 725.

[24] Congressional Quarterly, *CQ Guide to Current American Government* (Washington, D.C.: Congressional Quarterly Press, 1982), p. 125; B. Schwartz, *Super Chief*, pp. 20–21; Woodward and Armstrong, *The Brethren*, p. 11.

[25] Woodward and Armstrong, *The Brethren*, pp. 11–12, 24.

[26] B. Schwartz, *Super Chief*, pp. 763–64.

[27] Woodward and Armstrong, *The Brethren*, p. 22.

[28] Robert Shogun, *A Question of Judgement: The Fortas Case and the Struggle for the Supreme Court* (Indianapolis: Bobbs-Merrill, 1972), p. 249; William O. Douglas, *The Court Years, 1939–1975: The Autobiography of William O. Douglas* (New York: Random House, 1980), pp. 358–59; B. Schwartz, *Super Chief*, pp. 760–62.

[29] Woodward and Armstrong, *The Brethren*, p. 56.

[30] Ibid., p. 74.

[31] Ibid., p. 75.

[32] Douglas, *The Court Years, 1939–1975*, pp. 256, 359.

[33] Woodward and Armstrong, *The Brethren*, pp. 86–88.

[34] Ibid., p. 88.

[35] Alpheus T. Mason and William M. Beaney, *American Constitutional Law* (Englewood Cliffs, N.J.: Prentice Hall, 1972), pp. xxii–xxiv.

[36] Ibid., p. xxiv.

[37] Woodward and Armstrong, *The Brethren*, pp. 400–402, 428.

[38] *CQ Guide to Current American Government*, pp. 129–30.

[39] Woodward and Armstrong, *The Brethren*, pp. 33–34.

[40] Bickel, *The Least Dangerous Branch*, p. 16.

[41] 401 U.S. 222 (1971).

[42] *Oregon v. Haas*, 420 U.S. 714 (1975).

[43] *Michigan v. Mosley*, 423 U.S. 96 (1975).

[44] *Baker v. Carr*, 369 U.S. 186 (1962); *Reynolds v. Sims*, 377 U.S. 533 (1964); *Wesberry v. Sanders*, 376 U.S. 1 (1964).

[45] *Abate v. Mundt*, 403 U.S. 182 (1971).

[46] *Washington v. Davis*, 426 U.S. 229 (1976).

[47] Laughlin McDonald, "Has the Supreme Court Abandoned the Constitution?" *Saturday Review* (May 28, 1977), p. 10.

[48] *Roth v. U.S.*, 354 U.S. 476 (1957).

[49] *Miller v. California*, 413 U.S. 15 (1973).

[50] *Rostker v. Goldberg*, 453 U.S. 57 (1981).

[51] *Dames & Moore v. Regan*, 453 U.S. 654 (1981).

[52] *Kramer v. Chemical Construction Co.*, 460 U.S. 241 (1982).

[53] *Plyer v. Doe*, 457 U.S. 202 (1982).

[54] *Mississippi University for Women v. Hogan*, 458 U.S. 718 (1982).

[55] *Bob Jones University v. U.S.*, 461 U.S. 574 (1983).

[56] *Nixon v. Fitzgerald*, 457 U.S. 731 (1982).

[57] *Lynch v. Donnelly*, 465 U.S. 668 (1984).

[58] *U.S. v. Leon*, 468 U.S. 897 (1984).

[59] Stuart Taylor, "Justice Stevens Is Sharply Critical of Supreme Court Conservatives," *New York Times* (August 4, 1984), pp. 1, 17.

[60] Linda Greenhouse, "Searching the Past Court Term for Burger's Stamp," *New York Times* (July 20, 1982), p. 35.

[61] Linda Greenhouse, "High Court Faces Issues of Religion," *New York Times* (September 29, 1984), pp. 1, 13; and Greenhouse, "High Court Agrees to Hear Appeals on Speech Rights," *New York Times* (October 1, 1984), pp. 1, 9.

[62] *Wallace v. Jaffree*, 472 U.S. 38 (1985).

[63] *Aguilar v. Felton*, 473 U.S. 402 (1985).

[64] *Garcia v. San Antonio Metropolitan Transit Authority*, 469 U.S. 528 (1985).

[65] Linda Greenhouse, "Rulings of High Court's Term Reaffirm Church-State Barriers," *New York Times* (July 8, 1985), p. 11.

[66] Stuart Taylor, "High Court's 1985–86 Term: Mixed Results for President," *New York Times* (July 11, 1986), pp. 1, 8.

[67] 478 U.S. 714 (1986).

[68] *Moran v. Burbine*, 475 U.S. 412 (1986).

[69] 478 U.S. 186 (1986).

[70] Taylor, "High Court's 1985–86 Term," p. 8.

[71] 476 U.S. 747 (1986).

[72] *Thornburg v. Gingles,* 478 U.S. 30 (1986).

[73] *Wygant v. Jackson Board of Education,* 476 U.S. 267 (1986); *Local 28 v. Equal Employment Opportunity Commission,* 106 S. Ct. 3019 (1986); and *Local 93 v. Cleveland,* 106 S. Ct. 3063 (1986).

[74] "Addition of Scalia's Vote Unlikely to Alter Rulings," *New York Times* (July 11, 1986), p. 52.

[75] "The Third Branch Upheld," *New York Times* (July 13, 1986), p. 26.

[76] Ibid.

[77] Rodney A. Smolla, "One Judge, One Vote," a review of Herman Schwartz, *The Burger Years,* in *New York Times Book Review* (January 10, 1988).

[78] David M. O'Brien, "The Supreme Court from Warren to Burger to Rehnquist," *PS* (Winter 1987), pp. 13–15.

[79] Vincent Blasi, ed., *The Burger Court: The Counter-Revolution That Wasn't* (New Haven: Yale University Press, 1983). See Lawrence Baum, "Explaining the Burger Court's Support for Civil Liberties," *PS* (Winter 1987), pp. 21–28.

[80] Baum, "Explaining the Burger Court's Support for Civil Liberties," p. 25.

[81] Ibid., pp. 24–26.

[82] Stephen Gillers, "Burger's Warren Court," *New York Times* (September 25, 1983), p. 56.

[83] Quoted in Herman Schwartz, *The Burger Years,* p. xii.

[84] *New York Times* (July 4, 1971), p. 1.

[85] Tribe, *God Save This Honorable Court,* p. 122.

[86] O'Brien, "The Supreme Court from Warren to Burger to Rehnquist," pp. 16–17.

[87] Tribe, *God Save This Honorable Court,* pp. 111–21.

[88] *U.S. v. Leon,* 468 U.S. 897 (1984).

[89] Tribe, *God Save This Honorable Court,* p. 121.

[90] 476 U.S. 79 (1986).

[91] Herman Schwartz, *The Burger Years,* p. xii.

The Supreme Court in the Judicial System

An Ultimate Tribunal

THE STRUCTURE OF THE JUDICIAL SYSTEM

The United States Supreme Court is the final arbiter of America's constitutional issues. Of course, constitutional issues form only a small fraction of the legal problems daily presented before federal and state courts, and not even every constitutional issue is raised before the Supreme Court for resolution. Sooner or later, though, nearly every constitutional issue of policy significance has its day before the Supreme Court, and when that day comes, the Court has the last legal word. It sits atop an overcrowded and overarching federal judicial system that is itself superimposed on 50 distinct and separate state judicial systems. An understanding of the Supreme Court's place in these systems requires an awareness of their structures. We will begin with the structures of the state courts.

When the U.S. Supreme Court was created by the Constitution of 1789, well-developed judicial systems already existed in each of the 13 original states. After nearly 200 years of development and expansion of the federal court system, state court systems, just as state governments in general, have become less important to national policy making. Nevertheless, the 50 state court systems of today remain viable institutions and retain a considerable autonomy, especially in norm enforcement and private law cases.[1]

The 50 state court systems differ widely in structure, nomenclature, and procedure, but a few generalizations can be made.[2] (See Figure 2–1.)

FIGURE 2-1   Prototype of State Court Structure

STATE'S HIGHEST APPELLATE COURT

(Variously Named Supreme Court, Court of Errors, Court of Appeals)

INTERMEDIATE APPELLATE COURTS

(in about Half the States)

MAJOR TRIAL COURTS

such as

Common Pleas Courts, District Courts, Superior Courts, Domestic
Relations Courts, Probate Courts

MINOR TRIAL COURTS

such as

Justice-of-the-Peace Courts, City Courts, Police Courts, Night Courts,
Traffic Courts, Juvenile Courts, Small Claims Courts

Every state has several tiers of trial courts (courts of first instance to which new cases are initially brought for hearing) and at least one appellate court (a higher court in which trial court decisions can be reviewed). There is normally a division between minor trial courts (for example, municipal courts and small claims courts) and major trial courts (for example, county common pleas courts) in which the jurisdictional distinction is based on the amount of money in controversy (in civil cases) or the maximum possible term of incarceration (in criminal cases). About half the states have intermediate appellate courts that sit above the trial courts but beneath the state's supreme court. Every state has a supreme court that, like the United States Supreme court, is the court of last resort, the ultimate tribunal for the state's legal system. If, however, a case that has arisen in a state court system involves a substantial federal question requiring an interpretation of the United States Constitution, a federal law, or a treaty, the usual autonomy of the state court may give way to appellate review by the federal courts. This can happen in one of two ways. First, federal district courts (described later in this chapter) can grant a habeas corpus review to defendants in state criminal proceedings if they allege their constitutional rights are being violated by the state courts. One possible result of such a review is a federal injunction against the state court proceeding. However, adhering to the general principle of "comity," by which one court defers as a matter of legal courtesy to another court that has already begun proceedings in a case, the federal courts rarely grant such reviews. Indeed, while such federal court review of allegedly faulty state criminal proceedings was not uncommon during the Warren era,[3] the Burger Court of the 1970s and 1980s and the current Court have expanded the concept of comity, thereby reducing substantially the actual instances of such reviews.[4] Consequently, unless the U.S. Supreme Court later agrees to a direct review of the matter after the state supreme court affirms the conviction (a review rarely granted in practice), federal court review of alleged violations of constitutional rights by state criminal courts is now nearly eliminated. Direct appeal from a state supreme court to the U.S. Supreme Court is the second way, then, that the autonomy of state courts is occasionally weakened. This happens when a case decided by a state supreme court involves a federal question and all possible remedies have been exhausted at the state level. (A complete analysis of the methods and channels of U.S. Supreme Court review is presented in Chapter Four.) In an average year, however, the U.S. Supreme Court agrees to hear only 7 percent of the cases appealed to it from all the state supreme courts. For the most part, then, the jurisdictional lines between the state and federal courts are respected and the state and federal judiciaries remain distinct systems. This separation is preserved largely because state courts are preoccupied with the relatively narrow problems of private law (for example, disputes between private parties involving property, contracts, or torts), whereas the federal courts deal far more frequently with public law questions (for example, constitutional construction and the interpretation of congressional statutes). Benjamin Cardozo, who served on both the supreme court of New York state and the U.S. Supreme Court, contrasted the two as follows: "[the state supreme court] is a great common law court; its problems are lawyers' problems. But the Supreme Court is occupied chiefly with statutory construction . . . and with politics."[5] We turn now to a description of the federal judicial system over which the Supreme Court presides.

Standing at the base of the national court system and serving as its workhorses are the United States district courts. Originally thirteen in number, there are now a total of ninety-four U.S. district courts staffed by a total of 577 district court judges. The ninety-four district courts sit at locations designated by congressional statute. There is at least one district court in each state. Many states have two or three districts; a few have four. Many districts are subdivided into a number of locations where the court will hear cases.[6] The number of judges in a district varies considerably with the amount of judicial business in the territory: Idaho, Rhode Island, and the Northern District of West Virginia have only one judge; the Southern District of California (centered in Los Angeles) and the Northern District of Illinois (centered in Chicago) have twelve judges; and the Southern District of New York, including Manhattan, has twenty-five judges.[7] In districts with more than one judge, the most senior member of the court presides as its chief judge until he or she reaches 70 years of age. Judges over 70 years old may remain on the court but must relinquish the chief judgeship.

The U.S. district courts are the federal judiciary's general jurisdiction trial courts. They can hear all criminal and civil cases for which Congress has provided by statute. Their jurisdiction is in part exclusive and in part overlapping with state trial courts. Basically four types of cases are heard by the U.S district courts. First, all prosecutions of violations of national criminal statutes are initiated on the district level by the U.S. attorney for the district. Traditionally, however, most criminal law enforcement is done on the state and local level. Federal jurisdiction over criminal cases thus exists only when Congress has specified criminal offenses by statute. The major area of criminal jurisdiction for the U.S. district courts are robbery, assault, burglary, narcotics offenses, and immigration violations.[8] Since the mid-1960s, federal criminal jurisdiction has expanded as national concern over organized crime and drug abuse resulted in the passage of the Omnibus Crime Control and Safe Streets Act of 1968 and the Drug Abuse and Prevention Control Act of 1971. In an average year approximately 40,000 criminal cases are initiated in the ninety-four U.S. district courts, and we can expect federal district court jurisdiction over criminal cases to continue to grow as long as the Congress enacts criminal statutes.

Civil actions in which a party attempts to protect a right or seek payment for a wrong make up the other three types of cases heard by U.S. district courts. The first of these are suits brought under congressional statutes such as Antitrust, Civil Rights, Social Security, and Truth in Lending. Suits of this type have increased in recent years with congressional passage of various social welfare policies and other laws protecting sundry civil rights, privileges, and immunities. In an average year approximately 85,000 civil actions of this nature are initiated in the U.S. district courts. The second type of civil case heard by the U.S. district courts are those involving "federal questioning." A federal question exists when a party alleges an injury in excess of $10,000 has resulted from application of a federal law, a treaty, or the Constitution. Approximately 60,000 such cases are initiated in an average year. Finally, the U.S. district courts hear so-called diversity cases. These are civil actions that do not involve federal law but are suits in which the sum in controversy exceeds $10,000 and the parties are citizens of different states ("diversity of citizenship").[9] The purpose of this jurisdiction is to guarantee that when the dispute divides citizens of different states, and even though state law will be used to resolve the dispute, the parties will have access to a neutral federal forum. However, concerned over the heavy workload of the district courts, many judges and court administrators have urged that this diversity jurisdiction be eliminated. In doing so, they point out, about 35,000 cases would be removed from the overcrowded dockets of the district courts, about a 16 percent reduction in their total annual workload of 220,000 cases. It should be emphasized that the average annual workload of 220,000 cases in the 1980s represents an increase of about 175 percent since 1970.

United States district court cases are normally heard by one judge. Occasionally, however a three-judge panel will hear a case on the district level when, under guidelines provided for in congressional statutes, one of the parties convinces the court that an important question of constitutional law is involved in the case and that a proper disposition will require some sort of constitutional construction. At least one of the three judges must be a U.S. court of appeals judge from the circuit (described below) in which that particular district court is located and any appeal that follows the decision must be directed to the Supreme Court rather than to the court of appeals for that circuit as would be the practice in single-judge cases. However, "to relieve the burden of the three-judge court cases [which have] caused considerable strain on the workload of federal judges,"[10] Congress passed legislation in 1976 abolishing three-judge panels except in legislative reapportionment cases or unless specifically provided for in federal laws such as the Civil Rights Act of 1964.[11] Even before this legislatively mandated restriction, however, to limit its own workload the Supreme Court had tended to interpret strictly the various laws providing for three-judge cases because appeals from three-judge panels go directly to the Supreme Court as a matter of right.[12]

For all practical purposes most U.S. district court decisions are final. They either are not appealed or, if appealed, are sustained.[13] Of the 220,000 federal district court filings in an average year, only about 11 percent are appealed to the U.S. courts of appeals. These appeals make up about 85 percent of the annual workload of the federal judiciary's intermediate appellate courts. It is to the structure of these courts that we next turn our attention.

Intermediate appellate courts have existed on the national level from the beginning. The Judiciary Act of 1789, which created the original 13 U.S. district courts, also created three "circuit courts" to sit between the district courts and the U.S. Supreme Court. Each circuit court had three judges—one district court judge from the circuit and two Supreme Court justices. (There were originally only six Supreme Court justices, two assigned to each of the three circuits.) The term *circuit* stemmed from the medieval English practice by which royal justices were sent out to different parts of the realm. This practice was imitated in the original national judiciary when Supreme Court justices literally "rode circuit" in pursuit of their intermediate appellate court assignments. Although Supreme Court justices no longer ride circuit, the term continues to be used to designate the geographical areas served by the U.S. courts of appeals and, loosely, as a synonym for those courts themselves.[14]

Presently, there are thirteen U.S. courts of appeals, one for each of 11 numbered circuits, one with general jurisdiction for the District of Columbia, and one with specialized jurisdiction (over patent appeals and claims against the United States) called the Court of Appeals for the Federal Circuit. Each of the 11 numbered circuits covers several states. The First Circuit (Massachusetts, New Hampshire, Maine, and Rhode Island) is the smallest, with only four judges. The Ninth Circuit (Alaska, Hawaii, California, Oregon, Washington, Idaho, Montana, Nevada, and Arizona) is the largest, with twenty-three judges. There are now a total of 156 authorized judgeships for the courts of appeals, a 61 percent increase over the 97 authorized by law prior to the 1978 Judgeship Act. There are twelve judges on the special Court of Appeals for the Federal Circuit, which is a relatively new court created in 1982. Courts of appeals normally hear cases in panels consisting of three judges; but in particularly important cases or when there is substantial disagreement among various members of the court, the judges may sit *en banc,* that is, as a complete group on the bench. Normally, this happens only after a three-judge panel has heard the case.

In the 1980s about 30,000 cases were docketed per year in the U.S. courts of appeals. This represents an increase of about 220 percent since 1970. About 25,000 of these (85 percent) are appeals from the U.S. district courts. Losing litigants in U.S. district courts can appeal to the court of appeals of the circuit in which the district court is located merely by filing a notice of appeal with the district court within 30 days after judgment was reached. There are no restrictions other than the time factor,[15] and the courts of appeals must hear all cases brought to them.[16] Appeals from the district courts can bypass the courts of appeals and go directly to the Supreme Court in only three instances: (1) appeals of decisions by three-judge panels (as described above), (2) appeals of decisions declaring an act of Congress unconstitutional, and (3) appeals of decisions regarded as so important as to require immediate resolution.[17]

The remaining 5,000 cases docketed in an average year in the courts of appeals are reviews of decisions made in the quasi-judicial processes of such federal administrative agencies as the National Labor Relations Board (NLRB), the Internal Revenue Service (IRS), the Interstate Commerce Commission (ICC), and the Securities and Exchange Commission (SEC). Some of these cases are heard in the numbered appeals court for the circuit in which the controversy arises. Most are heard by the Court of Appeals for the District of Columbia, where the agency's headquarters are located. Some, such as certain Federal Communications Commission (FCC) and Environmental Protection Agency (EPA) cases are required by statute to be heard by the D.C. Circuit Court.[18]

It is very important to note that the U.S. courts of appeals are for all practical purposes the courts of last resort in the overwhelming majority of federal cases. Normally less than 20 percent of their decisions are appealed; and the Supreme Court, with its great discretion to hear or not hear appeals, reviews less than 10 percent of the decisions appealed. Thus, well over 90 percent of the decisions reached by the U.S. courts of appeals become final judgments.

Before describing the structure and workload of the U.S. Supreme Court itself, we must observe that there are a few specialized federal courts, not yet mentioned, whose decisions are, but only rarely, appealed to the Supreme Court. As we learn later in this chapter, the U.S. district courts, U.S. courts of appeals, and U.S. Supreme Court are generally referred to as "constitutional courts" because they are created by Article III of the Constitution to exercise the federal judicial power. The Supreme Court is expressly created by Article III, and the district and appellate courts are created by Congress under authority granted to it in Article III. There are in addition, however, some other national courts generally referred to as "administrative" or "legislative" courts that Congress has created under authority granted to it in Article I. One example is the U.S. Tax Court created by Congress under its authority to levy taxes (Article I, Section 8, Clause 1). This institution, composed of a chief judge and 15 associate judges, is an independent executive agency that adjudicates controversies involving excessive or deficient payment of income taxes, estate taxes, gift taxes, and excess profits. Its judgments are reviewable by the Supreme Court. A second example is the U.S. Court of Military Appeals created by Congress under its authorization to "make rules for the . . . regulation of the land and naval forces" (Article I, Section 8, Clause 14). This institution, located in the Defense Department and composed of three civilian judges appointed for 15-year terms, hears appeals from the decisions of court martials in which a general or admiral has been convicted or in which any armed forces personnel have been sentenced to death. Again, its judgments are reviewable but in practice are rarely reviewed by the Supreme Court.

Finally, we reach the U.S. Supreme Court itself, the nation's highest court and the only national court created directly by the Constitution. Although Congress is thus presumably obligated to maintain a Supreme Court, it need not provide the Supreme Court with funds and it controls the Court's appellate jurisdiction. Congress also controls the number of justices on the Court. Originally set at six, the number has been changed to five (1801–02), to seven (1802–37), to nine (1837–63), to ten (1863–66), to seven (1866–69), and finally to nine again in 1869, where it has remained since. Six justices constitute a quorum. The Court is headed by the chief justice of the United States, who, though not always its predominant member, is its presiding officer. His formal authority consists of presiding over the open sessions of the Court and over the judicial conferences (closed meetings in which the justices discuss and decide cases), assigning the writing of opinions when he is a part of the majority and supervising judicial administration for the entire national court system.[19]

An elaborate consideration of the methods and channels of review by which the Court hears cases, including detailed analyses of access, justiciability, and standing to sue, is reserved for Chapter Four. Here we will describe the sources from which the Court receives its cases and its average annual workload. (See Figure 2–2.) The Supreme Court is primarily an appellate court, but not a "workaday appellate tribunal" obligated to hear every mundane or detailed legal question put to it. Indeed, the general tenor of twentieth-century congressional legislation regulating the Court's jurisdiction has been to give the Court almost complete discretion

FIGURE 2–2   Structure and Workload of the Federal Judicial System

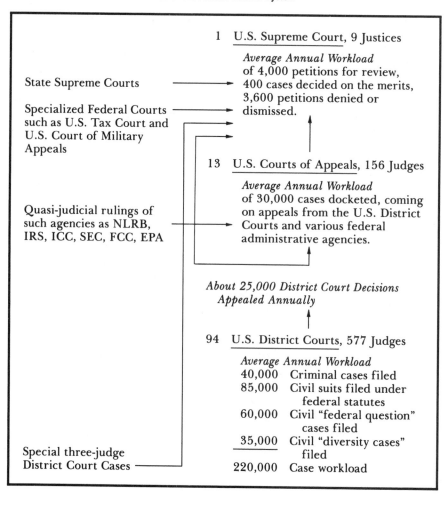

to pick the cases it will hear. These are generally cases of wide public interest or great constitutional importance. In short, the court has nearly complete freedom to play a "selective policy role."[20] It receives petitions for review from five sources: (1) direct appeals from the U.S. district courts, for example, when the district court has invalidated an act of Congress or when the United States is a party to the dispute; (2) appeals from three-judge district court panels; (3) appeals from the U.S. courts of appeals; (4) appeals from the specialized federal courts; and (5) appeals from state supreme courts. In an average year the Supreme Court receives approximately 4,000 petitions for review. It will normally agree to hear and make a decision on the merits (a substantive decision) in only about 8–10 percent (325–400) of these cases. About 150 of these are decided with a full written opinion explaining the Court's decision; the remainder are decided by per curiam opinions (short, unsigned opinions written "by the Court" rather than by one justice) and by memorandum orders (short notices) vacating (annulling or setting aside) the lower court decisions. The rest of the petitions for review (90–92 percent in an average year) are denied or dismissed.

THE SUPREME COURT'S PLACE IN THE JUDICIAL SYSTEM

From the beginning the existence of the dual court system has produced a struggling relationship between national and state courts. The creation of the initial national judiciary (consisting of district and circuit courts) by the Judiciary Act of 1789 constituted a victory in the first Congress for those fighting for a strong central government because it meant that the new national government would not have to depend on the cooperation of the already existing state courts to enforce its laws. At the same time, however, the state governments did retain their own courts, thus attesting to their continued autonomy and creating the complex and struggling relationships between national and state courts suggested here. From the outset the national courts have appeared to have the better of this struggle. According to the supremacy clause of the Constitution, the "Constitution, and the Laws of the United States which shall be made in pursuance thereof, and all Treaties . . . shall be the supreme law of the land, and the judges in every state shall be bound thereby, anything in the constitution or laws of any state to the contrary notwithstanding" (Article VI, Section 2). To help guarantee this supremacy of national law over state law, Congress wrote Section 25 into the Judiciary Act of 1789, thus giving the Supreme Court power to review and, if need be, overturn any state court decisions that had held against any claim made under the Constitution, laws, or treaties of the United States. When the validity of Section 25 was challenged in *Martin v. Hunter's Lessee*[21] in 1816, the Supreme Court held that (1) Section 25 is valid; the Supreme Court can review any state court decision that denies a claim based on the Constitution or national law or treaty; (2) although state courts, too, can initially rule on such matters, they are not "coequal" with the Supreme Court in authority—the Supreme Court is the final arbiter of constitutional issues; and (3) state courts are bound by Supreme Court decisions on these issues. Thus, by constitutional provision, by congressional statute, and by Supreme Court decision the supremacy of the Supreme Court over state judiciaries appeared secure as early as 1816.[22]

The judicial *power* of the Supreme Court, that is, its *general* authority to hear and decide cases, is conferred by the Constitution directly. According to Article III, Section 2, Clause 2, the court's power extends to

1. all cases in law and equity arising under the Constitution, laws, and treaties of the United States;
2. all cases affecting ambassadors, other public ministers, and consuls;
3. all cases of admiralty and maritime jurisdiction;
4. controversies between two or more states;
5. controversies to which the United States is a party;
6. controversies between a state and citizens of another state;
7. controversies between citizens of different states;
8. controversies between citizens of the same state claiming lands under grants of different states; and
9. controversies between a state or its citizens and foreign states, citizens, or subjects.

The *jurisdiction* of the Supreme Court, that is, its *particular* authority to hear certain kinds of cases, is of two types: its "original jurisdiction" (to hear cases of first instance as a trial court), which is also conferred directly by the Constitution; and its "appellate jurisdiction" (to hear cases on an appeal from state and lower federal courts), which is conferred by the Constitution but *subject to congressional regulation.* Because the Court's place in the judicial system as well as its power in the political system are so utterly dependent on this matter of jurisdiction, we will address the problems associated with it here, though leaving technical dimensions and current controversies to later chapters.

One of the few unambiguous provisions of the Constitution is the "original jurisdiction" clause (Article III, Section 2, Clause 2). This clause states that the Supreme Court can hear as a trial court, that is, without prior consideration by another court, only two types of cases: those involving diplomatic representatives of foreign states and those in which a state of the Union is one of the parties. Because this jurisdiction is precisely provided for in the Constitution, it can be changed, contracted, or enlarged only by constitutional amendment. Congress alone cannot tamper with it. For a variety of reasons, however, the Court hears very few cases under its original jurisdiction. Indeed, in its entire history, the Court has adjudicated less than 200 such cases. The source of the great bulk of the Court's work, and that which gives the Court both its towering legal stature and its prodigious political clout, is its appellate jurisdiction. But the "appellate jurisdiction" clause is anything but unambiguous. It states that in all cases other than those over which it has original jurisdiction, "the Court shall have appellate jurisdiction . . . with such exceptions, and under such regulations as the Congress shall make." Technically, then, the Constitution grants appellate jurisdiction to the Court; Congress is merely empowered to limit that jurisdiction. Perhaps if Congress had never made any exceptions, the Court under Article III alone could hear cases on appeal under whatever rules it wanted to establish for itself. This is now immaterial, however, because Congress has from 1789 regulated the Court's appellate jurisdiction, and the Court has acquiesced in these regulations. Thus, in law the Constitution positively grants appellate jurisdiction to the Court, and the Congress has only a negative, limiting power to make exceptions to it. In practice, though, the Congress positively grants the authority. But what does this mean? Does it mean that Congress has the power to cut off the Court's appellate jurisdiction in part? Or totally? Could a Congress in which the majority disapproves of abortion remove from the Court's jurisdiction the power to review a state supreme court's decision to uphold a state anti-abortion law? Could a Congress in which the majority favors school prayer remove from the Court's jurisdiction the power to review a state supreme court's decision to uphold a state or local school prayer policy? Is the Congress governed by constitutional requirements of due process when it regulates the Court's jurisdiction, or could it flagrantly defy the Constitution by making appeals to the Court depend on the race, religion, or partisan affiliation of the appellant? Or, on the contrary, does the "exceptions and regulations" clause mean that the Congress has no control over the substantive legal issues the Court can hear but merely has the authority to regulate the Court's docket with reasonable housekeeping measures (such as the legislation described earlier that has given the Court wider and wider discretion to hear only those cases it regards as of great constitutional importance)? Certainly most constitutional scholars would agree that the Congress may not use the exceptions and regulations clause to interfere with the Court's "essential functions." But it is a historical fact that the Congress did use its control over the Court's appellate jurisdiction for policy purposes in 1869 when, fearing the court would invalidate the Reconstruction Acts, Congress prevented the Court from determining their validity by withdrawing the Court's jurisdiction established under the Habeas Corpus Act of 1867. Although the Supreme Court itself upheld this regulation of its jurisdiction,[23] it did so under the dire circumstances of the Civil War and Reconstruction. Most legal scholars conclude that this 100-year-old precedent would not stand today. Still, this precedent for substantive Congressional control over the Court's appellate jurisdiction is being invoked today in support of similar court-curbing proposals now pending in Congress. (We will deal with these in Chapter Nine).

What the foregoing discussion is designed to emphasize is that the Supreme Court's judicial power and its appellate jurisdiction are at once the source of its political strength and limited by political factors. Not only are *substantive political issues* decided in this storm center of American politics, but also the Court is the center of stormy *procedural debates* over the kinds of issues it should hear and the conditions under which it should hear them. In Chapters Seven and Eight we will examine the history of its handling of substantive political issues, and in Chapter Nine we will consider a variety of interpretations regarding its proper role. We now conclude this chapter with a preliminary consideration of the political factors that shape the Court's role in the judicial system.

THE IMPACT OF POLITICAL FACTORS ON THE SUPREME COURT'S PLACE IN THE SYSTEM

Political factors have shaped the Supreme Court's place in both the judicial system and the political system from the beginning. As we have seen, the very creation of the federal judiciary by the first Congress was a political victory for those favoring a strong national government. For over 100 years thereafter the expansion of the federal judiciary was affected by the politics and political ideologies of nationalism versus localism.[24] To a large degree the extent to which state courts have remained vital institutions is attributable to the unabashed efforts of state court judges to preserve their independence from the national judiciary. Studies indicate, for example, that when state court judges can find no precise precedent in their own state's law, they are much more likely to cite precedents from the courts of other states than they are to cite precedents from the national courts. The very existence of a dual court system creates a strategic environment in which state courts are encouraged to struggle for continued autonomy. Duality creates alternative forums from which plaintiffs can choose. Indeed, there is considerable evidence that different forums produce different outcomes, particularly when state courts strive to evade Supreme Court rulings.[25] Even today political preferences among Supreme Court justices for deference to state courts motivate debates within the Court over the principle of comity. The relationship of the Court to lower courts, both federal and state, and the Court's role in policy making are determined largely by differing political preferences among the justices regarding access to the Court. Some justices believe the Court's highest mission is to

conserve its judicial credibility by remaining aloof from political controversy. To them, this should be done by stern "gatekeeping"—deference to
the decisions of lower courts and denial of access to those raising political
issues. Others believe that it is abdication for the Court to close its doors to
those who believe their constitutional rights have been violated. To them,
the Court is the one and only place where relief can be obtained, and they
would grant access to the Court's powers to both individuals and groups
who want to act as "private attorneys general" seeking to protect constitutional liberties. Indeed, the entire operation of the Court can be viewed as a
political circle: (1) Political factors shape the appointment of the Court's
justices, who are selected largely because they have been active in politics,
they support the right political party at the right time, and their political
ideologies comport with those of the appointing authority;[26] (2) their appointments are frequently the subject of political controversy; (3) political
interest groups bring political issues to the Court's attention; (4) the Court's
justices often decide these issues according to their political preferences;
(5) their decisions generate political conflict within the judicial system and
within society at large; and (6) the justices are in turn both applauded and
criticized for their politics.[27]

Of course, this is just another way of stating that the Supreme Court is,
above all else, a political institution. This is not a new revelation despite the
best efforts of most justices to be modest about it.[28] All the Court's decisions, including those to deny access and thereby not decide in a particular
case, are political decisions. To defer to other courts and other branches is
merely a procedural form of substantive power. Decisions made according
to what some justices might call "neutral principles," that is "objective decisions" that transcend the immediate result, inevitably involve taking sides.
And "judicial restraint" is just one form of "judicial activism" because a
judicial "hands-off" position has the practical effect of preserving the political status quo.[29] In short, the Supreme Court is a political institution whose
justices are political actors and whose decisions are often a product of policy
preferences.

It should not be surprising, then, that the Court would encounter
political opposition. Even restricting our chronicle of such opposition to the
twentieth century yields numerous examples. In 1913 a successful effort
was made to circumvent the Court by constitutional amendment. This occurred when the Sixteenth Amendment overturned a politically unpopular
decision to invalidate a federal income tax.[30] (A full discussion of efforts to
circumvent the Court via constitutional amendment and the possibility of a
Court counterattack attempting to circumvent the amendment process via
judicial activism is presented in Chapter Nine, which deals with the Court-
curbing proposals of the late 1980s.) Political attacks on the Court have
come from liberals as well as conservatives. When the Court struck down
many pieces of progressive social legislation early in the twentieth century

(for example, minimum wage, maximum hour, and child labor laws), liberals introduced legislation in Congress calling for the popular election and recall of the Court's justices. When the Court struck down liberal New Deal legislation in the 1930s, President Roosevelt proposed a bill increasing the Court's membership, hoping to "pack" the Court with political allies who would favor his legislative program. When the Court banned racial segregation in the public schools in 1954, conservatives introduced legislation in Congress proposing to remove desegregation cases from the Court's jurisdiction. When the Court required that legislative districts be equal in size (the "one man, one vote" decisions) in 1962, conservatives introduced legislation to remove reapportionment decisions from the Court's jurisdiction. Finally, in the late 1960s, as conservatives grew increasingly unhappy with Warren Court decisions, there came a proposal to create a "Court of the Union," composed of the chief justices of the 50 state supreme courts, to review U.S. Supreme Court decisions.[31]

The Court's highly politicized character clearly distinguishes it from the highest court of law in virtually all other countries, including other democracies. Its politicized character is directly attributable to its centrality to the making of public policy. The one thing that enables it to be a policy maker more frequently than the high courts of other countries is its power of *judicial review,* which permits the Supreme Court to consider and, if necessary, invalidate acts of Congress and actions of the president. The origins of this power, its policy-making potential, and debates regarding its propriety are fully considered in subsequent chapters. It must be emphasized here, however, that it is the power of judicial review that makes the Supreme Court much more than just a court of law. Judicial review enables the Court to play the roles of "council of elders" and "schoolmaster" of the Republic. It necessarily involves the Court in the policy process and inevitably subjects the Court to political controversy. (1) *The Court can override the will of the majority expressed in acts of Congress.* It has done so more than 100 times in our history, including such relatively recent decisions as those invalidating sections of the Fair Labor Standards Act, which extended minimum wage protections to the employees of state and local governments,[32] and invalidating certain provisions of the Social Security Act for discriminating unfairly between men and women.[33] Indeed, in 1980 the justices gave themselves a pay raise by invalidating sections of the Legislative Appropriations Act, which had rescinded two cost-of-living increases in federal judicial salaries.[34] In 1986 the Court invalidated a crucial provision of the Gramm-Rudman budget-balancing law.[35] (2) *The Court can generate legitimacy and support for hastily enacted or politically unpopular acts of Congress by upholding them when their legality is challenged.* Recent examples of this legitimating power include the Court's decision to uphold an act of Congress restricting the use of federal funds for abortions,[36] its holding that Congress can exclude women from the draft registration law,[37] and its decision to sustain a congressional requirement that strip-mined lands be carefully restored.[38] (3) *The Court can forcefully remind the president that he, like other Americans, is not above the law,* as the Court's ruling in the famous "Watergate Tapes" case dramatically demonstrated.[39] (4) *The Court can mandate the redistribution of political power in every state of the nation,* as it did in the reapportionment cases. (5) *The Court can tell the public that the fabric of society must be rewoven into new patterns,* as it has in the various abortion, pornography, and criminal justice cases described earlier in this book.[40]

Scholars have long debated the propriety of the Supreme Court's power of judicial review. That debate, though usually intense, is largely irrelevant. As Wilfred E. Binkley and Malcolm C. Moos have written, the power of judicial review has been "woven into the warp and woof of our constitutional fabric so completely that the garment could not scarcely endure its elimination."[41] Politically, the power of judicial review has never been seriously threatened, and the Supreme Court has become the most powerful court the world has ever known. We live under the Constitution, but as Chief Justice Hughes once remarked, the Constitution means what the United States Supreme Court says it means. In Chapter Three, we will examine the evolution of the Court and its Constitution in American history.

NOTES

[1] Herbert Jacob, *Justice in America* (Boston: Little, Brown, 1978), pp. 149–51.

[2] William C. Louthan, *The Politics of Justice* (Port Washington, N.Y.: Kennikat Press, 1979), pp. 41–46.

[3] *Fay v. Noia,* 372 U.S. 391 (1963); and *Henry v. Mississippi,* 379 U.S. 443 (1965).

[4] *Stone v. Powell,* 428 U.S. 465 (1976).

[5] Robert H. Jackson, *The Supreme Court in the American System of Government* (Cambridge: Harvard University Press, 1955), p. 54.

[6] Jerome R. Corsi, *Judicial Politics* (Englewood Cliffs, N.J.: Prentice Hall, 1984), pp. 181–82.

[7] Stephen L. Wasby, *The Supreme Court in the Federal Judicial System* (New York: Holt, Rinehart & Winston, 1984), p. 33.

[8] Howard Ball, *Courts and Politics: The Federal Judicial System* (Englewood Cliffs, N.J.: Prentice Hall, 1980), pp. 91–97.

[9] Louthan, *The Politics of Justice,* p. 47.

[10] Ball, *Courts and Politics,* p. 71.

[11] Wasby, *The Supreme Court,* p. 35.

[12] C. Herman Pritchett, *The American Constitution* (New York: McGraw-Hill, 1977), pp. 92–93.

[13] Wasby, *The Supreme Court,* p. 34.

[14] Louthan, *The Politics of Justice,* p. 49.

[15] Ball, *Courts and Politics,* p. 99.

[16] Wasby, *The Supreme Court,* p. 44.

[17] Corsi, *Judicial Politics,* p. 186.

[18] Wasby, *The Supreme Court,* p. 43.

[19] Louthan, *The Politics of Justice,* p. 51.

[20] Kenneth J. Richardson and Richard N. Vines, *The Politics of the Federal Courts* (Boston: Little, Brown, 1970), p. 32.

[21] 1 Wheaton 304 (1816).

[22] Louthan, *The Politics of Justice,* pp. 39–40.

[23] *Ex Parte McCardle,* 74 U.S. (7 Wall.) 506 (1869).

[24] Ball, *Courts and Politics,* pp. 275–76.

[25] Stuart Nagel, "Sociometric Relations among American Courts," *Southwest Social Science Quarterly* 43 (1962), pp. 136–42; Note, "State Court Evasion of United States Supreme Court Mandates," *Yale Law Journal* 56 (1967), pp. 574–83; and Louthan, *The Politics of Justice,* pp. 40–41.

[26] Ball, *Courts and Politics,* p. 280.

[27] Lawrence Baum, *The Supreme Court* (Washington, D.C.: Congressional Quarterly Press, 1981), pp. 1–2.

[28] Robert H. Birkby, *The Court and Public Policy* (Washington, D.C.: Congressional Quarterly Press, 1983), p. 1.

[29] Laurence H. Tribe, *American Constitutional Law* (Mineola, N.Y.: Foundation Press, 1978), pp. iv–v.

[30] *Pollock v. Farmer's Loan and Trust Company,* 158 U.S. 601 (1895).

[31] Irving R. Kaufman, "Congress vs. the Court," *New York Times Magazine* (September 20, 1981), pp. 44–54.

[32] *National League of Cities v. Usery,* 426 U.S. 833 (1976), though this decision has since been reversed.

[33] *Califano v. Wescott,* 443 U.S. 76 (1979).

[34] *United States v. Will,* 449 U.S. 200 (1980).

[35] *Bowsher v. Synar,* 106 S. Ct. 3181 (1986).

[36] *Harris v. McRae,* 448 U.S. 297 (1980).

[37] *Rostker v. Goldberg,* 453 U.S. 57 (1981).

[38] *Hodel v. Indiana,* 452 U.S. 314 (1981).

[39] *U.S. v. Nixon,* 418 U.S. 683 (1974).

[40] Congressional Quarterly, *The Supreme Court and Its Work* (Washington, D.C.: Congressional Quarterly Press, 1981), pp. 1, 52–53.

[41] Wilfred E. Binkley and Malcolm C. Moos, *A Grammar of American Politics: The National Government* (New York: Knopf, 1958), pp. 519–20.

III

The Supreme Court in American History
A Council of Elders

THE SUPREME COURT IN THE EIGHTEENTH CENTURY

The Supreme Court was created neither out of practical necessity nor because the role envisioned for it was indispensable, but because the framers of the Constitution felt theoretically compelled to arrange for a separation of powers and a system of checks and balances. Indeed, there is little evidence that the framers had any clearly formulated ideas about the Court's role.[1] The paramount tasks in the new government were to be legislative and administrative. The court's role, ambiguous at best, was to be comparatively minor.[2] Although most of the influential framers of the Constitution evidently assumed the Court would exercise the power of judicial review in cases properly before it, they failed to place a flat written statement of that power in the document. The Congress, which in its first session provided for judicial review of state court rulings, did not grant a parallel authority to the Court to nullify acts of Congress or actions of the president. Consequently, during its first decade of operation (1790–99) the Supreme Court got off to a very slow start.

In the beginning the Court was to hold two sessions each year, commencing in February and August. However, only three of the original six justices showed up for the Court's first session on February 1, 1790, in the Royal Exchange Building in New York City, the first capital. The second session, in August, lasted only two days. When the capital moved to Philadelphia in 1791, the Supreme Court shared a room with the mayor's court in the new city hall. But the Court decided no cases in either 1791 or 1792. The Court continued to meet in Philadelphia until 1800, but its August sessions were cancelled three times because of yellow fever epidemics.[3] During its entire first decade, in fact, the Court decided fewer than 50 cases.[4]

At the end of its first decade, then, the Supreme Court was not yet a significant actor in national policy making, and its relative unimportance was reflected in personnel matters. Robert Hanson Harrison, one of President Washington's six appointees to the first Court, declined the nomination apparently because he thought his post as chancellor of Maryland was more important. His replacement, James Iredell, served only until 1799, when he resigned. John Rutledge, a second of the original nominees, never attended a session of the Court and resigned in 1791 to take a state judgeship in South Carolina.[5] His replacement, Thomas Johnson, served less than two years, resigning in 1793. John Blair, a third of the original appointees, attended only irregularly and resigned for reasons of poor health in 1796. The chief justice, John Jay, spent much of his time out of the country on various diplomatic missions. After negotiating Jay's Treaty with Britain in 1798, Jay resigned from the Court to become governor of New York. The fifth of Washington's initial appointees, James Wilson, died in office in 1798. Thus, among Washington's first six choices for the court, only the sixth, William Cushing, served into the nineteenth century.[6]

Although the Supreme Court was not yet a powerful independent branch of government, a few of its pre–nineteenth-century decisions were notable. One was so controversial that it became the first Court decision to be directly overturned by constitutional amendment. Another assumed the power of judicial review though the law involved was upheld. A third suggested an approach, later adopted, by which the justices could write into the law their own views of right and wrong. We will examine each of these cases briefly.

The first major case of the decade was *Chisholm v. Georgia*, decided in 1793.[7] This case involved the administration of an estate whose assets were held by Georgia, a state of the Union. The plaintiffs, executors of the estate, were citizens of South Carolina. The broad issue presented was whether Georgia, as a "sovereign state," could be sued in the federal courts by citizens of another state without its consent. The Supreme Court's resolution of the matter was strongly nationalist in tone. The Court read the language of Article III literally where it states that the federal judicial power shall extend to controversies between a state and citizens of another state. When Georgia joined the Union, she gave up a portion of her sovereignty. "As to the purposes of the Union," Georgia is not a sovereign state. It is "causes" not "parties to causes" which come before the Court. Thus, Georgia is amenable to the jurisdiction of the national judiciary and suable in the federal courts by a citizen of another state.

This case is notable for several reasons. First, it shows that the Court is not infallible. Most of the framers of the Constitution were still alive in 1793, and they made it clear that they had intended nothing like what the Court had ruled. Second, it shows that if there were those in the early Republic who expected the Court to be a minor institution, they now had to recognize that although this Court might not be politically unassailable, it was a force to be taken seriously and reckoned with. Third, it shows that the Court can be overruled. The decision shocked most state governments, which saw it as leading to their financial ruin. Thus, just five years later the Eleventh Amendment was added to the Constitution, directly overturning *Chisholm* by exempting from federal judicial scrutiny suits against a state initiated by citizens of another state.[8]

A second major case of the decade was *Hylton v. U.S.*[9] decided in 1796. In a strict legal sense, this case merely presented a narrow technical question requiring the Court to define what the Constitution meant by "direct taxes." The Constitution clearly stated that direct taxes must be apportioned among the states by population, but it did not otherwise define direct taxes or provide examples. The Court became involved when Congress, in 1794, levied a $16 tax on carriages and the constitutionality of the tax was challenged. The challengers claimed the tax was a direct tax and must be laid in proportion to the census, but the Supreme Court ruled that direct taxes are only those on land and on individuals; thus the carriage tax was not a direct tax and was not subject to the apportionment requirement. In short, the carriage tax law was valid. The broader significance of the *Hylton* case, however, is its implication that the Supreme Court possessed the power of judicial review. *Hylton* had brought to the Court the first clear challenge to an act of Congress as unconstitutional. The Court had upheld the law, but the very fact that the Court conducted the review at all, the very process of considering the validity of the law, implied the power to invalidate if necessary.

A third notable case of the decade, and one whose long-term significance is commonly overlooked, was the 1798 case of *Calder v. Bull.*[10] As in *Hylton*, the legal issue presented appears to be narrow and technical, this time involving a matter of probate law. In March 1793 a probate court in Hartford, Connecticut, disapproved a will under which Bull would have benefited. Under state law Bull had 18 months during which he could appeal the decision. He did not. Thus, by the spring of 1795 Calder, who had prevailed under the 1793 probate decision, had every reason to feel secure in his property rights under the contested will. However, in May 1795 the state legislature in Connecticut passed a law setting aside the original probate decree and granting a new hearing at which Bull won. Calder eventually appealed to the United States Supreme Court, arguing that the state law setting aside the earlier decision was invalid under the Constitution's provision against *ex post facto* laws. The Supreme Court held, however, that the *ex post facto* clause prohibits the retroactive application of criminal laws only, not civil laws. This was a significant holding because it would mean that the *ex post facto* clause could not be used to protect personal rights of property or contract. Though significant, the decision was not unexpected, nor has it been changed or even attacked during the nearly 200 years since it was handed down. Thus, the long-term significance of *Calder v. Bull* lies not in the legal issue presented but in the *warning* issued by Justice Samuel Chase in his opinion. Chase, appearing almost apologetic for the Court's decision against Calder, said that in the future, legislative provisions adversely affecting property rights might be invalidated by the Court, if no Constitutional provision was available to invalidate them, on the grounds that they violated general principles of liberty or abstract principles of justice as found in the collective natural law consciences of the justices. Although such an approach to adjudication did not catch on immediately, Chase's warning proved prophetic when, under the doctrine of "substantive due process" described later in this chapter, the Court began in the 1890s to supervise control of legislation in precisely the manner Justice Chase had advocated in the 1790s.

Still, prior to the nineteenth century, the Court was not yet capable of playing the role of full partner in national policy making. Nor was it yet strong enough to resist and overturn the policy making of the other branches of the national government. With a new century all that was to change.

A NEW CENTURY: JOHN MARSHALL, JUDICIAL REVIEW, AND NATIONAL SUPREMACY

From its inception in 1789 until 1800, the national government was controlled by the Federalist party of Presidents George Washington and John Adams. The Federalists occupied the presidency, held majority control of Congress, and appointed and confirmed the justices of the Supreme Court. Indeed, the only opposition held the hardly stirring label of anti-Federalists. But in 1800 Adams was defeated in his reelection bid by the opposition party's leader, Thomas Jefferson. Jefferson's party, now calling itself the Democratic-Republicans, also took control over Congress. In 1801 the capital was moved to Washington, D.C., where construction was begun on the Capitol Building for Congress and a temporary residence was found for Jefferson. For its deliberations the Supreme Court was allotted a small committee room in the as yet unfinished Capitol. Jefferson was eventually sworn in on March 4, 1801, but political machinations of long-term significance had occurred between the 1800 election and March 1801. Indeed, the year 1801 would become a political watershed, dividing not just two centuries but also two parties and two very powerful leaders,

President Thomas Jefferson and his lifelong political foe, the new chief justice of the United States, Federalist John Marshall.[11]

The story begins in the immediate aftermath of the election of 1800. John Adams was now a lame duck. By March 1801 both the presidency and the Congress would be controlled by the opposition Democratic-Republican party. The federal judiciary, however, still populated by Federalists appointed for life, would remain out of Jefferson's control. Adams acted quickly, using what little time he had left, to shore up Federalist control of the national courts. First, on January 20, 1801, Adams appointed his secretary of state, John Marshall, to the position of chief justice. Marshall was confirmed on January 27 and sworn in on February 4, 1801, at the beginning of the Supreme Court's first term in Washington. Then, also in February 1801, the outgoing Federalist Congress passed several judiciary acts, including the Circuit Court Act, which doubled the number of federal judges, and the Organic Act, which authorized the appointment of 42 justices-of-the-peace in the District of Columbia. The Judiciary Act of February 1901 also reduced the number of Supreme Court Justices from six to five and shifted the Court's sessions from February and August to June and December. Jefferson saw clearly that all this legislation was a Federalist ploy to enable Adams to entrench a Federalist judiciary and to protect the Supreme Court from any quick changes through appointments by the new president. Adams did little to discourage this interpretation when he filled the new judgeships and justice-of-the-peace positions with Federalist party loyalists. However, after Jefferson became president on March 4, 1801, the new Congress acted to undo as much as it could of Adams's manipulation of the judiciary. The Circuit Court Act Repeal Bill was passed in early 1802, as was a measure providing that the Supreme Court would have a single annual term (rather than two sessions) beginning each year in February. Because this latter measure was enacted after February 1802, it delayed the commencement of the next term until February 1803. As a result the Supreme Court did not meet during the 14-month period from December 1801 to February 1803. In effect, the Congress had cancelled the Court's 1802 term.[12]

These machinations provided the crucible in which Chief Justice John Marshall managed to forge a strong and independent Supreme Court. The process began with the most celebrated case in American constitutional history, *Marbury v. Madison*.[13] Though decided in 1803, this case arose from the circumstances of political change described above. Simply, William Marbury was one of the persons whom Adams had appointed to one of the justice-of-the-peace positions created by the Organic Act of 1801. His commission of appointment was prepared and signed but not delivered (by the secretary of state, whose job it was in those days to deliver commissions of appointment) before the end of the Adams administration at midnight March 3, 1801. The new president, Jefferson, ordered his secretary of state, James Madison, to withhold delivery of the commission. Marbury then filed an original suit with the Supreme Court requesting that the Court order Madison to deliver the commission. Since the 1802 term of the Court had been cancelled (by Jefferson's Congress to forestall the Federalist challenge to the constitutionality of the Repeal Act in the Supreme Court until the political power of the new administration had been strengthened), the case was not decided until February 24, 1803.

As a matter of law and logic Marshall's work in deciding *Marbury v. Madison* is flawed craftsmanship. As a matter of politics and power, however, it is pure artistry. Marshall ruled that Marbury had a legal right to the commission, which had been properly prepared and signed, and that Marbury had a legal remedy, since there was no discretion in the office of secretary of state to withhold delivery of the commission. Thus, the Court could issue judicial orders to Madison, a member of the president's cabinet, to perform his duty. However, Marbury had brought his case directly to the Supreme Court in its original jurisdiction, presumably because Section 13 of the Judiciary Act of 1789 seemed to authorize such suits. But Marshall pointed out that the Court's original jurisdiction extends only to cases involving states or foreign diplomats and that Section 13 was therefore unconstitutional, an impermissible expansion of the Court's original jurisdiction. Thus the case was improperly before the Court, which was therefore powerless to order Madison to deliver Marbury's commission.

Although this case may seem to involve only an obscure historical figure's attempt to assume a relatively unimportant judicial office, and to turn on extremely technical grounds, the fact is that the case had great legal and political significance. First, Marshall established the power of judicial review, elaborated on the reasons for its necessity, and made the doctrine for the first time an explicit part of a legal record. Second, Marshall asserted that the Court had the power, though in the end not exercised in this case, to invade the presidential prerogative by issuing orders to a cabinet officer acting by direction of the president.

Let us examine the law and logic of the case. First, it is now commonly acknowledged that Marshall could have construed the language of Section 13 in such a way as to avoid considering its constitutionality.[14] It is clear that he chose to invalidate *this* law at *this* time in order to firmly establish the great doctrine of judicial review in a case that worked to the advantage of his political opponents.[15] After all, the concrete immediate result of Marshall's decision was to leave his fellow Federalist, Marbury, without his commission. Marshall's reasoning in support of judicial review, however, was weak. He used the supremacy clause to reason that if the Constitution is supreme, then any law repugnant to the Constitution is invalid. However, this arguments begs the question, Who has the power to decide whether or not a particular law *is* repugnant to the Constitution? Marshall also reasoned that the justices should have the power of judicial review because they had taken an oath to support and defend the Constitution. It would be difficult to understand, he argued, how the justices could be compelled to take such an oath but not be empowered to invalidate laws that are repugnant to that which they have sworn to support. But this so-called oath argument is also flawed, and for two reasons. First, this oath is not peculiar to judges but is taken indiscriminately by every officer of government. It no more proves that the power of judicial review resides in this Court than it proves that it resides in the president. Second, even if the oath were taken only by Supreme Court justices, it relates only to the official duties of the job. Thus, if those duties do not include judicial review, and Marshall did not otherwise or elsewhere prove that they do, then neither does the oath. These rebuttals to Marshall's various arguments were made in the most trenchant criticism of *Marbury* by Justice John Bannister Gibson of the Pennsylvania supreme court in 1825.[16] They are commonly accepted today. The language of the Constitution does not preclude the Court from exercising the power of judicial review, but neither does it grant that power. Marshall never managed to explain why such an important power was granted by implication rather than by flat statement.[17]

But if in the handling of *Marbury v. Madison* Marshall was not a very good lawyer, he was nevertheless an astute politician. He was in the enviable position to refuse and to accept power in the same breath. He knew that and acted accordingly. He established the Court's power in two extremely important ways while avoiding confrontations with the president and Congress that, probably, he could not have won. First, he established the great power of judicial review in a case that benefited his political opponents. The law he invalidated was a Federalist, not a Democratic-Republican, enactment. Further, Marshall left Jefferson and his Congress with no active method of repudiating judicial review. The ruling in *Marbury* established the doctrine of judicial review but did not require, under the circumstance, that Marshall order anyone to do or to refrain from doing anything. Thus, there was nothing to defy. There was "no immediate means available for undermining the doctrine by acting contrary to it."[18] Second and similarly, Marshall announced the power of the Court to issue orders to members of the president's cabinet, but in circumstances in which he did not actually have to issue such an order. Since this case was improperly before the Court, Marshall did not have to issue an order to Madison, an order which in all likelihood would have been ignored, thus weakening rather than strengthening the Court. Jefferson was actually angrier, at the time, about the Court's establishment of this second power than about the establishment of judicial review. But again, since no order had been issued, though the power to do so had been established, there was nothing for Jefferson, Madison, and the Congress to defy. Marshall had won two important political battles. He had established the Supreme Court's power and independence. He then assumed a posture of quiescence during most of the remainder of Jefferson's presidency. His political objective was to use the Court to consolidate strong national power. Once Jefferson was gone and the opponents of centralization became fewer and more diffuse, Marshall could begin to construe the Constitution in such a way as to expand national power at the expense of the states.[19]

In general, the period between 1800 and the Civil War (1861–65) was one in which the Supreme Court's docket was dominated by cases obliging the Court to balance state and federal power. During roughly the first half of this period, Marshall led the Court in a nationalist direction. The power to invalidate acts of state legislature, never really in doubt, was formally established in 1810.[20] The power to review and invalidate state court decisions was established in 1816[21] and reaffirmed in 1821.[22] Then, firmly in command, Marshall moved to broaden federal power, assist national economic growth, and unify the nation. The two major rulings of the Marshall era establishing national power, supremacy, and unity were *McCulloch v. Maryland* (1819)[23] and *Gibbons v. Ogden* (1824).[24]

Narrowly stated, the issue presented in *McCulloch v. Maryland* was whether or not Congress is empowered to create and charter a national bank. Since that power is not expressly granted to Congress in the Constitution, the broader question presented was whether Congress has any power in addition to those expressly enumerated. Marshall used the opportunity to convert the political theory of nationalism into the "master doctrine of American constitutional law."[25] It is true, he argued, that the national government possesses only those powers delegated to it in the Constitution. But these delegated powers are of two types: those expressly enumerated (the "expressed powers") and those delegated by way of implication (the "implied powers"). And where is that implication made? It is made in the "necessary and proper" clause (Article I, Section 8, Clause 18), which provides that in addition to the expressly enumerated powers Congress shall have the power to pass any law necessary and proper for carrying into executive those enumerated powers. Thus, for example, since Congress does have as one of its expressly enumerated powers the power to raise money through taxation, that enumerated power implies the power to hold that money safely and invest it wisely. So that while Congress is not *expressly* authorized to create and charter a national bank, it is *implicitly* granted that power. The word *necessary* is not a means of limiting national power; it does not mean "indispensable" but merely "convenient," "useful," and "calculated to produce an end." We should know this, Marshall argued, for two reasons. First, *necessary* cannot possibly mean the same thing as *absolutely necessary*; and whereas there are provisions of the Constitution in which *absolutely* is prefixed to the word *necessary*, there is no such prefix to the necessary and proper clause. Second, the necessary and proper clause appears in that part of the Constitution in which powers are granted, not in those in which limitations on powers are stated. Thus the doctrine of implied powers was firmly established, and the necessary and proper clause became the "elastic" clause of the Constitution that, over the years, would allow the powers of the national government to expand far beyond those expressly delegated in the document.

A similarly broad and nationalist interpretation of the "commerce" clause is what makes *Gibbons v. Ogden* (1824) the second major ruling of the Marshall era on federalism. This case involved the unpopular New York "steamboat monopoly" created some 20 years earlier by a New York state statute granting a Fulton-Livingston partnership the exclusive right to navigate steamboats on state waters. By assignment Ogden secured the right to navigate between New York City and New Jersey. Meanwhile, Gibbons was attempting to operate, between New York and New Jersey, two steamboats enrolled under an early congressional law providing for the licensing of vessels in the coastal trade. Although the Constitution expressly granted Congress the power to regulate commerce among the states, except for this licensing law Congress had not exercised its power to any great degree during the early years of the Republic. Now, however, there appeared to be a clear-cut conflict between the state monopoly law and the federal licensing act. On the one side, Ogden and the state contended that only the state could regulate its internal waterways; Congress had no jurisdiction over the internal waterways or commerce of a state. On the other side, Gibbons and the challengers of the state monopoly asserted that the monopoly interfered with the federal power to regulate commerce among the states because it excluded from New York waterways vessels licensed under federal law. Marshall could have solved the case with little elaboration simply by holding that both state and nation had acted within their powers, but that since the state law conflicted with the federal law, it must give way. Instead, before finding that conflict and coming to that conclusion, Marshall chose to examine in detail the nature of the commerce power, thus setting in motion the long process of determining the great reach of the federal commerce authority.

Commerce, said Marshall, is more than just buying and selling. It is more than mere traffic. It is "every species of commercialized intercourse," and it includes navigation. Congress has the plenary power ("complete in itself") to regulate all such commerce that is "among" the states. The word *among*, said Marshall, means "with" or "intermingled with." Commerce between two states cannot begin and end outside of each. Thus, Congress's power to regulate commerce can be introduced into the interior of the states. And what is left to the states? Only those transactions "between man and man within a state, or between different parts of the same state." And even then, only those that do not "extend to" other states because interstate commerce (commerce "among" the states) is *any* commerce that concerns more states than one.

Gibbons v. Ogden was in a sense the first great "antitrust" decision in our history. The immediate importance of the case was that it demolished a great monopoly against which many had been struggling for years. The monopoly had provoked great interstate animosity and had threatened to destroy the fledgling national commercial network.[26] Not appreciated at the time were economic results of a more far reaching nature. *Gibbons* opened the way for interstate communication by both steam and rail and for the cheap transportation of coal by water. In short, *Gibbons* was "the emancipation proclamation of American commerce."[27] Perhaps even more far reaching was Marshall's broad definition of the term *commerce,* which a century and a half later would prove to be the constitutional basis for such seemingly unrelated legislation as the Civil Rights Act of 1964.

John Marshall died in 1835 and was replaced the following year by Roger B. Taney, who was to serve as chief justice for 28 years until 1864. On the whole, Taney and his Court were much less inclined toward centralization than the Marshall Court. Unlike Marshall, whose "national supremacy" position was based on the assumption that the Constitution is an "ordinance of the people," Taney held to a position of "dual federalism" based on the assumption that the Constitution is a "compact among sovereign states." The era remained one in which federal-state relationships dominated the Court's docket; and as his opinion in the "License" cases[28] shows, Taney generally held to a states' rights position. The definition of commerce was narrowed to exclude manufacturing and agriculture, thus limiting the congressional commerce power to the regulation of transportation of commercial goods.[29] But those who expected the Taney Court to frequently overturn Marshall Court doctrines outright were wrong. The record was, rather, one of mere modification and refinement of Marshall court rulings.

It is safe to say that Taney and his Court will be longer remembered for the decision in the famous *Dred Scott* case.[30] Here the Court held that black slaves, who according to the Constitution of the era were "property," not "persons," were disabled from attaining citizenship. Congress, the Court held, could not halt the spread of slavery, and the law known as the Missouri Compromise was unconstitutional. The *Dred Scott* decision so divided southern and northern Democrats that the Republicans won the presidency in 1860.[31] Supreme Court decisions do sometimes, as this case shows, influence the outcome of elections. Yet there is an even greater lesson to be learned from the *Dred Scott* case about the political role of the Court. The Court is at its best when supporting the major policies of the dominant political alliance in the legislative and executive branches. In the absence of consensus within that alliance, the Court can rarely strike out on its own to make policy. Most attempts to do so meet with disaster.[32] (The Court's behavior over the last 30 to 40 years, however, may challenge this generalization, as we shall see.) The decision in *Dred Scott* weakened the

Court as a viable political institution for a generation. In the final analysis, the Taney Court had little lasting significance. When compared with other Court eras, before and after, the Taney Court was "peculiarly unphilosophical," its power depleted by the pressure of sectional conflict.[33]

FROM THE CIVIL WAR TO 1937: ECONOMIC REGULATION AND THE DOCTRINE OF SUBSTANTIVE DUE PROCESS

The first major period of struggle in the Court's history, a struggle of nationalism versus localism, ended with the Civil War. It ended with Chief Justices Marshall and Taney having provided the legal basis of a strong national government. The second major period of struggle, commencing with the early stages of industrialization and growth in the power of business, was one in which the Court was called upon to decide whether any government, national or local, could regulate private economic behavior. The issues now dominating the Court's docket were issues of political economy, and the disputes over these issues lasted until 1937.[34]

During the second half of the nineteenth century, both the state governments and the national government began to adopt laws regulating business activities. State laws sought to regulate the railroads and the liquor business. National laws sought to break up trusts and regulate commerce. Both state and national laws sought to improve the conditions of employment. While the Court's decision making early in this period was mixed, by the turn of the century it became increasingly laissez-faire, distinctly unfriendly to regulatory policies. To combat state regulations, the Court developed the doctrine of "substantive due process." To combat federal regulations, the Court construed congressional power under the Constitution very narrowly.[35] We will begin with the Court's response to state regulations.

At various points in its history the Supreme Court has made what in the end might be called bald and bold grabs for power.[36] But jurisprudentially, its attempts to establish jurisdiction and power have seldom been in leaps and bounds. Usually first have come slow, gingerly-taken steps and then a painfully gradual accumulation of precedents.[37] Such is the history of the evolution of substantive due process.

There is little evidence that before the Civil War the concept of due process meant anything more than a summary description of a fairly tried action at law, a test only of *how*, not *what*, legislative power could be exercised. There are only a few contrary examples. It is true that the Fifth Amendment's due process clause was invoked to protect property rights in the *Dred Scott* case. One of Taney's central arguments in that case was that Congress could not, without violating the due process clause, regulate slavery because to do so would interfere with an owner's right to acquire and hold property in slaves. And on the state level, the New York Supreme Court invalidated a state dry law on the grounds that it violated the property rights of brewers and sellers of beer and liquor. That case, *Wynehamer v. New York,* [38] was decided the same year as *Dred Scott* and invoked the same concept as rationale. The dry law violated a due process clause in the state constitution by depriving the brewers and sellers of the economic interest in their product. But it must be emphasized that *Dred Scott* is the only federal substantive due process decision prior to the Civil War, and that although *Wynehamer* stands for the same proposition, courts in other states were, contemporaneously with *Wynehamer,* deciding similar issues in precisely the opposite way. In any event, prior to the Civil War there was no due process clause in the U.S. Constitution aimed at state legislative power. That, however, was to change.

With the addition of the Fourteenth Amendment in 1868, the Constitution had two due process clauses, phrased the same, one directed at the national government and one directed at the states. Simply, the national government (Fifth Amendment) and the state governments (Fourteenth Amendment) may not deny to anyone within their jurisdiction "life, liberty, or property without due process of law." The Supreme Court struggled fitfully for the next 30 years to make "due process" an instrument for the protection of the substance of vested economic interests, a bulwark of laissez-faire political economics.

Early on the effort was unsuccessful. In 1873 a Louisiana law granting a monopoly to a slaughter house company was challenged by butchers left out of the state-created monopoly. Exercising its police powers to pass laws promoting the public health, safety, morals, and welfare, the state had created a monopoly to remove noxious slaughter houses and large collections of animals from densely populated areas. Those slaughter houses left out of the monopoly were thereby effectively put out of business. In the "Slaughter House" cases[39] they claimed, among other things, that the state monopoly law violated the Fourteenth Amendment's due process clause by denying them the economic interest in their property. Although the Supreme Court was divided on the question, its majority held that it knew of no interpretation under which the monopoly law would be held lacking in due process. The Court went on to say that any ruling that due process limited *what,* not *how,* legislatures legislated would improperly make the Court a "perpetual censor upon all legislation of the states." Four years later, in *Munn v. Illinois,* [40] the Court continued its hands-off position but left a hint of things to come. This case involved an Illinois law fixing rates for grain elevators. Munn, the owner and operator of a warehouse and grain elevator, refused to adhere to the law, contending that the fixed maximum rates denied him the full value of his economic interest in his business. The Court upheld the law and Munn's conviction for violating it. In doing so the Court fashioned the "business affected with a public interest" test. The Court reasoned, "When a man devotes his property to a use in which the public has an interest, the property ceases to be private; it becomes affected with a public interest and hence subject to a greater degree of regulation." The implication was, however, that businesses not so "affected" might be free from regulation. Then a decade later the Court again refused to strike down a law as violating substantive due process but issued a warning. This came in another dry-law case, *Mugler v. Kansas*.[41] Here, state law prohibited the manufacture and sale of liquor. Mugler, the owner of a brewery, was convicted for violating the law. The Court upheld the law and the conviction on the grounds that no property right secured by the Constitution had been violated. But it warned: "It does not at all follow that every statute enacted ostensibly for the promotion of . . . [health, safety, morals, and welfare] is to be accepted as a legitimate exertion of the police powers of the state. The courts are not bound by mere forms, nor are they to be misled by mere pretenses. They . . . [must] look into the substance of things."

Finally, in 1897 the Court began to "look into the substance of things." In *Allgeyer v. Louisiana*[42] the Court struck down a Louisiana state law prohibiting the effectuation of insurance policies entered into outside of Louisiana with insurance companies not approved by state law. This was the first time the Court, through a reasoned decision, specifically held that the substance of economic legislation violated due process. Over the next 40 years it would do so again and again. Laws providing for maximum hours of employment[43] and minimum wages,[44] laws designed to prevent fraud,[45] and a vast array of other progressive social legislation were invalidated as a violation of substantive due process. Not until the "Court Revolution" of 1937 (described below) did the Court recede from making economic policy.

During the same period described above, the Court tended to combat national economic regulation by construing the powers of Congress narrowly. The first major efforts by Congress to use its commerce power to achieve broad regulatory objectives came with the passage of the Interstate Commerce Act (1887) and the Sherman Anti-Trust Act (1890). Other social regulations, such as child labor laws, were passed relying on the commerce power. Congress also began to use its taxing power to achieve regulatory objectives. Although the Court's response to challenges to these laws was mixed, it managed to develop doctrines by which these measures could be invalidated. Once the New Deal legislation came to the Court in the mid-1930s, these doctrines of congressional limitations were available for applications by the Court's conservative but activist majority.

The development of these doctrines began before the turn of the century in the famous "Sugar Trust" case (1895).[46] Here, the federal government sought to obtain a Court order cancelling agreements by which the American Sugar Refining Company had purchased control of several other refining companies, including E.C. Knight Company. American

Sugar already controlled a majority of the refining companies in the country, and the government argued that these new purchases constituted a restraint of trade in violation of the Sherman Act. The Supreme Court, however, refused to allow the government to break up this "sugar trust." Rejecting the broad definition of commerce provided by Marshall in *Gibbons v. Ogden,* the Court asserted that "commerce means primarily transportation—the physical movement of goods following manufacture." It is true, the Court went on to say, that goods are manufactured only in order to be sold, but "this affects commerce only indirectly." Accordingly, private contracts aimed at controlling manufacturing are beyond the reach of congressional regulation. Thus, the Court developed the so-called mechanical test to determine "when commerce begins" and hence what can be regulated. Manufacturing (and presumably also, therefore, such things as mining and agriculture) "precede commerce" and are not subject to congressional regulation under the commerce clause. This same reasoning was later applied in the first "Child Labor" case[47] in 1918. Here, the Congress had sought to discourage the use of child labor by prohibiting the interstate shipment of goods produced with child labor. The Court held, however, that the "evil" of child labor occurs during production that is "antecedent" to commerce and cannot therefore be regulated by Congress. At the same time the Court did uphold congressional efforts to regulate lotteries[48] and Interstate Commerce Commission orders prohibiting discriminatory railway rates.[49] It also upheld the Pure Food and Drug Act[50] and the Mann Act,[51] which attempted to deal with the national problem of white slavery. Each of these had been passed under the Congress's commerce authority. However, when New Deal legislation was challenged in the 1930s, the Court returned to the mechanical test and restrictive views of congressional power. This approach culminated in 1936 in the case of *Carter v. Carter Coal Co.*[52] Here, under its commerce power, Congress had attempted to remedy the problems of the coal industry by stabilizing production and marketing. It had passed the Bituminous Coal Conservation Act, which placed a penalty on coal producers who did not conform to the wage and hour provisions of the law. Clearly, the validity of the law turned on whether its regulatory aspects were within the commerce authority of Congress. Just as clearly, under the ruling in the child labor case the law was invalid because the use of the commerce power to regulate mining is analogous to the use of the commerce power to regulate manufacturing. President Roosevelt had, however, told his New Deal Congress that the need was urgent and the benefits would be immediate, and he had urged the Congress to pass the law without worrying about its possible invalidation. The Court responded with the restrictive rationale developed in the "Sugar Trust" and "Child Labor" cases. The "local" character of manufacturing, agriculture, and mining is a "fact" irrespective of what may be done with the products after they have been manufactured, grown, or mined. Their "effect" on commerce is "indirect," "remote," "mediate," and "collateral." Mining, like manufacturing and agriculture, is intercourse for the purpose of "production not trade." It is therefore beyond the reach of the Congress's commerce power. The law was invalidated.

Similar attempts by Congress to use its taxing power to achieve regulatory objectives encountered similar responses from the Court prior to 1937. While not every regulation achieved under the taxing power was invalidated,[53] the Court tended to be restrictive in its interpretations. In the second "Child Labor" case[54] the Court refused to allow the Congress to regulate child labor under its taxing power. Here, thwarted in its attempt to regulate child labor under its commerce power, Congress passed essentially the same law but attempted to enforce it not as a prohibition on the interstate shipment of the products of child labor but by imposing a tax on the net income of employers of child labor. The Court ruled that the power to tax is designed primarily for the purpose of raising revenue. It does not empower Congress to achieve regulatory objectives, though any tax might have an incidental restraining effect on production. In this instance, the tax on the employers of child labor is clearly designed not principally to raise revenue but as a "penalty" to achieve compliance with a policy of regulation. Congress had therefore exceeded its power. Just as with the treatment of the commerce authority, this approach culminated in 1936 in the battle over New Deal legislation. In *U.S. v. Butler*[55] the Court was called upon to consider the validity of the Agriculture Adjustment Act's processing tax on wheat, corn, and cotton. The funds accumulated were paid out to farmers as an inducement to reduce their acreage. The purpose of the law was to raise farm prices by reducing production. But the Court held that Congress could not use its taxing and spending authority to seek regulation of activities outside its policy-making power. Congress has no independent authority to force producers to curtail production. Thus, Congress cannot use its taxing power to produce revenue to purchase compliance with a policy of curtailment.

A striking new period in constitutional development was about to occur, however. This new period was to commence with the so-called Court Revolution of 1937.

THE MAGICAL YEAR, 1937: "THE SWITCH IN TIME THAT SAVED NINE"

As noted earlier, vacancies on the Court have on the average occurred about every two years. The chances are one in five that a president will be able to make one appointment to the Court in less than one year in office, one in two that one appointment can be made within two years, and three in four that one appointment can be made within three years. Franklin Roosevelt had unusually bad luck. He had to wait five years (until the first year of his second term) to make his first appointment. The odds against such a long wait are four to one.[56] Meanwhile, of course, Roosevelt and his New Deal Congress, having come into power in 1933, inherited the Supreme Court's conservative "Nine Old Men," all appointed by Roosevelt's predecessors and inclined, in the majority, to strike down progressive legislation.

As the presidential election of 1936 approached, the Court had invalidated six pieces of New Deal legislation. Even state laws aimed at a program of economic recovery had been invalidated or only narrowly upheld. And new tests were coming. The National Labor Relations Act and the Social Security Act would surely be challenged, as would replacement legislation for the laws already overturned. Most of the challenged laws had been invalidated by 5-4 or 6-3 votes. Just a few changes in the Court's personnel would make a big difference. The 1936 election gave Roosevelt a landslide victory that he construed as a mandate to prevent the Court from standing as an obstacle to the popular will. On February 5, 1937, he proposed the so-called Court-Packing Plan. Specifically, he proposed a law enabling him to appoint an additional justice for each justice then sitting who was over 70 years of age. This would result in the appointment of as many as six new justices, certainly enough to undo what Roosevelt thought had been a reactionary reading of the Constitution by the Court's majority. In the end, however, the Court-Packing Plan became unnecessary. In 1937 the case of *NLRB v. Jones & Laughlin Steel Corp.*[57] came to the court. At issue was the National Labor Relations Act of 1935, which was designed to protect the right of workers to organize and to encourage collective bargaining procedures. Jones & Laughlin Corporation had refused to cease certain unfair labor practices and the National Labor Relations Board sought to have its order enforced. The Court upheld the law and directed the enforcement of the board's order. The distinction between "direct" and "indirect" effects on the interstate commerce is a difference of degree, not difference of kind, said the Court. The threat of labor disturbance, strikes, and industrial warfare is "immediate" and "possibly catastrophic," not remote. Industrial strife has a most "serious economic effect" upon interstate commerce. Congress, the Court conceded in conclusion, has the power to protect the "lifelines" of the national economy. There had been nothing in the facts of the case or in the oral arguments or in the cited authorities to distinguish this case from *Carter v. Carter Coal Co.* There had been no changes in the Court's personnel. Why had Chief Justice Hughes and Justice Roberts, whose swing votes produced the outcome, changed their minds? Perhaps it was because a series of strikes had educated them to the close connection between labor strife and interstate commerce.[58] "But the consensus among lawyers speculating on the Court's sudden reversal was that the Chief Justice and Mr. Justice Roberts believed that the continued nullification of the legislative program demanded by the people and their representatives . . . would lead to acceptance of the President's Court plan, and that this would seriously undermine the independence and prestige of the . . . Supreme Court."[59] In any event, the Court-Packing Plan shortly thereafter died in the Senate Judiciary Committee. The sudden reversal in *Jones & Laughlin Steel* became the "switch in time that saved nine." The year 1937 also saw the Court bring an end to substantive due process in the *West Coast Hotel Co. v. Parrish.*[60] Here, the Court upheld a state minimum wage law against the claim that it violated the due process clause of the Fourteenth Amendment. In justification the Court argued that "liberty" can be infringed by forces other than government, and "infringement by those forces may require the affirmative action of government for its protection." Finally, also in 1937, the Court upheld the unemployment compensation provisions[61] and the old age pension provisions[62] of the Social Security Act. *Butler's* restrictive interpretation of the taxing and spending power was thus effectively overturned. Congress could now use its taxing and spending power to induce compliance with a policy which, through expressed delegation of power alone, it could not command, but which, at the same time, is not expressly prohibited.

These sudden reversals in 1937 were accomplished, as mentioned above, without any changes in the Court's personnel. And because they were achieved by the narrowest of majorities, there was no reason, in 1937, to predict that these decisions would not themselves be overturned in the future. But then what had been President Roosevelt's bad luck in having no vacancies to fill on the Court during his first term turned to good luck. By 1940 all four dissenters in *Jones & Laughlin Steel* and *West Coast Hotel Co. v. Parrish* were gone. Justice Butler died in 1937; and Justice Van Devanter (in 1937), Sutherland (in 1938), and McReynolds (in 1940) retired. Indeed, by 1941 only Justice Roberts (who had changed his mind on most of the highly contested issues) remained from the Hoover era. The "Nine Old Men" had become the "Roosevelt Court," and the "Court Revolution" of 1937 was confirmed in case after case over the next three decades. The Fair Labor Standards Act, containing minimum wage and maximum hour guidelines, was upheld unanimously as a proper exercise of the commerce power in *U.S. v. Darby*[63] in 1941. The Agricultural Adjustment Act, which sought to stabilize commodity prices by limiting farm production, was upheld the next year.[64] By the 1960s the modern Court's conception of a broad commerce power led it to uphold application of the 1964 Civil Rights Act not only to establishments serving interstate travelers[65] but also to local restaurants serving food that had "moved" in commerce among the states.[66] Similarly, in the realm of the taxing power the Court continued to uphold congressional regulations through taxation in areas beyond its expressly granted regulatory powers.[67] And the shift against "substantive due process" in *West Coast Hotel Co.*

v. Parrish was unanimously confirmed in the 1940s[68] and again in the 1960s.[69] By then, of course, the liberal Warren Court was firmly in command. Having already described its record in Chapter One, we should place that record in its historical context here.

THE WARREN ERA

Although after the retreat of 1937 the Supreme Court continued to hear cases involving economic regulation, this area of litigation became a less significant part of its work and a far smaller source of its major decisions. The emphasis turned to civil rights and liberties. During the Warren era (1953–69), the Court became a more activist libertarian body, more uniformly supportive of civil liberties, than any other Court in our history.[70] For the first time in American history civil rights and liberties received systematic judicial protection. "The de facto Council of Elders for issues of political economy became one of social ethics."[71] The Warren Court's major decisions in school desegregation, reapportionment, school prayer, and criminal justice are reviewed in Chapter One. A more extended consideration of the Warren Court's policy making in civil liberties follows.

The Warren Court "detonated political dispute throughout its tenure."[72] In the 1950s it began a constitutional revolution in civil rights; in the 1960s it became even more aggressive in its pursuit of a just society, especially more aggressive in seeking a uniform or national standard of justice. At the start of the 1960s little of the Bill of Rights applied to the states except for the First Amendment freedoms of speech, press, religion, and assembly. By the end of the decade, however, most of the provisions of the Bill of Rights were "incorporated" into the due process clause of the Fourteenth Amendment, thus extending most federal protections to the states. In addition to incorporating the Bill of Rights, the Court had a number of new things to say about the meaning of these rights and of due process. Freedom of expression, especially new forms of political expression, were given protection. Peaceful demonstrations[73] and "sit-ins"[74] were determined to be protected forms of communication. Even some types of political "action," such as the wearing of antiwar black armbands in the public schools, were construed to be "symbolic speech" and thus protected by the First Amendment.[75] The Court also gave attention to other forms of expression not historically protected by the First Amendment. The press was given a fairly free hand in its coverage of public officials. Public officials who thought they had been libeled by the press could collect damages only if they could prove "actual malice," that is, that the press knew what it had printed was false or had shown a reckless regard for the truth. For all practical purposes this made the press immune from libel suits brought by public officials.[76] This doctrine was later extended to "public figures" as well as "public officials."[77]

In the area of criminal justice the *Miranda* case,[78] requiring that suspects be informed of their rights to remain silent and to legal counsel, will long be remembered as the most controversial of Warren Court rulings. In fact, however, the *Miranda* case was just one piece, though probably the centerpiece, of the "revolution" in the "rights of the accused" produced by the Warren Court. As a part of its attempt to "nationalize" the Bill of Rights and produce a uniform standard in criminal cases, the Warren Court required that the states, like the national government, must exclude illegally obtained evidence from criminal trials,[79] guarantee rights against self-incrimination[80] and double jeopardy,[81] and protect the criminal defendant's rights to counsel,[82] confrontation of opposing witnesses,[83] jury trial,[84] and speedy trial.[85] The Court also made wiretapping subject to constitutional limitation.[86]

The Warren Court's rulings in the civil rights area were not limited to school desegregation. The Court also prohibited gerrymandering as a means of diluting the political influence of black voters.[87] It invalidated state laws forbidding mixed marriages.[88] Also, it broadened the definition of "state-action," suggesting that even private discrimination might run afoul of the Constitution. In *Reitman v. Mulkey*[89] the Court ruled that whereas a state may by law seek to protect a claim to equal rights, such as the right to purchase property without discrimination, it may not by law seek to protect the right of an owner to sell residential property to whomever he chooses. Further, the Warren Court was occasionally willing to apply the equal protection clause to economic as well as social inequalities.[90] The Court applied the equal protection clause to the poor when it invalidated state residency requirements for welfare recipients[91] and when it ruled that if appellate procedure in criminal litigation requires the submission of a trial transcript and the defendant cannot afford one, the transcript must be provided without charging a fee.[92]

THE BURGER ERA

The Burger Court, as we learned in Chapter One, at least in its first decade (the 1970s), was not as uniformly conservative as many Court-watchers had predicted. It did significantly dilute and occasionally overturn important Warren era decisions in the areas of criminal justice, legislative apportionment, and obscenity/pornography. All in all, however, its record in the 1970s was one not of conservative uniformity but of little uniformity of any kind. It was, in short, quite unpredictable. The Burger Court became the first Supreme Court to hold sex discrimination to be a violation of equal protection when it invalidated a state law preferring males to females when two persons were otherwise equally entitled to be the administrator of an estate.[93] In addition, the Burger Court surprised just about everyone when it invalidated laws prohibiting abortions.[94] Indeed, a number of early Burger Court decisions in gender discrimination cases were decided in favor of the female litigant. But at the same time the Burger Court refused, and continues to refuse, to make gender, like race, a "suspect classification."[95] Thus, under Burger gender-based legislation, unlike race-based legislation, is not "presumptively invalid" even today. In the area of school desegregation the Burger Court of the 1970s appeared to endorse bussing as one tool of desegregation plans, at least when *de jure* segregation existed in the past or exists presently in at least part of a school system.[96] But the Court then said no when the issue was whether, having found a given school district to be *de jure* segregated, courts can order a multidistrict, areawide busing remedy absent a finding that the other school districts involved were segregated or affected segregation in other districts.[97] This latter ruling came in a case involving the *de jure* segregated and largely black Detroit school system. A lower court had found that to integrate the Detroit system with a mix proportionate to Detroit's population would still result in an identifiably black system. Thus, the lower court had ordered integration by busing with 53 neighboring suburban districts. The Burger Court, however, rejected the multidistrict remedy because there was no evidence that the suburban districts were *de jure* segregated or "affected segregation" in Detroit.

As the 1980s commenced, the Burger Court became more clearly conservative, although, as noted in Chapter One, its record was still mixed. In the early 1980s, however, the conservatives on the Burger Court became dominant. A number of major cases in the areas of criminal justice, religion, and civil rights were decided in a manner consistent with the Reagan administration's conservative urgings. In *U.S. v. Leon*,[98] as mentioned in Chapter One, the Court placed significant new limits on the rights of criminal defendants when it allowed the admission of evidence obtained on the basis of a search warrant that later proved defective. The Court thus created a "good faith exception" to the exclusionary rule prohibiting the use of illegally obtained evidence at trial. As the Court said in a second, similar criminal justice case, illegally obtained evidence can be admitted if the prosecutor can prove that the evidence would "inevitably" have been discovered by lawful means.[99] In the area of religion the Court ruled that a city may include a nativity scene as part of an official Christmas display without violating the First Amendment.[100] And in the area of civil rights the Court appeared to choose seniority over affirmative action when it ruled that a court may not order an employer to protect the jobs of recently hired blacks at the expense of white employees who have more seniority.[101] The new conservative domination, so obvious in the mid-1980s, was largely attributable to the role played by Justice O'Connor, who was no longer a mere conservative ally but an influential strategist of the Court's right wing and to Justice White's change in status from "swing" vote to conservative ally.[102]

While reversing the Supreme Court's direction was a high Reagan administration priority since Reagan's first election in 1980, a renewed and even more prominent emphasis was placed on this objective during Burger's last two years (1984–85, 1985–86) as chief justice. However, at least in the 1984–85 term, the Court rebuffed the Reagan administration's position in the important cases. All in all, it was a quiet term. The Court's docket contained few opportunities to make new law, and a number of potentially important cases were decided on narrow grounds.[103] In the two areas in which the administration was active in urging its views on the Court and in which important decisions were made, the outcome was not responsive to the administration's pleas. These two areas were freedom of religion and federal regulation. In the religion cases the Reagan administration was quite vocal in articulating its view that the Constitution affirmatively mandates a special status for and an accommodation of religion, not just a mere tolerance of it. But the Court, basing its rulings on the long-standing proposition that the government must pursue a course of complete neutrality toward religion, rejected the administration's position. The Court invalidated a state law providing for a moment of silent prayer in the public schools,[104] overturned another state law giving employees an unqualified right to a weekly day off for religious observance but not for other purposes,[105] and rejected yet other state programs that sent public school teachers into parochial school systems to provide remedial instruction and enrichment courses.[106] In the area of federal regulation the Court made one of its most important decisions ever. In a strong blow to advocates of states' rights and clearly overruling its own recent precedent of only nine years, the Court ruled that state and local governments must pay their employees according to federal minimum wage and hour standards.[107] This decision, however, occurred in a context of widespread judgment that the case of precedent had been wrongly decided in the first place.

The most significant aspect of Burger's last term (1985–86) was an even bolder and more accelerated effort by the Reagan administration to induce the Court to accept its arguments on key issues of constitutional law. Especially with Edwin Meese III replacing William French Smith as attorney general, and Charles Fried replacing Rex Lee as solicitor general, the administration, as we saw in Chapter One, urged the Court to depart from its own precedents to achieve the administration's policies. These efforts to influence the Court, perhaps the most intense efforts of any administration in 50 years, may have backfired. A more subtle approach, some critics claimed, may have won more cases. In the end the Court responded with some decisions consistent with administration urgings, but in most of the cases offering the Court an opportunity to promote Reagan's so-called social agenda, the Court looked the other way.[108]

As we learned in Chapter One, the Court did reaffirm presidential power when it invalidated the automatic mechanism for spending cuts that was at the core of the Gramm-Rudman budget-balancing act. The Court's decision in this case rested on the conclusion that the invalidated provision of the law gave executive power to an official (the U.S. comptroller general) who is subject to removal from office by Congress, thus unconstitutionally encroaching on presidential authority to estimate, allocate, and order spending cuts. Even in this case, however, some commentators saw the mere continuation of a ten-year trend toward strengthening the presidency vis-à-vis Congress, not the endorsement of Reagan's distinctive concept of separation of powers.[109]

Burger's last year yet again produced mixed results in cases involving social policy and civil liberties. Decisions regarded generally as liberal were handed down in the areas of abortion, affirmative action, women's rights, and voting rights. In *Thornburg v. American College of Obstetricians and Gynecologists,* the Court reasserted its support for broad abortion rights that the administration had asked it to abandon. Here the Court declared unlawful a state law requiring physicians to provide women requesting abortions with detailed information about the risks and alternatives, to file reports with the state, and to do whatever they could to guarantee live births in late-term abortions. The Court was more unyielding than ever in its insistence that states not interfere with abortion rights.[110] In the area of affirmative action, the court reasserted its support for the limited use of racial preferences in employment practices for minorities if specific past job discrimination has been demonstrated. Indeed, the Court went so far as to say that a public employer (for example, a school board) may attempt to redress its own past discrimination through the use of numerical hiring goals favoring members of minorities.[111] In *Local 28 v. Equal Employment Opportunity Commission,*[112] the Court sustained a lower court decree requiring a union to eradicate its own "egregious" discrimination by meeting a specific "membership goal" of 29.23 percent.[113] In an important women's rights case[114] the Court ruled that sexual harassment of an employee by a supervisor which is so "severe or pervasive" as to create "a hostile or abusive work environment" violates Title 7 of the Civil Rights Act of 1964. This case was the first one on sexual harassment ever heard by the Supreme Court. Women's groups hailed the decision as a victory for working women and as a defeat for the Reagan Justice Department, which had supported the employer in the case.[115] Finally, in the first significant test of the 1982 Amendments to the Voting Rights Act, the Court held that minority voters (black voters in this case) may successfully challenge a legislative apportionment scheme if it "operates to minimize or cancel out their ability to elect their preferred candidates."[116] The concrete result in this case was the invalidation of four election districts in North Carolina. Again, the administration's position was rejected by the Court.

Death penalty cases decided in Burger's last year underscore the Court's continuing division. A decade after Burger's Court had reinstated the death penalty under rigid procedural rules, many complicating components continued to confound the Court in 1986. In one particularly interesting case the Court ruled that the Constitution prohibits the execution of persons who have become so insane that they do not know they are about to be executed or the reason for it.[117] The defendant in this case had been convicted of murder while robbing a restaurant in 1974. He had never claimed he was not responsible for his crime because he had been insane at the time of the murder. Rather, the argument advanced by his lawyer was that he had gradually gone mad while on death row for over a decade. Preaching to us as only the Court as schoolmaster can do, Justice Thurgood Marshall wrote for the Court's majority, "For centuries no jurisdiction has countenanced the execution of the insane . . . , [for centuries] execution of the insane has been condemned as savage and inhuman . . . , [we must] seriously question the retributive value of executing a person who has no comprehension of why he has been singled out and stripped of his fundamental right to life." Indeed, he added, we need to "protect the dignity of society itself from the barbarity of exacting mindless vengeance."[118] However, less than two months before this decision a different Court majority dealt opponents of the death penalty a major defeat when it upheld the exclusion of committed death penalty opponents from juries in capital cases irrespective of whether their exclusion increases the likelihood of conviction.[119]

This last death penalty decision is an example of what happened during Burger's last year when the Court's more conservative justices were able to mold winning coalitions. Decisions regarded generally as conservative were also handed down in criminal justice and some so-called privacy cases. In *Moran v. Burbine*[120] the Court continued its practice, begun in the early 1970s and described in Chapter One, of diluting the *Miranda* rules, which require that law enforcement officers inform suspects of their rights to remain silent and to have an attorney present before commencing an interrogation. Controversy over the *Miranda* decision had raged for 20 years after its enunciation in 1966. As Burger's last term began in October 1985, Attorney General Edwin Meese III added fuel to the flames when he asserted in an interview published in *U.S. News & World Report* that *Miranda* was an "infamous" decision. When asked whether innocent people should have the protection of the *Miranda* rules (well known to everyone who has seen an arrest on television), Meese responded, "Suspects who are innocent of crime should. But the thing is, you don't have many suspects who are innocent of crime." To this he added his conclusion that the practical effect of *Miranda* is "to prevent the police from talking to the person who knows the most about the crime—namely, the perpetrator . . . *Miranda* only helps guilty defendants."[121] Meese's comments drew outraged responses from many legal scholars and civil libertarians. Harvard law professor Laurence Tribe said that Meese "obviously does not believe in the presumption of innocence. . . . Mere accusation does not transform one into a criminal." University of California law professor Paul Hoeber said, "It's dangerous to have the Attorney General spouting such nonsense. . . . Obviously, many people are suspected who turn out to be innocent of crime. The fact of suspicion is not the equivalent of guilt." And Arthur Spitzer, legal director of the Washington, D.C., office of the American Civil Liberties Union, said that Meese "should be ashamed of himself. . . . The Bill of Rights is meant to protect those innocent people who become suspects."[122] These remarks by Meese and his critics took on added significance during Burger's last year because the *Burbine* case was scheduled for consideration by the Court. In this case, the suspect *was* given his "Miranda warnings" and three times rendered written waivers of his rights and at no point requested the presence of an attorney. He then made incriminating statements when questioned by police. However, without the suspect's knowledge his sister had retained a lawyer for him, and the lawyer had called the police and received assurance that the suspect would not be questioned until the next day. The police withheld this information from the suspect and proceeded to question him until he made the incriminating statements. The suspect was later convicted and sentenced to prison. On appeal the Supreme Court held that neither the Sixth Amendment right to counsel nor the Fifth Amendment right against self-incrimination operated to invalidate voluntary statements made by the suspect in police custody even though a lawyer had been retained by his sister. In short, the Court ruled that the police may use deception to keep a defense lawyer away while they question a suspect, and the police need not tell the suspect that a lawyer is trying to reach him. This decision was undoubtedly the biggest win for the Reagan Justice Department before the Supreme Court in the criminal justice area.

A similarly big victory, against the core of Reagan's "social agenda," came in *Bowers v. Hardwick*.[123] As noted in Chapter One, the Court held here that nothing in the Constitution prevents the prosecution of homosexual relations between consenting adults, even in the privacy of their own homes. The case arose when Michael Hardwick was arrested in his bedroom while having sex with another man. The police said they had gone to Hardwick's home to arrest him for failing to pay a fine for drinking in public. In his argument before the Supreme Court the state's attorney asserted that there is no constitutional right to "engage in homosexual sodomy," that "our legal history and our social traditions have condemned this conduct," and that constitutional law "must not become an instrument for a change in the social order." Mr. Hardwick's lawyer argued, on the other side, that the government must have a better reason than "majority morality" to justify "regulations of sexual intimacies in the privacy of the home," and that the Supreme Court has a "duty" to protect constitutional rights, especially two of the most precious of such rights, the right to private sexual relations and the right to be free from governmental intrusions into private homes.[124] Writing for the majority, Justice Byron White agreed in large measure with the state's position. Using history as his guide, White wrote that prohibitions of homosexual activity have "ancient roots." Sodomy, he wrote, was "forbidden by the laws of the original thirteen states when they ratified the Bill of Rights. In 1868, when the Fourteenth Amendment was ratified, all but five of the thirty-seven states in the Union had criminal sodomy laws. In fact, until 1961, all fifty states outlawed sodomy." Further, commenting on the Court's proper role, White asserted that the Court should not "discover new fundamental rights" because to do so subjects it to attack from the political branches.[125] In dissent, Justice Harry Blackmun took the opposite position with respect to both the nature of the right asserted by Mr. Hardwick and the proper role of the Court. Blackmun wrote that this case was "about the most comprehensive of rights and the right most valued by civilized men, namely, the right to be let alone." As to the Court's proper role and the majority's reliance on social history, Blackmun, quoting from an opinion by Justice Oliver Wendell Holmes earlier in the century, wrote, "It is revolting to have no better reason for a rule of law than that it was laid down in the time of Henry IV. It is still more revolting if the grounds upon which it was laid down have vanished long since, and the rule simply persists from blind imitation of the past."

American University law professor Herman Schwartz has subsequently characterized Justice White's majority opinion as "cruelly traditionalist,"[126] and Yale professor Paul Gewirtz has criticized the Court's majority for failing "to acknowledge in any way the human dimension of the issue . . . that this case involves human beings who have need for intimacy, love and sexual expression like the rest of us."[127] But the telling point for those interested most in the role of the Supreme Court as guardian of the Constitution and as schoolmaster of the Republic far transcends the outcome of this particular case. That point is that few, if any, Supreme Court justices truly believe in judicial self-restraint. Although those justices in the majority in *Hardwick* stressed the need for restraint, they engaged in judicial activism in other cases decided during the same term. In fact, the Burger Court's entire record is one of activism. So it has always been. And, probably, so it will always be.[128]

BRIEF SUMMARY

The Supreme Court's role in the American political system was ambiguous in the minds of the framers of the Constitution. In its first decade the Court played a minor role relative to the legislative and executive branches. Under the leadership of Chief Justice John Marshall (1801–35), however, and with a few modifications under the leadership of Chief Justice Roger B. Taney (1836–64), the Supreme Court's power and political prominence grew greatly. After the Civil War the Court became an increasingly attractive forum for resolving political conflict, and gradually its penchant for activism became increasingly evident as it sought to promote national uniformity in the face of disharmonious state laws. In the late nineteenth century—but especially after 1925—the Supreme Court gained greater and greater discretion in picking and choosing the cases it would decide. As mentioned in Chapter Two and detailed in Chapter Four, the general tenor of twentieth-century congressional legislation regulating the Court's jurisdiction has been to give the Court increasing freedom and leisure to hear cases it believes to be of great constitutional importance or wide public interest, that is, an increased freedom to play a selective policy role. *In short, the administrative and procedural machinery with which the Supreme Court works today facilitates judicial activism irrespective of policy goals and without reference to ends.* Thus the key question is, *Activism to which end?* We will attempt to answer that question in Chapters Seven and Eight, where we examine the Court's policy-making role, both as it allocates power within the political system and as it protects individual rights.

NOTES

[1] Julius Goebel, Jr., *History of the Supreme Court of the United States: Vol. I, Antecedents and Beginnings to 1801* (New York: Macmillan, 1971), p. 206.

[2] Robert G. McCloskey, *The American Supreme Court* (Chicago: University of Chicago Press, 1960), pp. 3–9.

[3] Congressional Quarterly, *The Supreme Court and Its Work* (Washington, D.C.: Congressional Quarterly Press, 1981), p. 4.

[4] Laurence Baum, *The Supreme Court* (Washington, D.C.: Congressional Quarterly Press, 1981), p. 18.

[5] McCloskey, *The American Supreme Court*, p. 4.

[6] Congressional Quarterly, *The Supreme Court and Its Work*, pp. 4–5.

[7] 2 Dall. 419 (1793).

[8] Mary M. Walker, *The Evolution of the United States Supreme Court* (Morristown, N.J.: General Learning Press, 1974), pp. 4–5.

[9] 3 Dall. 172 (1796).

[10] 3 Dall. 386 (1798).

[11] Congressional Quarterly, *The Supreme Court and Its Work*, pp. 6–8.

[12] Ibid.

[13] 1 Cr. 138 (1803).

[14] William Van Alstyne, "A Critical Guide to *Marbury v. Madison,*" 1 *Duke Law Journal* (1969), p. 15.

[15] Charles Warren, *The Supreme Court in United States History,* Vol. I (Boston: Little, Brown, 1922), pp. 242–43.

[16] *Eakin v. Raub,* 12 S&R. 330 (Pa. 1825).

[17] McCloskey, *The American Supreme Court,* pp. 8–9.

[18] Walker, *The Evolution of the United States Supreme Court,* p. 5.

[19] Ibid., pp. 5–6.

[20] *Fletcher v. Peck,* 6 Cr. 87 (1810).

[21] *Martin v. Hunter's Lessee,* 1 Wheat. 304 (1816).

[22] *Cohens v. Virginia,* 6 Wheat. 264 (1821).

[23] 4 Wheat. 316 (1819).

[24] 9 Wheat. 1 (1824).

[25] McCloskey, *The American Supreme Court,* p. 67.

[26] *The Supreme Court and Its Work,* pp. 11–12.

[27] Warren, *The Supreme Court,* Vol. I, p. 616.

[28] 5 How. 504 (1847).

[29] *Veazie v. Moor* 55 U.S. 568 (1853); See Walker, *The Evolution of the United States Supreme Court,* pp. 8–10.

[30] *Dred Scott v. Sandford,* 19 How. 393 (1857).

[31] *The Supreme Court and Its Work,* p. 18.

[32] Robert A. Dahl, "Decision-Making in a Democracy: The Supreme Court as a National Policy-Maker," 6 *Journal of Public Law* (1958), pp. 35–36.

[33] Carl B. Swisher, *History of the Supreme Court of the United States: Vol. V, The Taney Period, 1836–1864* (New York: Macmillan, 1974), pp. 973–74.

[34] Arthur S. Miller, *Toward Increased Judicial Activism: The Political Role of the Supreme Court* (Westport, Conn.: Greenwood Press, 1982), p. 45.

[35] Baum, *The Supreme Court,* p. 20.

[36] Miller, *Toward Increased Judicial Activism,* p. 45.

[37] McCloskey, *The American Supreme Court,* p. 227.

[38] 13 New York 378 (1857).

[39] 83 U.S. 36 (1873).

[40] 94 U.S. 113 (1877).

[41] 123 U.S. 623 (1887).

[42] 165 U.S. 578 (1897).

[43] *Lochner v. New York,* 198 U.S. 45 (1905).

[44] *Adkins v. Children's Hospital,* 261 U.S. 525 (1923).

[45] *Jay Burns & Co. v. Bryan,* 264 U.S. 504 (1924).

[46] *United States v. E.C. Knight Co.,* 156 U.S. 1 (1895).

[47] *Hammer v. Dagenhart,* 247 U.S. 251 (1918).

[48] *Champion v. Ames,* 188 U.S. 321 (1903).

[49] *The Shreveport Case,* 234 U.S. 342 (1914).

[50] *Hipolite Egg Co. v. U.S.,* 220 U.S. 45 (1911).

[51] *Hoke v. U.S.,* 227 U.S. 308 (1913).

[52] 298 U.S. 238 (1936).

[53] See *McCray v. U.S.,* 195 U.S. 27 (1904).

[54] *Bailey v. Drexel Furniture Co.,* 259 U.S. 20 (1922).

[55] 297 U.S. 1 (1936).

[56] Dahl, "Decision-Making in a Democracy," pp. 39–40.

[57] 301 U.S. 1 (1937).

[58] William B. Lockhart, Yale Kamisar, and Jesse H. Choper, *Constitutional Law* (St. Paul: West Publishing Co., 1980), p. 127.

[59] Robert L. Stern, "The Commerce Clause and the National Economy, 1933–46," 59 *Harvard Law Review* (1946), pp. 681–82. Quoted in Lockhart, Kamisar, and Choper, *Constitutional Law*, p. 127.

[60] 300 U.S. 379 (1937).

[61] *Steward Machine Co. v. Davis*, 301 U.S. 548 (1937).

[62] *Helvering v. Davis*, 301 U.S. 619 (1937).

[63] 312 U.S. 100 (1941).

[64] *Wickard v. Filburn*, 317 U.S. 111 (1942).

[65] *Heart of Atlanta Motel, Inc., v. U.S.*, 379 U.S. 241 (1964).

[66] *Katzenbach v. McClung*, 379 U.S. 294 (1964).

[67] *U.S. v. Kahriger*, 345 U.S. 22 (1953).

[68] *Olsen v. Nebraska ex rel. Western Ref. & Bond Ass'n.*, 313 U.S. 236 (1941).

[69] *Ferguson v. Skrupa*, 372 U.S. 726 (1963).

[70] Baum, *The Supreme Court*, pp. 21–23.

[71] Miller, *Toward Increased Judicial Activism*, p. 45.

[72] Walker, *The Evolution of the United States Supreme Court*, p. 43.

[73] *Edwards v. South Carolina*, 372 U.S. 229 (1963).

[74] *Brown v. Louisiana*, 383 U.S. 132 (1966).

[75] *Tinker v. Des Moines School District*, 393 U.S. 503 (1969).

[76] *New York Times v. Sullivan*, 376 U.S. 254 (1964).

[77] *Curtis Publishing Co. v. Butts*, 388 U.S. 131 (1967).

[78] *Miranda v. Arizona*, 384 U.S. 436 (1966).

[79] *Mapp v. Ohio*, 367 U.S. 643 (1961).

[80] *Malory v. Hogan*, 378 U.S. 1 (1964).

[81] *Benton v. Maryland*, 395 U.S. 784 (1969).

[82] *Gideon v. Wainwright*, 372 U.S. 335 (1963).

[83] *Pointer v. Texas*, 380 U.S. 400 (1965).

[84] *Duncan v. Louisiana*, 391 U.S. 146 (1968).

[85] *Klopfer v. North Carolina*, 386 U.S. 213 (1967).

[86] *Katz v. U.S.*, 389 U.S. 247 (1967).

[87] *Gomillion v. Lightfoot*, 364 U.S. 339 (1960).

[88] *Loving v. Virginia*, 388 U.S. 1 (1967).

[89] 387 U.S. 369 (1967).

[90] Walker, *The Evolution of the United States Supreme Court*, p. 55.

[91] *Shapiro v. Thompson*, 394 U.S. 618 (1969).

[92] *Griffin v. Illinois*, 351 U.S. 12 (1956).

[93] *Reed v. Reed*, 404 U.S. 71 (1971).

[94] *Roe v. Wade*, 410 U.S. 113 (1973).

[95] *Frontiero v. Richardson*, 411 U.S. 677 (1973).

[96] *Swann v. Charlotte-Mecklenburg Bd. of Educ.*, 402 U.S. 1 (1971); and *Keyes v. School District*, 413 U.S. 189 (1973).

[97] *Millikin v. Bradley*, 418 U.S. 717 (1974).

[98] *U.S. v. Leon*, 468 U.S. 897 (1984).

[99] *Nix v. Williams*, 467 U.S. 431 (1984).

[100] *Lynch v. Donnelly,* 465 U.S. 668 (1984).

[101] *Firefighters v. Stotts,* 467 U.S. 561 (1984).

[102] Linda Greenhouse, "Conservatives on Supreme Court Dominated Rulings of Latest Term," *New York Times* (July 7, 1984).

[103] Linda Greenhouse, "Rulings of High Court's Term Reaffirm Church-State Barriers," *New York Times* (July 8, 1985).

[104] *Wallace v. Jaffree,* 472 U.S. 38 (1985). See Linda Greenhouse, "High Court Upsets Alabama Statute on School Prayer," *New York Times* (June 5, 1985).

[105] *Thornton v. Caldor,* 472 U.S. 703 (1985). See Linda Greenhouse, "High Court Voids Connecticut Sabbath Law," *New York Times* (June 27, 1985).

[106] *Grand Rapids v. Ball,* 473 U.S. 373 (1985); and *Aguilar v. Felton,* 473 U.S. 402 (1985). See Linda Greenhouse, "Public Teachers Can't Hold Class in Church Schools," *New York Times* (July 2, 1985).

[107] *Garcia v. San Antonio Metropolitan Transit Authority,* 469 U.S. 528 (1985). See Linda Greenhouse, "Justices Enhance Federal Powers over the States," *New York Times* (February 20, 1985).

[108] Stuart Taylor, Jr., "High Court's 1985–86 Term: Mixed Results for President," *New York Times* (July 11, 1986).

[109] Ibid. See also Stuart Taylor, Jr., "High Court Voids Major Step in Law That Cuts Deficit," *New York Times* (July 8, 1986).

[110] 476 U.S. 747 (1986). See also Stuart Taylor, Jr., "Justices Uphold Abortion Rights by Narrow Vote," *New York Times* (June 12, 1986).

[111] *Wygant v. Jackson Board of Education,* 476 U.S. 267 (1986). See also Stuart Taylor, Jr., "High Court Bars a Layoff Method Favoring Blacks," *New York Times* (May 20, 1986).

[112] 478 U.S. 421 (1986).

[113] Stuart Taylor, Jr., "Affirmative Action Upheld by High Court as a Remedy for Past Job Discrimination," *New York Times* (July 3, 1986).

[114] *Meritor Savings Bank, FSB v. Vinson,* 477 U.S. 57 (1986).

[115] Stuart Taylor, Jr., "Sex Harassment on Job Is Illegal," *New York Times* (June 20, 1986).

[116] *Thornburg v. Gingles,* 478 U.S. 30 (1986).

[117] *Ford v. Wainwright,* 478 U.S. 95 (1986).

[118] Commentary and analysis provided in Stuart Taylor, Jr., "Court Curbs Executions of the Insane," *New York Times* (June 27, 1986).

[119] *Lockhart v. McCree,* No. 84-1865 (1986). See Stuart Taylor, Jr., "Justices Reject Broad Challenge in Capital Cases," *New York Times* (May 6, 1986); and Taylor, "Death Penalty Ruling: No Sharp Increase in Executions Seen Soon," *New York Times* (May 7, 1986).

[120] 475 U.S. 412 (1986).

[121] Quoted in Stuart Taylor, Jr., "High Court Faces Political Issues as Session Begins," *New York Times* (October 6, 1985).

[122] Quoted in "Outrage Follows Meese's Remarks on Miranda Rule," *The Columbus Dispatch* (October 10, 1985).

[123] 478 U.S. 186 (1986).

[124] Stuart Taylor, Jr., "Privacy of Sexual Acts Contested," *New York Times* (April 1, 1986).

[125] Linda Greenhouse, "Privacy Law and History," *New York Times* (July 1, 1986).

[126] Herman Schwartz, *The Burger Years: Rights and Wrongs in the Supreme Court, 1969–1986* (New York: Viking/Elisabeth Sifton Books, 1987), p. xvi.

[127] Ibid., quoting from Paul Gewirtz, "The Court Was 'Superficial' in the Homosexuality Case," *New York Times* (July 8, 1986).

[128] Schwartz, *The Burger Years,* p. xx.

The Supreme Court at Work

The Cult of the Robe

HOUSING THE COURT

On the first Monday in October 1935 the Supreme Court held its first session in its newly constructed "marble palace" at One First Street Northeast in Washington, D.C. The Court's move into its new building ended 145 years of nomadic existence during which the Court occupied a variety of incommodious quarters commonly shared with others or bequeathed by others who left for superior accommodations.[1] The tradition of sharing space began with the Court's first session in February 1790 when the Court occupied a second floor meeting room in the Royal Exchange Building in New York, the first capitol city. This building had been designed as an open-air market, and the butchers had to be relocated so as not to disrupt the work of the Court. When in the next year the capitol was moved to Philadelphia, the Court was expected to meet in the new city hall, but its construction was incomplete when the Court convened in February 1791. Thus, the Court met briefly in the unheated Independence Hall. When the construction of the city hall was completed, the Court shared space with the mayor's court, and on some occasions was forced to meet on the second floor because the mayor's court had preempted use of the courtroom. When the government was moved to the new capitol city in the District of Columbia in 1801, the Court began a 135-year stay in various rooms in the Capitol Building. Between 1801 and 1810 the Court occupied a half-finished, sparsely furnished committee room in the bowels of the lower level of the Capitol. In 1810 the Court was moved to a different room in the Capitol, the first chamber especially designed for it. There the Court remained until 1860, except for a brief period (1814–17) when it was forced to meet in a local tavern while the damage done by the British burning of the Capitol during the War of 1812 was repaired.[2] It was in this room in the basement beneath the Senate chambers that the Court heard the *Dred Scott* case while arguments over the same volatile issues of slavery and sectionalism were being exchanged in the Senate upstairs in the same building.[3] In 1860 the Court moved from this basement room to the old Senate chamber on the first floor. There it remained until its move to the new building in 1935. Its various accommodations in the Capitol had been inadequate for a number of reasons. There was only little space for the Court's records and library, and that space defied expansion. The clerk had only a tiny office. The justices had none. The acoustics, however, according to Justice Douglas's account in his autobiography, were better in the Capitol than in the new building.[4]

The new building was designed by architect Cass Gilbert, also famous for his work on the Woolworth Building in New York and the building housing the Department of Commerce. Gilbert modeled the new building on a classical Greek temple. Scholar Bernard Schwartz provides one of the better descriptions of the building:

> Its physical scale is truly impressive. Both longer and wider than a football field, it is four stories high, and is constructed almost entirely of marble. At the main entrance are sixteen huge Corinthian columns, topped by a pediment; in its center, Liberty Enthroned, holding the scales of justice, guarded by Order and Authority on either side. The interior of the building is as impressive as its exterior. . . . Openwork gates, elevator doors, even the firehose cupboards are of gleaming bronze. Two spiral marble staircases, self-supporting marvels of engineering, soar from garage to the top floor, five levels up. . . . The new building also has abundant office space, both for Justices' chambers and Court staff, and a magnificent courtroom—as well as ample amenities, including a mini-gymnasium and basketball court on the top floor, which Court personnel like to call 'the highest court in the land.'[5]

Variously characterized as a "Grecian temple," "marble palace," and "marble mausoleum," the Supreme Court Building has been both acclaimed and criticized. Admirers emphasize its beauty, simplicity, and dignity. But Chief Justice Stone thought it "bombastically pretentious." Another justice claimed the Court is "nine black beetles in the Temple of Karnak."[6] And Justice Douglas never stopped complaining about the acoustics in the Courtroom itself. In response the ceiling was lowered and red velvet curtains were placed behind and on the sides of the bench to stop the echo of voices. However, according to Douglas, these changes did not greatly improve the situation.[7] Today a loudspeaker system and the installation of a recording machine to tape oral arguments have largely corrected the conditions of which Douglas complained. One thing is certain: The building is strong and secure. The floors, doors, and walls are of oak and mahogany. The roof is made of Roman tile over lead-coated copper set on a slab of watertight concrete. It has been observed that the "Court might succumb to a political storm, but it will never be driven out by any kind of inclement weather."[8]

TRADITIONS OF THE COURT

Tradition has always played an important role in the operations of the Supreme Court. Among the major traditions are those of *secrecy, courtesy, seniority,* and *dissent.*[9]

    The tradition of secrecy applies mainly to the Court's formal deliberations but also contains the norm of nondisclosure of personal disagreements and ill will between and among the justices. The rule precluding the presence of all except the justices from the Court's conferences is age old. A number of leaks in the 1970s, described below, in 1979 led the court to reformulate and reissue rules governing press access to the Supreme Court Building. News leaks are regarded by every department and agency of government as both regrettable and unavoidable, but at the Supreme Court they are regarded as an infringement of a sacred trust. As a result, the Supreme Court is undoubtedly the most leakproof of government institutions. Nevertheless, some leaks do occur. They tend to be created in one of three ways: (1) informants provide information to an inquisitive press; (2) justices make disclosures in their speeches and writings; (3) scholars produce studies based on the private papers of the justices and intra-Court memoranda. In the first category, informants have ranged from justices themselves to low-level Court employees. Considerable evidence indicates, for example, that Justice John McLean leaked to the *New York Tribune* a running account of the Court's secret deliberations in the *Dred Scott* case. McLean, who dissented in the case, sympathized with the *Tribune's* antislavery position. More recently, *Time* magazine accurately predicted both the outcome and the 7-2 vote in the surprising *Roe v. Wade* abortion case more than a week before the results were announced. It was widely assumed that the vote had been leaked by a law clerk. Chief Justice Burger immediately ordered that all clerks refuse to talk with or even be seen with reporters. In 1979 ABC TV reported the result of an important case involving freedom of the press, again well before it was announced. Chief Justice Burger concluded that the leak had come from a linotyper who worked in the Court's basement printing shop. The typesetter, who would have access to the opinion before it was printed and announced, denied that he had leaked the information. Within a week, however, Burger fired him. In the second category, the best historical examples of justices revealing in speeches and writings the internal workings and disagreements are Justices Stone and Brandeis. As reported in earlier chapters, though, Justices Stevens and Blackmun criticized their colleagues in public speeches as well. It appears that this second category of leaks providing glimpses of the Court's inner workings is most common during periods when the Court is deeply divided and internal conflicts are at a peak. The third category, that of scholarly investigations using private papers of justices, was initiated in a large way in 1946 with Alpheus T. Mason's biography of Justice Stone. In this case, however, Stone had died and his widow had turned over the papers to Mason. Indeed, until recently, this mode of investigation, best represented by Walter Murphy's *Elements of Judicial Strategy,*[10] did not quote from the private correspondence of, or attribute motives to, any living or sitting justice. This explains the great stir of criticism produced by the 1979 publication of Woodward and Armstrong's *The Brethren.*[11] Written largely from interviews "on background" (meaning that the identity of the source is kept confidential) with justices and law clerks and from drafts of opinions and intra-Court memoranda, some thought to be purloined by the clerks, the authors not only describe the Court's decision-making process as one dominated by negotiation and bargaining but also attribute thoughts, feelings, conclusions, and motivations to justices based on the contents of documents the justices thought to be confidential. Although the publication of *The Brethren* may raise questions about the ethical standards of both the researchers and their law clerk informants, even Walter Murphy concludes that the general picture painted of the Court in *The Brethren* is accurate.[12]

The tradition of courtesy is based on a fervent but often feeble hope of fraternal harmony. Simply stated, the tradition of courtesy requires that justices refuse to allow legitimate differences of opinion to impair close interpersonal relations. Contrary examples are so numerous, however, that they first appear to be the norm. Justice Samuel F. Miller tells a friend that Chief Justice Waite is a "mediocre" and "small man" in the 1870s. Justice McReynolds, the hard-bitten conservative, snarls anti-Semitic hostility toward Justices Brandeis and Cardozo in the 1920s and 1930s. Justice Jackson, holding Justice Black responsible for blocking his elevation to the chief justiceship, manufactures allegations that Black is short on judicial ethics in the 1940s. Riven by battles of philosophical differences and driven by fierce egos, Justices Douglas and Frankfurter go at each other openly in the 1950s and 1960s. It is perhaps inevitable that strong-willed justices, pent up together for decades, will feud. They may walk to conference arm in arm, and formality may require that they shake hands with each other before each of their secret conferences, but there is little goodwill or humor in it. The Brethren, says Justice Powell, are like "nine one-man law firms."[13] Considering the potential for a bench of nine to walk off in nine different directions, the striking thing is the extent to which these tendencies toward open irritability and animosity are more frequently restrained than they are revealed.

The tradition of seniority affects the assignment of office space to the justices, seating in the courtroom, conference discussion and voting procedures, and the assignment and announcement of opinions. Only the chief justice is exempt from the seniority norm. Each of the justices has a three-room office, but two of these nine suites are off the public corridor outside the large bronze doors that seal off the justices from the public. Since office space is assigned according to seniority, it is normally the two most junior justices who occupy the office space outside the bronze doors. The only exception to this norm over the years is Justice Douglas, who chose to remain in suite 108, outside the bronze doors, from the time of his appointment in 1939 until 1962 when Justice Frankfurter died. Douglas then moved into Frankfurter's suite. Ten years later, however, the Court received funds from Congress to remodel the interior of the building to accommodate the swelling number of law clerks. Douglas promptly moved back to suite 108 because, adjacent to a stairway at each end, suite 108 was impossible to enlarge and Douglas wanted safety from expansion.[14] In the courtroom itself the chief justice occupies the center chair, with the senior associate justice to his immediate right and the second senior associate justice to his immediate left. The remaining six associate justices are then seated in alternating order of seniority. In the conference the chief justice is in a pivotal position that can enable him to exert great influence. The chief justice briefly summarizes the facts and issues of each case to be discussed and is then the first to state his view as to how the case should be decided. The associate justices in order of seniority then state their views. When it comes time to vote, the order is reversed. The most junior associate justice votes first, the most senior associate justice votes next to last, and the chief justice last. The assignment of opinions is also ordered by seniority. If the chief justice is a member of the majority, he assigns the writing of the opinion; if not, the assignment is made by the senior associate justice in the majority. Similarly, when the opinions are announced in the open Courtroom, all justices who wrote opinions (concurring and dissenting) in a given case announce them in reverse order of seniority.

Although the Court has always made its decisions by majority vote, the tradition of dissent as we know it today did not emerge until the Marshall era. During the Court's first decade each justice wrote his own opinions, which were then read by each justice seriatim in reverse order of seniority. Marshall, who wanted the Court to speak with one voice, quickly convinced his Federalist colleagues on the bench to adopt a practice of announcing an "opinion of the Court," which normally enabled him to write the opinion. However, this approach lasted only until President Jefferson was presented with his first opportunity to fill a vacancy on the Court with a Democratic-Republican appointee. In 1804 Jefferson appointed William Johnson to the

Court. Johnson did not hesitate to register his disagreement with his Federalist colleagues in written dissenting opinions, and he is now considered the "father of dissent" on the Court. Johnson served from 1804 until 1834 and wrote half of the 70 dissents during his 30 years on the Court. Justices are remembered as "great dissenters" for a variety of reasons. In some instances, it is not because they dissented regularly but because a particular dissent, under the circumstances, is historically quite notable. This would be true of Justice Benjamin Curtis, whose last opinion for the Court was his famous dissent in the *Dred Scott* case. Others are notable because later Courts vindicate their views as correct. This would be true of Justice Oliver Wendell Holmes, who although known as the "Great Dissenter," actually dissented less frequently than did the average of his colleagues during his tenure. The position taken by Holmes in dissent frequently became the law of the land later, however, because of the subsequent reversals of the Court's decisions. Others are notable mostly because of the great number of dissents filed. This would be true of Justice John Marshall Harlan, who wrote 380 dissenting opinions between 1877 and 1911. Not surprisingly, the tradition of dissent, like exceptions to the traditions of courtesy, tends to peak during periods of dissension and division on the Court. Of course, frequent dissent is had only at a cost, both to the Court as a whole and to the dissenting justice. Both judicial biographies and behavioral studies of judicial decision making suggest that justices are often disinclined to dissent, even if tempted, because they prefer to protect the institutional stability of the Court or to avoid personal isolation.[15] Chief Justice Burger is well known for switching sides to avoid personal isolation, leading his clerks to advance an easy rule of thumb for predicting his vote: "He will always be to the right, but never alone."[16]

SCHEDULING THE TERM

As we learned in Chapter Two, the Supreme Court receives approximately 4,000 requests for review each year. It hears and makes a decision "on the merits" (a substantive decision) in only 325–400 of these cases. Of these, the Court decides only about 150 with a "full treatment" of both oral argument before the Court and a full written opinion. The remainder of cases decided on the merits, frequently without oral argument, are decided *per curiam* (with short unsigned opinions written "by the Court" rather than by one justice), or are decided by memorandum orders vacating lower court decisions. In the remainder of the 4,000 cases filed (90–92 percent in an average year), the Court refuses to grant the review at all. Simply, the appeal is dismissed or the petition denied.

Since 1917 the Supreme Court has done its work in a single annual term that commences on the first Monday in October. In recent years the

October term, as it is called, which once ended in mid-May, has lasted until late June or early July. Appeals reach the Court at the rate of about 80 per week. Appeals received late in the term (March–July) and granted review are normally scheduled for argument during the next October term. Thus, a portion of a given term's agenda is set during the prior term. On the average about 40 cases (approximately three weeks of oral argument) are accepted at the end of a term for argument during the next term.[17] In addition, requests for review continue to arrive at the Court daily during the summer months. These requests normally await the return of the justices in the early fall for action.[18] Typically, the Court hears oral arguments and holds closed conferences to discuss and decide cases it has heard and to accept or reject requests for review in seven two-week sessions beginning in October and ending in early May. Two-week or three-week sessions normally separate these sessions, during which the justices work independently, largely in isolation, reading information about pending cases, doing research and preparing for oral arguments and conferences coming up in the next two-week session, and writing opinions in cases that have been decided.[19] Occasionally, important cases come up toward the end of the term and their resolution cannot be postponed until the next fall. In such instances the Court will postpone adjournment of its regular term until action is completed. Recent examples include the "Pentagon Papers" case,[20] in which the Court permitted the *Washington Post* and *New York Times* to publish purloined government documents on the Vietnam War, the "Nixon Tapes" case,[21] in which the Court ruled that President Nixon could not invoke executive privilege to withhold White House tapes of conversations allegedly containing evidence of wrongdoing, and the "Iran Settlement" case,[22] in which the Court sustained the arguments by which Presidents Carter and Reagan arranged for the release of the American hostages in Iran.[23]

According to Supreme Court Rule 3(1) the Court may, in addition to its annual October term, "hold a special term whenever necessary." Thus, if important matters arise after the October term has been adjourned and are sufficiently urgent that postponement until the fall is deemed impossible, the Court will hear the case in a special summer session. Such sessions are extremely rare, however, and in the Court's history only four cases have been decided in special session. Of these, probably the most important, or at least most dramatic, is *Cooper v. Aaron,* involving the desegregation of the public schools in Little Rock, Arkansas, in 1958.[24] A lower federal court had issued a desegregation order, but the order was actively opposed by both the governor and legislature of the state. Widespread public hostility fueled by the opposition to desegregation by state officials threatened the opening of the public schools scheduled for September 15, 1958. The local school board requested a delay in desegregation due to the heated public opposition. In special session the Supreme Court heard oral arguments on August 28 and September 11. The next day the Court unanimously upheld the lower court's desegregation order.[25]

REVIEWING CASES AND AGENDA SETTING

As we have learned, the Supreme Court has both original and appellate jurisdiction. That is to say, it can act both as a trial court and as an appellate court. In some instances the Court's jurisdiction is obligatory; that is, it is required to hear the case brought to it. In other instances, the vast majority, its jurisdiction is discretionary; it can, in other words, decline to hear a case brought to it. Thus to a large extent the Court sets its own agenda. In this section we will examine in detail the methods and channels of review by which cases are rejected or accepted for treatment.

The Supreme Court's original jurisdiction is limited to cases involving the diplomatic representatives of foreign states and to cases in which a state of the Union is one of the parties. These are the only two types of cases the Court can hear as a trial court. For a variety of reasons the Court hears very few cases under its original jurisdiction. In the first place, the Court's original jurisdiction is not exclusive. In other words, the U.S. district courts, which, as we have seen, are the trial courts for the federal system, are also empowered to hear these two types of cases and occasionally do so. Second, foreign ministers and ambassadors generally enjoy diplomatic immunity and are therefore rarely tried before American courts. Third, although original jurisdiction cases are technically obligatory, the Court has established procedures by which it can, and does, deny leave to file an original case. Finally, the kinds of cases states are likely to bring to the Supreme Court have dwindled in recent years. During America's early years under the Constitution disputes over state boundaries and river rights were more common, thus involving the Court in a relatively greater number of original cases. Today, however, there are very few original cases, limited largely to occasional disputes between western states involving the diversion of water resources.[26] Even this smaller number of original cases adds to the Court's heavy workload. Thus, when an original case is heard and questions of fact are in dispute, the Court appoints a "special master" to conduct a hearing on the facts to reduce the Court's time commitment to the case.[27]

Nearly all the Court's work in an average year, then, is done in appellate jurisdiction. As we learned in Chapter Two, the Court receives its appellate cases from five sources: (1) direct appeals from U.S. district courts when the district court has invalidated an act of Congress or when the United States is a party to the dispute; (2) appeals from three-judge district court panels; (3) appeals from U.S. courts of appeals; (4) appeals from specialized federal courts; and (5) appeals from state supreme courts. From these five sources, requests for review come in the form of *petitions for* certiorari, *applications for appeal,* or *requests for extraordinary writs* such as habeas corpus. The first of these make up the bulk of the Court's workload. Certiorari is an entirely discretionary jurisdiction. Petitions for certiorari are filed by losing parties in lower courts setting out the reasons why review should be granted. The Court is not mandated to hear the case. The Court yearly agrees to hear less than 10 percent of the cases petitioned. The Court makes this "cert. decision" as lawyers call it, by the so-called rule of four. If after reading the certiorari petition and studying related materials four justices agree to hear the case, it will be heard. Four is obviously not a majority of nine, but the reasoning is that if four U.S. Supreme Court justices conclude a case presents significant issues that should be resolved, the case should be heard. Individual justices may concur with or dissent from the "cert. decision," but all are eligible to participate on the merits whether they had originally voted to hear the case or not. In the entire history of the certiorari jurisdiction, only Justice Frankfurter seemed to hold the contrary view that there should be no dissents from the denial of certiorari and that a justice need not participate on the merits if he had voted to deny certiorari.[28] Students of the "cert. decision" have found as an empirical fact that since 1925, in all cases in which certiorari has been granted, the Court has overturned the lower court decision in slightly more than two-thirds of the cases. Some of these students have reasoned that such a high reversal rate may indicate that a denial of certiorari means that the court approves the lower court decision. The justices have steadfastly denied this, insisting that the decision to grant or deny certiorari is based exclusively on the importance of the case presented. In practice, of course, a denial of certiorari does have the effect of allowing the lower court decision to stand. Yearly about 90 percent of the cases decided have come to the Court through the certiorari route.

The second form of review, the application for appeal, is formally a review by right. The Court is required by statute to hear the case. This mandatory jurisdiction exists as follows:

FROM THE STATE COURTS

1. Where a state court has invalidated a federal statute or treaty provision.
2. Where a state court has upheld a state law or state constitutional provision allegedly in conflict with the federal Constitution, laws, or treaties.

FROM THE U.S. COURTS OF APPEALS

1. Where a federal law or treaty is held unconstitutional.
2. Where a state law or constitutional provision is held invalid because it is in conflict with a federal law, treaty, or constitutional provision.

FROM THE U.S. DISTRICT COURTS
(APPEAL DIRECT TO SUPREME COURT)

1. Where a federal statute with a criminal penalty is held unconstitutional.
2. Where judgment has been rendered in a suit to enforce the antitrust laws, the Interstate Commerce Act, or Title II of the Federal Communications Act.
3. Where three-judge courts grant or deny an injunction in suits to restrain enforcement of state statutes or federal statutes, or orders of certain federal agencies.[29]

Although formally constituting a mandatory jurisdiction, appeals are in practice often denied. This is partly because the justices believe the issues raised by a particular appeal are unimportant. It is also because the justices recognize that hearing all appeals would take up too much of their precious time. Accordingly, the justices may dismiss an appeal on the grounds that it raises an "insubstantial" issue or that its application includes procedural defects. Alternatively, the Court may grant a summary affirmance of the lower court decision. More than half of all appeal applications in an average year are in practice denied in one of these ways. The decision to grant an appeal, like the decision to grant certiorari, is made by the rule of four. But the summary dismissal or affirmance of a lower court decision in an appeal has a technically different legal result than a denial of certiorari. The denial of certiorari, while for all practical purposes leaving the lower court's decision standing, is not regarded as a Supreme Court precedent. Dismissal and affirmance on appeals are regarded legally as decisions on the merits of the case and technically carry some weight as precedents for future cases.[30] Appeals that are granted make up only about 10 percent of the cases decided annually by the Court.

Even so, some members of the Supreme Court have complained that in the 1980s the workload created by applications for appeal by right is overly burdensome. They have argued that their obligatory jurisdiction required them to give scant oral argument time to cases that are complex but of little importance. In turn, they have said, the Court has too little time for the more important cases, forcing the Court to decide some significant issues summarily and thus sowing confusion in lower courts. In June 1988, after prodding by Chief Justice Rehnquist, the Congress responded to these complaints by passing a bill abolishing the requirement that the Court decide certain classes of appeals. As a result, the Court now has nearly complete freedom to decide what cases to review. Rehnquist said that the abolition of the Court's obligatory jurisdiction had been "for many years . . . the primary legislative goal of the Court." Congressman Robert Kastenmeier, chair of the House Subcommittee on Courts, called the bill the "most significant jurisdictional reform affecting the High Court in over 60 years" and predicted that it would be of "substantial assistance to the Court in managing its heavy caseload."[31]

In addition to petitions for certiorari and applications for appeal, cases occasionally come before the Court on certain miscellaneous writs and by certification. The typical miscellaneous writ is the writ of habeas corpus by which prisoners challenge their convictions. Certification is a process by which a lower court, usually a U.S. court of appeals, asks the Supreme Court to rule on a stipulated question of law supposedly in professional doubt. Certification does not constitute a concrete case or controversy in the traditional sense. Miscellaneous writs and certification are, however, few and far between. Indeed, if one were to add together all the cases of certification the Supreme Court decides annually that have come to it in miscellaneous writs and original jurisdiction, the sum would rarely exceed 1 to 3 percent of its total workload. Of the roughly 4,000 requests for review received annually, then, the great bulk result from either petitions for certiorari or applications for appeal.

Obviously, deciding whether to grant or deny review to 4,000 cases per year is extremely burdensome and necessarily requires some kind of prescreening process. Through the 1980s and into the 1990s this process has taken the form of the chief justice's "discuss list." Although the decision to grant or deny review is made by the justices in conference, not every case filed is considered there. Once a case is filed and given a docket number, the justices and their law clerks have the responsibility of reviewing the case and deciding whether it merits the Court's consideration. Meanwhile, the chief justice and his law clerks review the cases on the docket and prepare a "discuss list" made up only of those cases the chief justice believes important enough to be considered. Appeals are placed on the "discuss list" automatically, but nearly three-quarters of the petitions for certiorari are normally denied a place. The list is compiled before the conference convenes. Thus in an average year about two-thirds of all cases are denied consideration without conference discussion, so the prescreening process is a significant one.[32] Once the conference convenes, any justice can have a case placed on the list simply by asking that it be done. When the "discuss list" is complete, the justices decide by the rule of four whether or not to grant review. On the Monday following the Court's conference an "orders list" indicating which cases have been accepted and set for oral argument later in the term and which cases have been denied review is announced in open court.

ORAL ARGUMENTS

For the many years the Court was housed in the Capitol, oral arguments in cases accepted for review with full treatment were held from 12 noon until 2 P.M. and from 2:30 P.M. to 4 P.M., with a 30-minute lunch break between. This schedule was probably set to coincide with that of the Congress, which in those days convened on weekdays at noon.[33] The present schedule—10 A.M. to noon and 1–3 P.M. on Monday, Wednesday, and Friday—was initiated in 1969. Since 1970, by the Court's own rule, most cases receive a maximum of one hour of oral argument apiece, 30 minutes to each side. Exceptions to the one-hour limit are granted only occasionally and only when requested and granted prior to the commencement of the argument. Thus, with four hours of argument three days per week, the Court can hear about 12 cases a week.[34]

Once the Court has announced it will hear a case, the clerk of the Court schedules the case for oral argument. A case is usually scheduled for argument about three months after it has been accepted for consideration. Under current rules only one attorney is heard for each party unless special permission is granted in advance to allow more than one lawyer to participate because several parties are on one side.[35] According to Rule 44, attorneys may not read from a prepared text during oral argument.[36] Indeed, there have been occasions when justices have interrupted lawyers reading from a brief to remind them of the rule. Normally, lawyers attempt to clarify and emphasize the main points contained in their written briefs, already submitted to the Court, by speaking from an outline or notes. Frequently, they will be interrupted by questions or remarks from the bench. Since the time allowed each side includes time for questions and remarks by the justices, each lawyer has in practice considerably less than 30 minutes to make a presentation. Questions consume about 10 minutes of the half hour allotted. Special permission may be granted to extend the half-hour limit, but only for the purpose of answering questions. According to one famous anecdote, Chief Justice Hughes, insistent upon adherence to the time limit, once informed a lawyer that his time had expired when the lawyer was in the middle of the word "if."[37]

Do oral arguments make a difference? Some critics contend they do not. According to this view, because the justices have read the written briefs submitted by each side prior to argument and have probably discussed the case with law clerks and possibly other justices, they have already made up their minds by the time the argument is heard. However, the justices themselves have contended that oral arguments serve a useful purpose. Representative of this view is Justice Brennan's position: "Oral argument is the absolute indispensable ingredient of appellate advocacy. . . . [M]y whole notion of what a case is about crystallizes at oral argument. This happens even though I read the briefs before oral argument."[38] The truth of the matter is that oral arguments do not of themselves generally win cases, but poorly argued points of law and evasive answers to questions from the justices have occasionally lost cases for attorneys and their clients.[39]

CONFERENCES

Whether or not to accept cases for consideration, as well as a determination of the disposition of cases heard in oral argument during preceding weeks, is discussed, and ultimately voted upon, in the justices' secret conferences. Prior to 1955, conferences were held in the evening or on weekends, depending on the workload. Presently the Court holds its conferences on Fridays and occasionally on Wednesdays during the weeks when oral arguments are scheduled. The day generally begins around nine in the morning and lasts until five or six in the evening. The justices are summoned to the conference by a buzzer rung by the chief justice, who has drawn up the agenda.[40] According to the conventional wisdom, first to speak on each matter to be decided is the chief justice, followed by the senior associate justice, and then by the other associate justices in order of seniority. Usually each justice speaks without time limitation and is rarely interrupted. Discussions tend to be probing and, with some exceptions, polite. When it comes time to vote, the junior justice, last in the order of discussion, votes first. The chief justice votes last. In theory the order of voting protects newer justices from the influence of their seniors.[41] "It is in the conference that the mettle of a Justice is tested, for here he must meet his colleagues in the rough and tumble of free discussion."[42]

This "two-stage" procedure—justices discussing a case in descending seniority followed by a vote in reverse order—has apparently been changed to a "single-stage" procedure—views and votes announced at the same time, beginning with the chief justice and continuing in descending order of seniority. However, there is disagreement between scholars and the justices themselves as to when the change occurred. (Indeed, some scholars continue to write as if the two-stage procedure were still used.) Political scientist Henry Abraham has recently written that several letters sent to him from justices sitting between 1970 and 1982 attest to the continuing use of the two-stage procedure during at least most of the Burger Court (1969–86). On the other side, political scientist David O'Brien has written that the two-stage procedure has not been used since the Chief Justiceship of Charles Evans Hughes (1930–41). Chief Justice Rehnquist has recently reacted to this dispute, asserting that the single-stage procedure has been employed during his entire tenure on the Court (beginning in 1971) and that Justice Brennan has told him that that procedure has been followed ever since he joined the Court in 1956. Justice O'Connor wrote to Abraham in 1988 confirming the current use of the single-stage mode. Thus, while we do not seem to know when the shift occurred, what motivated the change, what happened to the rationale for the two-stage procedure, or what impact the change has had on the interaction among the justices, we can safely assume that the single-stage procedure is now the status quo.[43]

Histrionics in conference are not uncommon. Justice Douglas has written as follows about his lifelong adversary, Justice Frankfurter:

> He often came in with piles of books, and on his turn to talk, would pound the table, read from the books, throw them around and create a great disturbance. His purpose was never aimless. His act was designed to get a particular Justice's vote or at least create doubts in the mind of a Justice who was thinking the other way. At times, when another was talking, he would break in, make a derisive comment and shout down the speaker.[44]

Although discussion in conference sometimes changes a justice's view of a case, that is not its principal function. The principal function is to discover the consensus. This is particularly important in the assignment of the opinions to write. When in the Court's early years each justice wrote an opinion in each case, consensus was less important. Then the vote determined the outcome but there was no single opinion for the whole Court or for its majority. Since the days of Chief Justice Marshall, however, the effort has been to produce as far as possible one opinion for the Court, or at least for its majority. Such opinions often have the effect of modifying or concealing sharp differences in the scope of the decision. Some Justices therefore feel compelled to write concurring opinions in which they acknowledge having voted with the majority but disagree in one or more respects with the majority opinion. Nevertheless, knowing the consensus of the conference is crucial to the assignment of opinions and to a reduction in the number of opinions.[45]

OPINION WRITING AND VOTE CHANGING

In the final phase of the Supreme Court's work, opinions are assigned and written. If in the majority, the chief justice assigns the opinion. Otherwise the opinion is assigned by the senior justice in the majority. Since, as suggested above, the opinion is an expression of the collegial thinking of the justices, the writer must take care to draft it in such a way as to keep the allegiance of at least four other justices until the formal announcement of the Court's decision and opinion in open court. Thus, preparation of the majority opinion necessarily involves much "give and take." While the majority opinion is being prepared, other justices may be drafting separate concurring opinions or dissenting opinions. Months may pass while dozens of drafts of these opinions—majority, concurring, and dissenting —are circulated to other justices. The wording and reasoning of opinions, especially of the majority opinion, may be changed many times to accommodate other justices. As justices read the circulated drafts, they may shift their votes from one opinion to another. Indeed, until the moment when the writer of the majority opinion announces it in open court, the justices are free to change their position. Occasionally, although rarely, a majority disappears and a circulated dissenting opinion picks up enough votes to become the Court's tentative majority opinion. Finally, the alignment of the justices becomes firm as they choose to "join" a majority or dissenting opinion. "Justices often view the timing, the sequence and the explanations offered for 'joins' as crucial to their efforts to put together and hold a majority."[46] When the Court's decision and opinion are announced in open court, only the final versions of the opinions are made public and published by the U.S. Government Printing Office in *United States Reports*, the official record of Supreme Court opinions.

It should be noted here that some Supreme Court scholars have advocated doing away with written opinions altogether. In part this argument is advanced on the grounds that abolishing the practice of writing opinions would save precious time. But the most ardent advocates of such a change are those who also advocate a more activist role for the Court and believe the change would give the justices more time for a more activist role. Arthur Selwyn Miller, for example, has argued that no one really believes written opinions explain the reasoning processes by which the justices have reached decisions. Further, he has concluded that decisions without opinions would, for the better, make lawyers more outwardly result oriented.[47] We must grant, however, that among the majority of judges and most legal scholars, Miller's position is a most unconventional and unacceptable point of view.

LAST STEPS

A party whose petition or application for Supreme Court review is rejected may ask for a *reconsideration* but rarely gets it. A party that has lost an argument may ask for a *rehearing*, which will be granted if the request is supported by any justice in the majority. Finally, the Court itself may, but rarely does, call for a *reexamination* of a case already decided.

However rare, such "last steps" can be momentous. This could hardly be clearer than in the Court's treatment of a major civil rights issue in 1988 and 1989. A dramatic development occurred on April 25, 1988, when the Court's majority requested that the attorneys in a pending job discrimination case (*Patterson v. McLean Credit Union*),[48] which the Court had already heard, make new arguments on whether the Court should overrule a major 1976 civil rights decision made in *Runyon v. McCrary*.[49] Specifically, the sequence was as follows. After the Civil War Congress passed a number of laws (for example, the Civil Rights Act of 1866 and the Voting Rights Act of 1870) now codified in Title 42 of the United States Code. Resurrecting these long-ignored laws in efforts to root out racial discrimination in the modern era has necessarily posed perplexing problems of statutory interpretation for the Court. Neverthe-less, in recent years the Court has ruled that Title 42 prohibits racial discrimination in the sale of private homes,[50] prohibits a private associa-tion from restricting the use of a swimming pool to white members,[51] and prohibits racial discrimination by private employers.[52] And in *Runyon v. McCrary* (1970), the Court ruled that Title 42 prohibits private, commer-cially operated schools from denying admission to blacks.[53] The reason-ing in *Runyon* was sufficiently broad to permit its application to racial discrimination in private transactions generally. Neither the Congress nor the public at large exhibited great discontentment with these deci-sions.[54] Indeed, despite many opportunities in the decade following the *Runyon* decision in 1976, the Congress had never even considered revis-ing the Court's interpretation of the statute.[55] Then in 1987–88 came the case of *Patterson v. McLean Credit Union.* Here, Mrs. Patterson claimed that her on-the-job supervisor at a credit union in Winston-Salem, North Carolina, had articulated racial slurs against blacks generally, had treated her personally in a hostile and degrading manner, and had ac-corded her less desirable job assignments than white employees. The Court agreed to decide the case on October 5, 1987. The issue the Court agreed to decide was whether an employee alleging racial harassment by her employer could sue the employer for damages under Title 42. Oral arguments were heard by the Court on February 29, 1988. The issue of whether the *Runyon* precedent should be reconsidered was not raised by either party to the *Patterson* case, not in their written briefs or in their oral arguments. Both sides were willing to assume the validity of the old law and contest only whether the old law applied to racial harassment in the workplace. Nor did any justice on the Court raise the issue of the validity of the old law with either of the attorneys at the oral arguments. Consequently, the 5-4 vote announced on April 25 was totally unex-pected. Specifically, the majority required that the *Patterson* case be "restored to the calendar for re-argument" and directed the attorneys for both sides to brief and argue "whether or not the interpretation [of Title 42] adopted by this Court in *Runyon v. McCrary* be reconsidered."

The Supreme Court thus ordered, in an uncommon but not unprece-dented fashion, the reargument of a case already heard. In this particular instance the potential policy impact of reargument was great. The major practical consequence of the *Runyon* interpretation of Title 42 had been to grant victims of job discrimination both expanded safeguards and more effective remedies than are furnished by more recent civil rights laws. The Civil Rights Act of 1964 (Title VII), for example, does prohibit job discrim-ination on grounds of race as well as gender, religion, and national origin. However, that law applies to large employers only and grants the victim reinstatement with back pay as the only remedy. On the other hand, since *Runyon,* Title 42 has been construed to apply to all private employers and, at least in instances of extreme violations, to provide victims with puni-tive damages. The five justices who voted to reconsider *Runyon* said at the time that there was no real cause for alarm as yet on the part of *Runyon* supporters because they had voted only to reconsider, they had not yet decided to overturn, and there is no harm in requesting argument on whether a particular precedent should be recast or overruled.[56] In other words, the majority seemed to be saying to potential critics, "Don't worry, the Court is merely thinking about overturning precedent, as it does every so often."[57]

But such a disclaimer tends to mislead both students of the Court and the public at large, both with regard to the substantive policy implications of this particular decision and with regard to the more general consider-ation of the Court's role in setting its own agenda. Substantively, over roughly the last half century the Court has advanced the cause of racial equality by encouraging attorneys to attack segregation. The Court has done so by agreeing to hear discrimination cases, whether in education or employment or voting or housing. The signal sent to civil rights lawyers has been largely positive. The Court's decision on April 25, 1988, how-ever, "suggested the emergence of an agenda of civil rights retrenchment and retreat. . . ; [it was] an invitation from the Court . . . [to opponents of civil rights] to challenge . . . settled principles that protect minority rights."[58] As things actually turned out, the Court's request for reargu-ment in the *Patterson* case was of large significance. After reexamination the Supreme Court in June 1989 unanimously upheld the *Runyon* prece-dent that construed the 1866 civil rights law as a bar to discrimination in private employment. *But* by a 5-4 vote the Court ruled that the law applied only at the point of initial hiring and thus could not be used, as by Mrs. Patterson in her fight against McLean Credit Union, to bring a lawsuit over racially biased treatment on the job. In other words, *Runyon* was technically saved as a precedent, but in practice sharp limits were placed on its application. Perhaps better than anyone else, Mrs. Patterson's attor-ney summarized the practical impact of a reexamination that results for-mally, as this one did, in a maintenance of the status quo but that, for all practical purposes, changes public policy. The unanimous decision uphold-ing *Runyon*, he said, is "a victory in a battle that never should have been fought"; but the 5-4 decision on the law's application "has the practical effect of denying to those who suffer the emotional pain and indignity of on-the-job racial harassment any effective remedy."[59] As we learned ear-lier in this chapter, the Supreme Court has virtually unlimited discretion in setting its own agenda. Columbia University law professor Jack Green-berg aptly summarizes both process and policy as they can be gleaned from this case study as follows: "By opinions, grants and denials of writs permitting review, and by actions like the April 25 decision, the Court instructs lawyers about what arguments may be successful in future cases.

This encourages the development of cases and ultimately of law in directions the Justices prefer."[60]

NOTES

[1] Catherine Hetos Skefos, "The Supreme Court Gets a Home," *Supreme Court Yearbook 1976* (Washington, D.C.: Supreme Court Historical Society, 1975), p. 27.

[2] Ibid.

[3] C. Vann Woodward, "A Dredful Decision," *New York Review of Books* (December 7, 1978), p. 30.

[4] William O. Douglas, *The Court Years, 1939–1975: The Autobiography of William O. Douglas* (New York: Vintage Books, 1981), pp. 4–5.

[5] Bernard Schwartz, *Super Chief: Earl Warren and His Supreme Court—A Judicial Biography* (New York: New York University Press, 1983), pp. 27–28.

[6] Quoted in Congressional Research Service, *The Supreme Court and Its Work* (Washington, D.C.: Congressional Quarterly, 1981), p. 98.

[7] Douglas, *The Court Years, 1939–1975*, p. 5.

[8] Wesley McCune, *The Nine Young Men* (New York: Harper & Brothers, 1947), p. 2.

[9] This section draws largely on the material provided in Congressional Quarterly, *Guide to the U.S. Supreme Court* (Washington, D.C.: Congressional Quarterly, 1979), pp. 714, 723–24, 741–47.

[10] (Chicago: University of Chicago Press, 1964).

[11] Bob Woodward and Scott Armstrong, *The Brethren: Inside the Supreme Court* (New York: Simon & Schuster, 1979).

[12] Walter Murphy, "Spilling the Secrets of the Supreme Court," *The Guardian* (January 13, 1980), p. 18.

[13] "Court at the Crossroads," *Time* (October 8, 1984), p. 30.

[14] Douglas, *The Court Years, 1939–1975*, p. 5.

[15] David N. Atkinson and Dale A. Neuman, "Toward a Cost Theory of Judicial Alignment: The Case of the Truman Bloc," *Midwest Journal of Political Science* 13 (1969), pp. 271–83.

[16] "Inside the Burger Court," *Newsweek* (December 10, 1979), p. 87.

[17] Linda Greenhouse, "From Here On, It's Uphill for the Supreme Court," *New York Times* (May 6, 1984).

[18] Howard Ball, *Courts and Politics: The Federal Judicial System* (Englewood Cliffs, N.J.: Prentice Hall, 1980), p. 250.

[19] Ibid., p. 253.

[20] *New York Times v. U.S.*, 403 U.S. 713 (1971); and *U.S. v. Washington Post*, 403 U.S. 713 (1971).

[21] *U.S. v. Nixon*, 418 U.S. 683 (1974).

[22] *Dames and Moore v. Regan*, 453 U.S. 654 (1981).

[23] Congressional Research Service, *The Supreme Court and Its Work*, pp. 58–59.

[24] 358 U.S. 1 (1958).

[25] Congressional Research Service, *The Supreme Court and Its Work*, pp. 58–59.

[26] William C. Louthan, *The Politics of Justice* (Port Washington, N.Y.: Kennikat Press, 1979), p. 52.

[27] Lawrence Baum, *The Supreme Court* (Washington, D.C.: Congressional Quarterly Press, 1981), p. 82.

[28] Glendon Schubert, *Constitutional Politics* (New York: Holt, Rinehart & Winston, 1960), p. 100.

[29] See United States Code, Chapter 81, Title 28, Section 1254.

[30] Baum, *The Supreme Court*, p. 82.

[31] Stuart Taylor, Jr., "High Court Expected to Gain Freedom in Selecting Its Cases," *New York Times* (June 9, 1988).

[32] Baum, *The Supreme Court*, p. 83.

[33] Douglas, *The Court Years, 1939–1975*, p. 5.

[34] Congressional Research Service, *The Supreme Court and Its Work*, p. 59.

[35] Ibid., pp. 61–63.

[36] Ball, *Courts and Politics*, p. 259.

[37] Congressional Research Service, *The Supreme Court and Its Work*, p. 64.

[38] Ibid., p. 63.

[39] Ball, *Courts and Politics*, p. 259.

[40] Ibid., pp. 253–54.

[41] Congressional Research Service, *The Supreme Court and Its Work*, p. 65.

[42] Loren P. Beth, *Politics—The Constitution and the Supreme Court* (New York: Row, Peterson, 1962), p. 41.

[43] Robert C. Bradley, "What is Actually Happening Behind Closed Doors? The Conference Proceedings of the Supreme Court," 6 *Law, Courts, and Judicial Process Section Newsletter* (Summer, 1989), pp. 1–3; and "Correspondence" from William Rehnquist and Henry J. Abraham, 7 *Law, Courts, and Judicial Process Section Newsletter* (Fall 1989), pp. 8–9.

[44] Douglas, *The Court Years, 1939–1975*, p. 22.

[45] Ibid., p. 34.

[46] Woodward and Armstrong, *The Brethren*, p. 3.

[47] Arthur Selwyn Miller, *Toward Increased Judicial Activism: The Political Role of the Supreme Court* (Westport, Conn.: Greenwood Press, 1982), pp. 25, 308.

[48] No. 87-107 (1988).

[49] 427 U.S. 160 (1976).

[50] *Jones v. Alfred H. Mayor Co.*, 392 U.S. 409 (1968).

[51] *Tillman v. Wheaton-Haven Recreation Association, Inc.*, 410 U.S. 431 (1973).

[52] *McDonald v. Santa Fe Trail Transportation Co.*, 427 U.S. 273 (1976).

[53] Laurence H. Tribe, *American Constitutional Law* (Mineola, N.Y.: Foundation Press, 1988), pp. 333, 333n16, 1479n31, 1508n52.

[54] Stuart Taylor, Jr., "One Vote Tips a Balance on Civil Rights," *New York Times* (May 1, 1988).

[55] Jack Greenberg, "Distressing Signals from the Court," *New York Times* (May 1, 1988).

[56] Stuart Taylor, Jr., "Court, 5-4, Votes to Restudy Rights in Minority Suits," *New York Times* (April 26, 1988).

[57] "Casting a Shadow over Civil Rights," *New York Times* (April 27, 1988).

[58] Greenberg, "Distressing Signals from the Court."

[59] Linda Greenhouse, "Court Upholds Use of Rights Law But Limits How It Can Be Applied," *New York Times* (June 16, 1989). See *Patterson v. McLean Credit Union*, ——— U.S. ——— (1989).

[60] Greenberg, "Distressing Signals from the Court."

Supreme Court Participants

THE JUSTICES: SELECTION, TENURE, RETIREMENT, AND IMPEACHMENT

Most prominent and prestigious among the various Supreme Court participants are obviously the justices themselves. Chapter One provided some understanding of their appointment and the surrounding politics of selection. Here we will address directly the Supreme Court selection process, and we will examine the tenure, retirement, and possible impeachment of our justices.

Although the Constitution in Article II, Section 2, provides that the president shall appoint Supreme Court justices by and with the advice and consent of the Senate, the Constitution stipulates no formal qualifications: none of residency, none of age, none of educational or professional background. Most students are surprised to learn, for example, that the Constitution does not require that Supreme Court justices hold law degrees. In large measure this is because law schools as we know them today did not exist until the last quarter of the nineteenth century. Indeed, until the period following World War I, apprenticeships in law offices remained the principal pathway of entry into the legal profession.[1] Thus, it surprises many to learn that it was not until 1957, when Stanley Reed was replaced on the High Bench by Charles Whittaker, that all sitting members of the Supreme Court held law degrees.[2]

In a very real sense Supreme Court justices constitute a kind of "secular priesthood," which "monitors the governmental process" and protects "substantive value choices."[3] Yet most Supreme Court scholars agree that the Court is not a "meritocracy" and that its justices are frequently appointed for political reasons, normally by presidents who hope to influence public policy for many years beyond their tenure as chief executive.[4] On most related questions regarding the Supreme Court selection process, scholars, other commentators, and, yes, even judges and justices disagree. Chief Justice Rehnquist has said that presidents have had only "partial success" when attempting to make a lasting impact by appointing justices who share their policy preferences. But, he has said, there is "no reason in the world why presidents should not" try to do so.[5] Judge Irving Kaufman, of the United States Court of Appeals for the Second Circuit, has disagreed. He argues that presidents can and have successfully "packed" the Court with justices who share their views on important matters of public policy but that it is clearly wrong for them to try to do so. Kaufman urges, rather, that presidents make appointments to the Court based on so-called neutral criteria of "intellectual acumen" and "proven excellence."[6] Disagreeing in part with both Rehnquist and Kaufman, Supreme Court scholar David M. O'Brien writes that although presidents may try to mold the Court to support their policy preferences, their appointees, once on the Court, frequently disappoint them.[7] Approaching the matter from a slightly different angle, political scientist Henry Abraham has specified six criteria presidents *should* use when making appointments to the Court: "demonstrated judicial temperament; professional expertise and competence; absolute personal and professional integrity; an able, agile, lucid mind; appropriate professional educational background or training, and the ability to communicate clearly both orally and in writing."[8] Disagreeing in part with all of the above, constitutional scholar Laurence Tribe has argued that as a matter of political reality presidents *will* try to influence the Court through their appointments, presidents regularly *make correct guesses* about the possible behavior of their appointees once on the bench and *are rarely surprised* by their views or votes; in any event, it is neither possible nor desirable to make appointments based solely on politically neutral principles. Once on the Court, justices cannot avoid making choices among competing visions and values. In other words, Tribe's view is that presidents can and do change the Court's direction by changing its membership.[9] With reference to the historical evolution of the appointment process, political scientist John Schmidhauser writes that it was virtually inevitable that the Court's justices would be chosen on the basis of political considerations within a broad societal context.[10]

Despite these widely divergent comments and conclusions, there are some facts, historical and empirical, we can agree upon. The selection, tenure, retirement, and impeachment of Supreme Court justices are not entirely unknown, mysterious, or otherwise ambiguous phenomena. The Constitutional Convention in 1787 seriously considered only four proposals for Supreme Court selection: appointment by the Congress, appointment by the president alone, appointment by the Senate alone, and finally the alternative actually adopted, appointment by the president with a majority vote confirmation by the Senate. Though mentioned at the Constitutional Convention by Benjamin Franklin, the notion of electing justices by popular vote was not treated seriously and never debated by the delegates. We have seen that no selection criteria were formally provided by the framers. However, the method of selection specified by the framers and the structure of the federal judiciary created by the first Congress set the stage for selections based on the criteria of the potential justice's party affiliation, political ideology, sectional background, and interest-group connections. Though mentioned by some delegates, professional training and judicial experience were not discussed seriously and never specified as a prerequisite of office.[11] Many formal proposals have been made over the years to alter the selection process and to introduce selection criteria. Such proposals have usually arisen during periods of political controversy over the Court's ideological composition, rivalry between Congress and the president, or "progressive" assertions of the need for a Court more responsive to popular will. Examples include a proposal to give the House of Representatives a confirmation role like that of the Senate, proposals to grant the sole power of appointment to the two branches of Congress, and various proposals to elect justices (for example, a proposal that voters in each federal circuit elect one associate justice with the chief justice then elected either nationally or by and from among the associate justices). There have been yet other proposals that would not alter the method of selection but would add qualifications of office. For example, one proposal made as recently as 1956 specified that Supreme Court nominees must have at least five years of experience as a judge on a lower federal court or on a state supreme court. None of these proposals, however, has met with either broad public support or widespread endorsement within Congress.

Before leaving our consideration of the selection process, we should take notice of two themes persuasively argued by Professor Laurence Tribe in his 1985 book *God Save This Honorable Court: How the Choices of Supreme Court Justices Shape Our Lives.* First, Tribe all but destroys the "myth of the surprised President" by demonstrating convincingly that presidents almost always get exactly what they want from the justices they appoint. Second, Tribe also explodes the "myth of the spineless Senate" by showing persuasively that the Senate not only has refused to be a rubber stamp but has rejected nearly one in five Court nominees, frequently on the basis of their political and economic philosophies. Regarding the first theme, Tribe points out that the idea that presidents are often surprised by the behavior of justices they have appointed is an idea resting largely on celebrated anecdotes famous mostly because they are exceptions to the general rule. Some authors have pointed out, for example, President Theodore Roosevelt's displeasure with his own appointment of Justice Oliver Wendell Holmes largely because of Holmes's votes and opinions against Roosevelt's antitrust policies. Even this author must plead guilty to being mislead by the myth because, in 1979, he wrote:

> It is true that [presidents] sometimes guess incorrectly about how judges will behave. The conservative President Eisenhower appointed Earl Warren expecting him to be a moderate to conservative chief justice. When Warren demonstrated his liberal leanings Eisenhower said of his choice: 'The biggest damn fool mistake I ever made!' The liberal President Wilson appointed James McReynolds thinking that McReynolds's record as a young trust-busting attorney indicated a liberal ideology. McReynolds turned out to have no other liberal bones in his body.[12]

Tribe has set the record straight. Holmes did sometimes write and vote against Roosevelt's antitrust policies. In the case that bothered Roosevelt most, Holmes's dissent supported a four-justice minority, totally unaffecting a 5-4 decision upholding Roosevelt's law. Yet in such policy areas as minimum wage and maximum hour legislation, child labor regulations, and labor union law, all vital to the president's preferences, Holmes almost uniformly supported Roosevelt's position.[13] Regarding Eisenhower's appointment of Earl Warren, it is undoubtedly the case that Warren turned out to be far more liberal than Eisenhower had expected, especially in cases involving civil rights and liberties. But Eisenhower's objectives in appointing Warren probably had little to do with how he expected Warren to vote once on the Court. Rather, Eisenhower had other political objectives in mind. He wanted to pay off his debt to Warren for delivering nearly all of California's delegate votes at the 1952 Republican National Convention (Warren had been governor of California at the time). Further, Eisenhower placed Warren on the Court to remove him from the California political scene, where his progressive politics and policies were a problem for the state's party leadership, which included Eisenhower's vice president, Richard Nixon. In other words, from the perspective of what Eisenhower hoped to achieve by appointing Warren, the president got what he wanted. Regarding Wilson's appointment of McReynolds, there is some reason to believe that Wilson did recognize that McReynolds was truly a conservative and chose to put him on the Court in order to get him off Wilson's cabinet, where he had served Wilson badly as attorney general. Even if Wilson did guess wrong about McReynolds, Tribe concludes that Wilson's surprise, if he was surprised, stands as only one dramatic example of an exception to the general rule.[14] From the beginning, presidents have consistently made appointments to the Court to achieve a variety of political and policy objectives, and generally they have been pleased with the results. Washington appointed the first six justices, and three were persons who had helped him produce the Constitution, while the three others had worked hard to guarantee state ratifications of the document. Washington's justices consistently supported the president's efforts to expand national governing authority. John Adams saw to it that his Federalist party's policies would survive the takeover of the executive and legislative branches by Jefferson's Democratic-Republican party with his eleventh-hour appointment of Chief Justice John Marshall. For 35 years thereafter Marshall attempted to do what Adams almost certainly had wanted. Andrew Jackson carefully appointed nominees who he hoped would help him redirect American politics along lines preferred by his Democratic party, especially with respect to the great battle over the legality and propriety of a central national bank. Jackson was not disappointed by his nominees. And the story goes on and on.[15] This is not to say that Supreme Court justices are mere automatons. As Tribe writes, if the myth of the surprised president means only that justices "are not minions of the Presidents who nominate them—then we can concede its undeniable truth because it is also irrefutably trivial." Surprises have occurred, but they are rare indeed. Moreover, "a President with any skill and a little luck can usually avoid them—and can, with fair success, build the Court of his own dreams."[16]

The second theme, the emptiness of the "myth of the spineless Senate," is similarly complex but important. First, we must distinguish between the Senate's influence on the nomination itself and its influence after the fact of nomination as it considers its confirmation vote. As to the former, there are a few examples of the Senate successfully pressuring the president to nominate a particular person. In 1862 all but four senators petitioned President Lincoln to appoint Samuel F. Miller. After Lincoln did so, the Senate voted to confirm the nomination in less than half an hour. In 1869 the Senate petitioned President Grant to nominate Edwin M. Stanton, a former secretary of war. Stanton was not Grant's personal first choice, but the president did make the nomination. Such examples are rare, however, and in general we can conclude that the Senate has not played a historically significant role in influencing nominations to the Court.[17] The story of the Senate's confirmation function, however, is quite different. Here it has played a crucial role. Of the 145 persons appointed to a seat on the Supreme Court, the Senate has rejected 28—nearly 20 percent.[18]

At least two important lessons can be learned by taking notice of what happened in 1969–70 when President Nixon attempted to fill a vacancy on the Supreme Court resulting from the resignation of Justice Fortas on May 16, 1969. As we learned in Chapter One, Nixon was rebuffed twice by the Senate when it rejected first the nomination of Judge Haynsworth and then the nomination of Judge Carswell. Nixon finally got his way with the nomination and Senate confirmation of Justice Balckmun, who took his seat on June 22, 1970. It must be granted, of course, that this series of events was unusual. There had not been a double rejection for the same seat since 1894, when President Cleveland's nominations of William Hornblower and Wheeler Peckham were rejected in succession by the Senate. The delay caused by that confirmation battle resulted in the Court operating for a full term without a full bench for the first time since the Civil War. More pertinent to our immediate concerns, however, is Nixon's assertion during the battle that Senate approval of Supreme Court nominees should be pro forma, and his argument that the rejections of Haynsworth and Carswell constituted a violation of the separation of powers by virtue of Senate encroachment on presidential power. Nixon's position, however, does not square with the expectations of the framers of the Constitution at least as described by Alexander Hamilton in the *Federalist Paper No. 76.* [19] Hamilton wrote that a president's nominee might well be rejected by the Senate. But, he added, the practical effect of such a rejection could "only be to make place for another nomination by himself. The person ultimately chosen must be the object of his preference, though perhaps not in the first degree." Thus, it would seem that the double rejection of Haynsworth and Carswell, although unusual, was entirely proper. From these facts we learn two lessons: (1) presidents do usually get what they want, at least in the end; and (2) the Senate is no rubber stamp, nor was it intended to be.

In any event, as Tribe writes, the simple fact is that the Senate has played a vigorous part in the confirmation process from the start, whether it *ought* to or not. The credibility of the spineless Senate myth has in recent years been supported by the relatively easy confirmations of Justices Blackmun, Powell, Rehnquist, Stevens, and O'Connor between the years 1970 and 1981. But this is to overlook what happened before Blackmun (the rejections of Haynsworth and Carswell in 1969–70) and, we might add, what has happened since (the failure of the Bork and Ginsburg nominations in 1987). The historical record from Washington's administration through Reagan's makes it clear that the Senate will scrutinize nominees and sometimes reject them. Washington's nomination of John Rutledge for the position of chief justice was rejected by the Senate largely because of Rutledge's opposition to Jay's Treaty, which the Senate's majority strongly supported. Rutledge's opposition to the treaty was thought to raise serious questions about his views on foreign policy generally; and since the treaty was so strongly and vocally supported by members of his own party in the Senate, Rutledge's opposition raised questions about his political judgment. Thus from the beginning the Senate has shown an inclination to inquire independently into a nominee's substantive beliefs. Its rejection of Madison's nominee, Alexander Wolcott, in 1811 was based mostly on the Senate's conclusions that by way of training, experience, and temperament Wolcott was not qualified to serve. However, other nominees have been rejected (or confirmed by only the narrowest of votes) largely for political reasons. In 1826 John Quincy Adams's nomination of Robert Trimble was confirmed only after a bitter battle because the Senate thought Trimble too deeply wedded to the Whig party's preference for federal power. When Trimble passed away just two years later, Adams failed to secure the nomination of John Crittenden for the same reasons. George Woodward was nominated by President Polk in 1845. When Woodward's advocacy of the so-called American Nativist agenda (which emphasized a limitation on immigration and discrimination against some ethnic groups) became the issue in the Senate confirmation fight, he too was rejected. In 1861 lame duck President Buchanan nominated Jeremiah Black, whose experience as U.S. attorney general and as chief justice of the Pennsylvania Supreme Court made him clearly qualified; but Black's opposition to the out-and-out abolition of slavery led to his rejection by the Senate. Twenty years later President Hayes failed to win confirmation of his nominees, Stanley Matthews, largely because Matthews, a corporate attorney, was perceived as being too extremely committed to business interests. The Senate simply ignored Hayes's nomination until he left office. President Garfield renominated Matthews shortly thereafter; and although he was confirmed, it was the narrowest of possible victories—24 to 23. In 1930 President Hoover's nomination of court of appeals judge John Parker was rejected by Senate vote essentially because of Parker's opinion favoring the legality of so-called yellow dog contracts, which require that employees pledge as a condition of employment not to join a union. In addition, as we have already seen, Judge Haynsworth was rejected in 1969 in part because of his perceived opposition to civil rights litigants. The point, as Tribe makes it, cannot be overemphasized: For better or worse, Supreme Court nominees are often judged by the Senate on the basis of what they believe. Although we might point to both periods of acquiescence and examples of abuse on the part of the Senate, the plain fact is that nominees are sometimes rejected on the basis of their socioeconomic, political, and judicial philosophies.[20]

Once on the Court, justices have tended to enjoy a relatively lengthy tenure, the average being around 15 years. Chief justices in particular seem to hang on forever. Marshall and Taney, two of the most revered, were 80 and 87 respectively when they departed. Among associate justices, Holmes stayed on past his 90th birthday. Many others have served on the Court into their eighties, including such distinguished jurists as Louis Brandeis, Hugo Black, and Felix Frankfurter, as well as more recently Justices Harry Blackmun, William Brennan, and Thurgood Marshall. (Marshall is fond of saying, "I was appointed for life and I intend to serve out my term.") This aging or "greying" phenomenon has necessarily led to some now famous "old Courts" in our history. The "oldest" Court—(defined by the average age of the sitting justices)—is the "nine old men" of the early New Deal era in the mid-1930s before President Franklin Delano Roosevelt's first appointment. Its average age was 72 years. Then, in order, comes the Burger

Court of 1986 (average age, just short of 72); the 1909 Court before President Taft's record-setting six appointments in one term (average age, 70); the 1861 Court prior to Lincoln's appointments (average age, 69); and the first "old" Court, which confronted newly elected President Andrew Jackson in 1828 (average age, 63).[21] The Court's potential influence in public policy, particularly the potential influence of chief justices of long tenure, is revealed in the fact that while we have had 41 presidents (through Bush), we have had only seventeen chief justices (through Rehnquist). Obviously, then, many chief justices have had influence well beyond the tenure of the president who appointed them. John Marshall was chief justice for nearly 35 years over the course of six different presidential administrations; Roger Taney for 28 years covered at least parts of nine different presidencies; Earl Warren, for sixteen years over four presidencies; and Warren Burger, for sixteen years also over parts of four presidencies.[22] Given the lengthy average tenure of Supreme Court justices, given the particularly lengthy residence of some chief justices, and given the resulting and inevitable "greying" of the Court as cohorts age together, presidents are occasionally presented with a "historic opportunity" to change the Court's direction by changing its membership. Thus, President Andrew Jackson made six nominations in eight years as chief executive (1829–37), Lincoln appointed five justices in only three years (1861–64), Taft made six nominations (1909–13)—the most ever in one term—and Franklin Roosevelt, after having to work out his first term with no vacancies, ultimately made seven appointments in a four-year period spanning his second and third terms. Obviously, the power of a president to influence public policy through judicial selection should not be underestimated. Presidents are, in fact, confronted with those "historic moments" when, with luck, they can seize the opportunity to appoint justices who share their values and their vision. As we have seen, those justices normally will vote just as the president who appointed them had hoped.[23]

Of course, Supreme Court justices do eventually retire. Neither the Constitution nor any existing congressional statute mandates retirement. Article III, Section 1, of the Constitution states only that justices "shall hold their Offices during good Behavior." Thus, Supreme Court justices are in effect appointed for life. The only available means of forced removal from the bench is impeachment (discussed below); but only one justice in our history has been impeached by the House, and none has been removed by conviction in the Senate. As we learned in Chapter Three, during the Court's early years prior to its emergence as a significant national policy maker, justices frequently resigned after brief service to take what seemed then to be more attractive positions in government. Eventually, however, and especially in the twentieth century, most justices would choose to serve until death or until advanced age accompanied by poor health led them to retire. There are, of course, exceptions to the general rule. Some justices have resigned as a matter of conscience. Examples include Justice John Campbell in 1861 (to return to his home in Alabama at the start of the Civil War) and Justice Benjamin Curtis in 1857 (because of his disagreement with the *Dred Scott* decision). Others have resigned in order to seek or take other jobs. Chief Justice John Jay resigned in 1795 to become governor of New York, Justice Charles Evans Hughes in 1912 to run for president, Justice James Byrnes in 1942 to become director of the Wartime Office of Economic Stabilization, and Justice Arthur Goldberg in 1965 to accept appointment as United Nations ambassador. Some have left the Court apparently because of simple job dissatisfaction. Notable examples are Justice John Clark in 1922 and Justice Charles Whittaker in 1962. There are yet other reasons for early resignation. Justice Tom Clark resigned in 1967 after the appointment of his son to the position of U.S. attorney general so that potential conflicts of interest would not create the appearance of impropriety. Indeed, impropriety, whether real or merely apparent, led Justice Abe Fortas to resign in 1969, as we learned in Chapter One.[24]

In some instances the Court's best interest may have been better served had certain justices resigned earlier than they did. In most such instances the justices had their reasons for staying on. Justice Gabriel Duvall, though in clearly failing health, refused to resign after President Jackson's reelection in 1832 because he feared Jackson would appoint a "radical" justice to replace him.[25] Chief Justice Taft, though also in poor health and aware of his ailments, refused to resign in 1929 because, as he put it, "I must stay on the Court in order to prevent the Bolsheviki from getting control."[26] More recently, justices of recognized ability during their prime stayed on despite nearly incapacitating infirmities. In the early 1970s Justices Hugo Black (senility), John Marshall Harlan (who was nearly blind), and William O. Douglas (severe stroke) continued to serve. At least in Douglas's case, the reason was the apparent hope that he could hold on until after the presidential election of 1976 so that his replacement might be named by a Democrat. Even though Douglas was induced to leave reluctantly in 1975, after his formal resignation he continued to come to the Court as if he were still a member.[27]

A recitation of the difficulties described above leads naturally to an interest in current Supreme Court retirement policies and proposals for their reform. We might also wonder exactly what early retirement policies and disciplinary actions, including impeachment, might be appropriate when a justice, though physically, mentally, or ethically infirm, finds resignation or retirement unpalatable. Current law provides that justices may choose retirement, with continuing compensation commensurate with their salaries, at age 70 after having served ten years or at age 65 after having served fifteen years. Further inducing "early" retirement is a provision allowing justices who are 70 and who have ten years' service to take partial retirement by sitting on lower federal courts and thus receive not only full pay as of their retirement date but also any subsequent salary increases. The current policy does not, however, deal with the difficult case of a justice who refuses to retire even though many, including upon occasion a majority of his colleagues, think he should. To address this and related circumstances, suggestions have been to add a mandatory retirement age (of 70 or 75) to the Constitution by amendment. Supreme Court scholar Charles Fairman has argued that at least two sound justifications exist for such an amendment.

> [F]irst, the actual impairment of mental and physical powers. . . . A second reason . . . involves considerations of a different order. Rigidity of thought and obsolescence of social outlook, though more objective, may be no less real than the waning of bodily powers. When a majority of the Court cling to views of public policy no longer entertained by the community or shared by the political branches of government, a conflict arises which must be resolved.[28]

To date, however, no mandatory retirement proposal has even come close to adoption.

The ultimate sanction against wayward Supreme Court justices is impeachment. Like other federal officials, justices can be removed from office upon a majority vote in the House to indict and a two-thirds vote in the Senate to convict for "treason, bribery, or other high crimes and misdemeanors" (Article II, Section 4). However, for reasons both historical and practical the removal of a Supreme Court justice through impeachment proceedings is today highly unlikely. The historical reasons are several. The first is provided by the only case in which the House has voted to impeach. In 1804 the House voted eight articles of impeachment against Justice Samuel Chase. The charges revolved around Chase's extrajudicial participation in the failed effort to reelect Federalist President John Adams in 1800, and around his misguided and highly partisan charges to grand juries in the treason trials of two Jeffersonian Republicans, John Fries and James Collender, in 1803. In fact, the impeachment proceedings against Chase were part of President Jefferson's attempt to use impeachment to win control of the Federalist judiciary he inherited after his election to the presidency in 1800. However, Chase was acquitted on all counts by the Senate on March 1, 1805. Jefferson himself admitted that the impeachment of Supreme Court justices was a "mere scarecrow" and "a farce which will not be tried again." In effect, the Chase case served to discount impeachment as a method of forcing justices out of office and to discourage its further use by convincing most persons that impeachment is a heroic device to be saved for the most serious of situations.

In recent years, therefore, no justice has faced the real possibility of impeachment. Chief Justice Warren, long the much-hated villain of the right-wing John Birch Society, faced calls for impeachment by that and other ultraconservative groups in the 1950s and 1960s, but no such pleas were taken seriously by the Congress. Liberal Justice William O. Douglas also faced calls for impeachment in 1970. The charges revolved around various alleged financial improprieties and around his off-the-court writings considered by some to be an endorsement of revolution. In fact, as we learned in Chapter One, the attempt to impeach Douglas was largely a politically motivated counteroffensive launched by the defenders of President Nixon's nominees to the Court, Haynsworth and Carswell. Angered by defeat, the House leader of this group, Gerald R. Ford, sought Douglas's impeachment and argued that an impeachable act is "whatever a majority of the House of Representatives considers it to be at a given moment in history."[29] The House subcommittee that took up the Douglas case did agree that the grounds for impeachment do extend beyond criminal acts to other, lesser offenses, but the subcommittee found nothing in the record to warrant further proceedings against Douglas. The attempt to impeach Douglas thus died in subcommittee on December 3, 1970. Finally, we have the case of Abe Fortas mentioned above and described in detail in Chapter One. Fortas, as we learned, resigned in 1969 amid allegations of financial wrongdoing. Some writers have argued that had Fortas not resigned, he almost certainly would have faced impeachment proceedings. If this is so, the effect is to make the impeachment of Supreme Court justices even less likely today because well aware of the Fortas case, justices are now very careful about their extrajudicial activities, investments, and connections to foundations that might cause conflicts of interest.[30]

In addition to the lessons of history, practical problems may well further discourage the use of impeachment against allegedly wayward justices. A number of unanswered legal questions exist. For example, can indictment of a justice on criminal charges precede or only follow an impeachment? If criminal indictment and conviction in the courts *can* precede impeachment, can imprisonment also precede impeachment?[31] These are not unimportant questions because, among other reasons, unless a justice is impeached, no rule prevents him or her from receiving full salary for life even if convicted of crimes. Then there are a variety of practical problems now leading to calls for some type of substitute for congressional impeachment of justices and other federal judges. For example, "What type of trial is the Senate supposed to conduct? What happens to the Senate's regular calendar during the days or weeks necessary to hear the evidence? If much of the work is delegated to a committee . . . does the Senate as a whole perform its constitutional duty?"[32] The framers of the Constitution contemplated a Senate of 26 members; a jury of 100 is clearly a different thing. Further, growing evidence suggests that members of today's Senate do not think of themselves as either prosecutors or jurors and are increasingly uncomfortable in those roles. Current debate on the subject of judicial impeachment may seem unnecessary, given the unlikely occurrence of an impeachment of a Supreme Court justice. But in 1985 Judge Harry Claiborne became the first federal judge in 50 years to be impeached, convicted, and removed from office. Impeachment proceedings were also initiated recently against two other federal judges, Alcee L. Hastings and Walter L. Nixon. And while the impeachment of lower federal court judges has always been more likely than the impeachment of a Supreme Court justice, the concerns now expressed as a result of recent and pending cases involving federal judges would also be raised should a matter of such seriousness arise that a Supreme Court justice would actually face an impeachment test. Current reform proposals range from those that would transfer the impeachment power to the Federal Judicial Conference (the policy-making body for the federal judicial system) to those that would create a special commission composed of judges, lawyers, and lay people—modeled on systems already in place in some states—to handle judicial discipline and removal from office. Proponents of change tend to cite the problems mentioned above in justification. Opponents tend to argue that no change, making removal easier, should be considered because the life tenure of our justices is the very thing that gives them the independence and the isolation from political forces so crucial to their function as guarantors of civil rights and liberties.[33]

THE LITIGANTS: INDIVIDUALS, THE GOVERNMENT, INTEREST GROUPS, TEST CASES, AND CLASS ACTIONS

The litigants are the parties who come to the Supreme Court with cases. Every case that comes to the Court has at least two formal parties, and often there are more than two parties on each side. Parties to Supreme Court cases consist of a comparatively disparate assortment of individuals and groups. The largest single type of individual litigant is normally the criminal defendant appealing a conviction, but individual litigants are also frequently before the Court as parties to disputes dealing with such diverse matters as civil rights and liberties, labor-management relations, and personal injuries. National, state, and local government may also be a party. Since roughly 30 percent of the civil cases initiated in federal district courts each year involve the national government as one of the two sides to the dispute, it should not be surprising that some of those are ultimately appealed to the Supreme Court. Such cases typically involve some sort of tax or contract dispute. Similarly, state and local governmental agencies are also parties to cases that come to the Court. Most Americans understand that criminal law governs the behavior of persons by prohibiting acts against society as a whole, and thus a criminal case is one in which the government prosecutes a defendant. In some instances appeals to the Supreme Court ultimately follow. Many Americans are often surprised to learn, though, that the government is also frequently a party to civil cases. The simple point is that most of the cases the Supreme Court finally hears, whether criminal or civil, have a public character.

Although it is difficult to generalize about Supreme Court litigants, Professor Lawrence Baum has developed a fairly simple typology that is useful to our understanding. Baum distinguishes the "ordinary" litigant from the "political" litigant. "Ordinary" litigants appeal cases to the Court to promote or protect a personal or institutional interest. "Political" litigants come to the Court to promote public policies they prefer (for example, environmental and consumer protection or civil and welfare rights).[34] Ordinary litigation typically terminates in federal or state lower courts. Indeed, in the civil area, evidence indicates that little more than 10 percent of all civil disputes ever reach trial. They are commonly concluded out of court at settlement or pretrial conferences. Those that are tried in court are frequently not appealed by the losing party—especially not "all the way to the Supreme Court"—because the cost is prohibitive or the likelihood of winning is minimal.[35] It has been estimated that it takes two to five years for a typical case to go all the way up to the Supreme Court. Costs, including the printing of the briefs and records, are very high.[36] Conversely, political litigation is usually taken to some level of appeal and not uncommonly to the Supreme Court itself.[37] This should not be surprising, since political litigants can achieve broad policy victories only by taking their cases to the highest possible echelon of the judicial system. Because major matters of public policy are at issue, political litigants commonly find financial support for their cases and causes from interest groups that share their objectives. (We will examine interest groups as litigants in detail below.)

Students of Supreme Court litigation differ on the proportion of cases they believe can be deemed "political" in Baum's typology. Clement Vose concludes that most Supreme Court cases are taken to the Court to achieve public policy objectives.[38] Nathan Hakman thinks that most Supreme Court cases are initiated as *ad hoc* private controversies; parties are drawn into the judicial process step by step and appeal by appeal. Judicial policy making may eventually occur, but not because the litigant consciously embarked on a journey with that destination in mind.[39] Samuel Krislov seems to agree.[40] Baum himself comes to what is probably the correct conclusion. If we count *all* the cases brought to the Court, as distinguished from those the Court in fact hears and decides on the merits with a full opinion, the majority are "ordinary" cases. They are criminal cases in which the government hopes only to sustain a conviction or a defendant hopes only to remain out of jail. Neither party has an intent to establish a great principle of constitutional or criminal law affecting all of society. Or they are tax or antitrust cases in which a person or corporation has a particular economic interest to protect. The cases actually heard and decided by the Court, on the other hand, tend more frequently to be those in which public policy objectives are paramount to at least one of the parties.[41] Even the justices seem to recognize the difference between these two kinds of cases, referring to the uninteresting, tedious, or technical cases as "dogs."[42] Baum uses two actual cases to further clarify the distinction between "ordinary" and "political" litigation. In 1978 the Supreme Court decided a case in which a white male applicant to a medical school sought to have his denial of admission reversed on the grounds that the school's preferential admission policy—affirmative action—denied him his legal rights. Here, the litigant Allan Bakke was not interested primarily in the long-range or widespread policy implications of a Supreme Court decision regarding affirmative action. It is true that both Bakke and the medical school were supported in the litigation by a variety of interest groups. However, Bakke's fundamental objective was to gain admission. Indeed, he even sought an out-of-court settlement to achieve his personal objective. Such a settlement would have had virtually no long-term policy significance. In other words, Bakke's principal objective was to gain admission to the medical school for himself, to achieve a personal interest, not to promote a public policy. In that sense, although the decision in Bakke's case was highly publicized and apparently important. (Bakke won when the policy that had excluded him was invalidated even though the Court said some other types of preferential admission policies are legal.) Allan Bakke himself was an "ordinary" litigant. By contrast, on two occasions Madalyn Murray O'Hair brought cases to the Supreme Court with primarily political goals in her mind. In one she sought successfully to obtain a Court ruling banning prayer in the nation's public schools. In the other she challenged a governmental tax exemption for religious property. She had nothing to gain personally from a favorable Court decision. In fact, her family was tormented by persons who opposed her views, and she lost her job as the result of her efforts. But because her primary intent was to achieve a policy objective, she was a "political" litigant.[43]

The Bakke and O'Hair suits did have one thing in common, however. They were costly. Indeed, the costs of individual litigation, whether "ordinary" or "political," are so considerable that individual cases have gradually given way in recent years to what Samuel Krislov calls "representational litigation."[44] By this designation Krislov is conveying an increasingly important fact about life in and around the Supreme Court: In many, if not the majority of, important cases before the Supreme Court, organized interest groups play a variety of significant roles. Interest groups may come before the Court directly as litigating parties with the purpose of advancing public policies in the interest of their members. In such cases the formal litigant is usually an individual member of the group, but the group provides necessary financial support. Seeking policy objectives before the Supreme Court is particularly attractive to minority groups or others so disadvantaged by their size or lack of electoral support that access to the Supreme Court comes far more easily than access to the Congress or to the executive branch bureaucracy.[45] Environmental activists, consumer protectionists, and welfare rights groups are good examples.[46] Since roughly the mid-1970s public interest law firms have increasingly provided legal counsel to groups whose resources are too limited to retain their own lawyers and to pursue their policy objectives before the Court entirely on their own.[47]

Interest-group involvement in cases before the Court may also occur in several indirect ways. This is important because groups cannot ordinarily advance their interests in the judicial arena in the same manner as they can in the legislative and executive branches of government. For example, our norms prohibit direct contact with judges (that is, button-holing judges in the traditional "lobbying" sense). However, interest groups have found alternative mechanisms. The four most common means of group access to the Supreme Court are passing information along to justices quite indirectly by writing articles for legal periodicals, submitting amicus curiae briefs, instituting test cases, and organizing class actions.

Only limited evidence suggests that justices read and are influenced by law review articles. Some observers have argued that "liberal" justices read and are influenced by articles in legal periodicals more frequently than "conservative" justices. If this is true, it may be because conservatives are less likely to find support for their views there. In any event, none of this evidence is very solid, and the impact of law review articles on Supreme Court decision making remains extremely difficult to measure.

Submitting amicus curiae briefs is a somewhat more direct means of influencing Supreme Court decisions. Technically intended to give to the Court information and arguments not otherwise presented, these briefs thus provide a broader basis for decision. They may simply complement the brief of a litigant, or they may advise the Court of the probable consequences of an adverse decision. In practice, of course, they enable interested parties to place their opinions and attitudes on the record; and in the sense that they rely principally upon the utility of information, they parallel most clearly the technique of lobbying before legislatures. There are, however, certain restrictions and costs. To file a brief an interested group must first receive permission from the litigants or the Court. Even if permission is granted, amicus curiae briefs may simply encourage similar briefs from the adversary. Nevertheless, interest groups do perceive the amicus curiae brief as a useful means of influencing the Court's decisions.[48] Between 1970 and 1980 more than half of all noncommercial cases decided by the Supreme Court with a full opinion had one or more amicus curiae briefs.[49] Any interested group may, in theory, file such briefs, yet most come from active civic organizations, organized interest groups, and from the federal government itself through the Office of the Solicitor General in cases to which the government is not a party.

Examples of groups now well known for filing amicus curiae briefs are the ACLU, the NAACP, the AFL-CIO, the American Jewish Congress, and Common Cause.[50] This may seem to be a list of "liberal" groups only, but groups pursuing "conservative" goals, either directly as litigants or indirectly as "friends of the Court," also abound.[51] Examples include Citizens for Decency through Law, Americans for Effective Law Enforcement, the National Right to Work Legal Defense Fund, the National Rifle Association, and the American Legion. Indeed, during the first decade of the Burger Court, 1969–80, a marked growth in the participation of conservative interest groups occurred. While the participation of both conservative and liberal groups grew during the decade, the participation of the conservative groups was more likely to be as amicus curiae than was that of liberal groups.[52] Not surprisingly, conservative groups appeared more frequently in economic regulation cases, liberal groups in civil liberties cases.[53] Although the participation of amicus curiae has long been a tactic of organized interests in litigation before the Supreme Court, little sound evidence supports the proposition that amicus curiae participation substantively affects the Court's final decision. However, increasing evidence does suggest that amicus curiae briefs submitted prior to the Court's decision on whether or not to hear a case do affect the Court's agenda even if not its ultimate decision. A recent statistical analysis demonstrates that the presence of amicus curiae briefs filed prior to the decision on certiorari significantly and positively increases the chances that the Court will give the case a full treatment.[54]

The test case is an even more direct means of obtaining favorable action from the Supreme Court. Ordinarily, the tactic is to violate a law intentionally in order to have "standing" in the courts and thus provide judges with an opportunity to interpret the law or the Constitution in a manner consistent with the group's goals. Although test cases have been used successfully in winning important policy changes, there are some obstacles. A group cannot institute a test case unless it first finds someone who is willing to violate the law. Even if such a person is found, he or she may tire of the case and back out or, more commonly, may lose standing before the case reaches its conclusion. This has been a problem, for example, in the area of school desegregation where the student is out of school before the case is decided and therefore no longer an aggrieved party. Finally, even if a litigant is found and does maintain standing, the Court may decide the case against or for the litigant, but on grounds other than those anticipated to solve the problem.[55]

Some of these difficulties, particularly the standing problem, have been overcome by using class action suits. A litigant can in some cases file a case not only for him- or herself, but also for all others "similarly situated." This can be an important technique for at least two reasons. First, if one litigant should lose standing, a substitute can stand in. Second, if the

Court decides the case consistently with the policy goals of the instigator, that decision will be assured a much broader application. Thus, for example, in a consumer protection case brought against a manufacturer of allegedly unsafe toys, if the manufacturer loses, the payment of damages under the terms of the court's judgment must be made not only to one plaintiff but to all members of the class. Obviously, a successfully executed class action provides a much broader remedy than is otherwise obtainable.[56] Celebrated examples of successful class actions include the school desegregation cases of 1954–55 and the legislative reapportionment cases of the early 1960s. However, although class actions may help some groups achieve a policy goal of broad applicability and stretch scarce resources (and, at the same time, help court avoid repetitive litigation), there are some related problems. The "easy-access days" of the 1950s, 1960s, and 1970s appear to be over, as the Supreme Court since about 1973 has, in case after case, limited the use of the class action suit.[57] Even when permitted, those within the class who may "disagree with the dominant class view are quite likely to be submerged."[58]

In short, interest groups of all types come to the Supreme Court to advance their interests and policy objectives. Many have succeeded. Nonetheless, there is little evidence that justices select cases for hearing because they are brought by particular interest groups.[59] According to "cue theories" developed by political scientists, the justices accept or deny cases for review based on the involvement in the cases of certain "cues" such as a civil liberties issue, disagreements about the law in lower courts, and the presence of the federal government as the petitioner. The most recent scholarship suggests that the clearest correlation between any of these "cues" and the justices' selection of a case is the involvement in the case of the federal government.[60] Thus, as mentioned in several connections before in this chapter, the federal government is frequently itself a litigant before the Court. Given the huge federal "jurocracy"[61] topped off by the U.S. solicitor general, it is useful to consider the federal government's role as a litigant within the context of lawyers as Supreme Court participants.

THE LAWYERS: THE SUPREME COURT BAR, PRIVATE ATTORNEYS, THE SOLICITOR GENERAL, AND OTHER GOVERNMENT LAWYERS

Although most lawyers are not directly involved in the making of public policy, legislative and administrative policy-making councils on both the national and state levels are dominated by lawyers. More than 23,000 lawyers are employed in one capacity or another by the federal government, and probably a figure approaching ten times that number is employed by the states. From the beginning of the American Republic, political leadership has been preempted by lawyers. Alexis deTocqueville considered lawyers to be an intellectual elite exercising a preponderant influence in the American polity, and with good reason. Of the 56 signers of the Declaration of Independence, 25 were lawyers, as were 33 of the 55 framers of the Constitution.[62] A substantial number of our presidents and secretaries of state have been lawyers, and lawyers have constituted a plurality of our members of Congress from the beginning. Today lawyers remain ubiquitous in policy-making councils, legislative, executive, and judicial. Even in the nonjudicial arenas, they are almost always a plurality.[63]

Here we will examine the particular roles played by lawyers as Supreme Court participants. Qualifications for those lawyers who aspire to practice before the Supreme Court were established by the "first" Court in 1790 in Rule 2: "It shall be requisite to the admission of attorneys and counsellors to practice in this court, that they shall have been such for three years past in the Supreme Court of the State to which they respectively belong, and that their private and professional character shall appear to be fair."[64] Admission to what is called the "Supreme Court Bar" continues today to require these same attributes of personal and professional character and qualification to practice before a state supreme court. Although a lawyer who is not a member of the Supreme Court Bar is permitted to work on a case, that lawyer may not enter an appearance in a case before the Court or even file a case with the Court unless sponsored by at least one member.[65] To gain admission to the Supreme Court Bar, a lawyer must present a certification of his or her qualification to practice before a state supreme court and a written personal statement endorsed by two justices who are not related to the applicant. Formal membership is then achieved either by oral motion in open court or, more commonly in recent years, by written motions without a personal appearance.[66]

Before the mid-nineteenth century there was a distinctive bar of the Supreme Court whose members frequently lived and ate in the same boarding houses as the justices. Prominent lawyers like Daniel Webster, Henry Clay, William Wirt, and John C. Calhoun were a part of this age when the Supreme Court Bar moved as the Court moved. Today, of course, no such conditions exist.[67] But there are other obvious differences between the Supreme Court Bar of the early years and that of the current era. To some, the most visible difference is the lack among current members of the "dramatic flair and oratorical genius that 19th century legal luminaries . . . exhibited."[68] To others

> the most striking difference between the argument of the 19th century and that of today is the difference in the lawyers themselves. In the 19th century there was a Supreme Court Bar, a group of lawyers in or about Washington for at least portions of the year to whom other lawyers sent their cases in the

same fashion that a New York lawyer today might send a piece of San Francisco business to a San Francisco lawyer.[69]

Given the awe that admission to the Supreme Court Bar inspires within the public, and given the greater ease of getting to Washington that modern transportation allows, the Bar of the Court's early days is now greatly dispersed. Indeed, many lawyers have gained admission to the Supreme Court Bar with no intent of actually handling a case before the Court. Up to 1807 only 60 persons had been granted admission to the Bar. In 1930 it was estimated that there were about 30,000 members. In the 1990s about 6,000 lawyers are admitted each year, and the total number of lawyers admitted since the start is estimated to exceed 150,000. To refer to these lawyers as members of the Supreme Court Bar is a bit misleading, however. They are, in fact, quite a heterogeneous collection of persons from all parts of the country, not an organized group or a bar with any formal leadership.[70]

If we narrow our focus to those private lawyers who actually bring cases to the Supreme Court, we find they become associated with those cases in differing ways and enter those cases at differing levels of litigation. For example, lawyers before the Warren Court in reapportionment cases got involved as a result of friendship with latent litigants, whereas those who brought civil rights cases to the Warren Court were normally there because of a group affiliation. Lawyers who ultimately argue a case before the Court are not necessarily those who handled the case at trial or upon the first appeal. In the reapportionment and loyalty-security cases of the late 1950s and early 1960s, 15 percent of the lawyers who appeared before the Court entered the litigation only at the Supreme Court level. In criminal justice cases argued before the Court during the same period, about 25 percent entered only once the case came before the Court. In civil rights cases, the number of lawyers becoming involved only at the Supreme Court stage reached around 35 percent.[71] In test cases of all kinds, however, in which the intent is to achieve a particular policy goal, the lawyers arguing before the Court tend to be involved in the litigation from the initial trial onward.[72]

One of the better studies of lawyers practicing before the Supreme Court is Jonathan D. Casper's book dealing with those lawyers who argued civil rights and liberties cases decided with opinion by the Supreme Court during the years 1957–66.[73] Casper uses the concept of "clientele" (that set of persons whom the lawyer perceives as being primarily affected by the outcome of the case in which he or she is involved) to develop a typology of lawyers that is then related to their recruitment, their goals, and the outcomes in various areas of litigation. (Some of the data cited in the preceding paragraph are drawn from Casper's study.) Three discrete clientele types are found to have theoretical utility. The "Advocate's" clientele is his or her client. "Advocates" are concerned only with winning their cases; their own policy preferences are irrelevant to their activity as lawyers, as are the ramifications of their cases for others in society. The "Group Advocate's" clientele is a group that may not be a formal party to the litigation but to which the lawyer perceives himself or herself as having some long-term commitment and whose goals the lawyer seeks to advance. Finally, the "Civil Libertarian's" clientele is all of society. "Civil Libertarians" are not interested primarily in their client but in their cases as a means to raise issues involving democratic principles, for example, free speech. Though the data collected for this study do not permit grand generalizations, the findings do raise provocative questions. As the group advocate and civil libertarian view their litigation more nearly as a means of raising issues than of protecting their clients' best interests, might they not be less amenable to a negotiated settlement than the advocate who wants only what is best for his or her individual client? Thus, in criminal cases will the defendant receive a better or a worse defense? Will the civil libertarian, concerned primarily with the establishment of principles, prefer to lose than to win on a technicality? Although Casper's study is merely "exploratory," it is one of the few studies, and one of the best, urging us to understand better the critical role played by private lawyers who appear as Supreme Court participants.

Relatively few private lawyers appear frequently before the Supreme Court. There were some private lawyers in the nineteenth Century who appeared so often (several over 100 times) that they might then have been thought of as something like a regular bar. Today, however, the most seasoned private lawyer may not argue more than a handful of cases before the Court in an entire career. There is, by contrast, considerably greater continuity in the staffs of the U.S. solicitor general and other government lawyers who appear regularly before the Court. We will now turn our attention to this breed of Supreme Court lawyer.

As we have learned, the federal government participates in many Supreme Court cases directly as a litigant or indirectly as amicus. The federal government's principal legal office is the Department of Justice headed by the U.S. attorney general. The attorney general supervises the prosecution of alleged violations of federal criminal law (though at the trial level in most criminal cases, litigation is directed by the U.S. attorney assigned to the district in which the case is being prosecuted). The attorney general also coordinates important civil litigation initiated to implement policies promoted by the president, such as civil rights and antitrust. Except in the most important of federal cases, however, the attorney general's supervision of litigation at the trial level is quite loose. A much tighter supervision is exercised when cases involving the federal government are appealed. These appeals, especially those to the Supreme Court, are centrally controlled by the U.S. solicitor general and argued on appeal, not by the U.S. attorney who appeared at trial, but by Justice Department staff lawyers. Both the attorney general and the solicitor general are presidential (and normally "political") appointees. Both are expected to be a member of the president's executive branch's team. Technically the solicitor general is subordinate to the attorney general, but traditionally each has labored more or less independently of the other. In a certain sense the metaphor of attorney general as "captain of the offensive team" and of solicitor general as "captain of the defensive team" is useful to an understanding of their actual operations. In any event, the job of the solicitor general is to supervise and coordinate the appeal of cases to the Supreme Court. The decision to appeal is usually based on the probability of winning, the probable damage resulting from a loss, and a concern to help reduce the Court's workload.[74]

When cases involving the federal government are appealed, they are more often won than lost. There are a number of obvious and not-so-obvious reasons. First, the government's lawyers are commonly career officials who specialize in only a few areas of litigation. Also, they have more experience arguing cases before the Supreme Court than do most private lawyers. Hence, they bring to the Court a relatively high level of expertise. Second, the solicitor general has an opportunity to survey a broad spectrum of cases then in the federal judicial system or likely to arise there. Thus the solicitor general can delay the appeal of some issue that the federal government cares greatly about until the time for appeal is propitious. Appealing the right case at the right time increases the likelihood of victory, and private lawyers rarely if ever have that luxury. Finally, and not to be overlooked, is the Court's much greater willingness to accept appeals made by the solicitor general than those made by private litigants, a willingness generally attributed to the Court's appreciation of the solicitor general's assistance in aiding the Court in limiting its workload.[75]

THE SUPPORTING PERSONNEL

An examination of the Supreme Court's supporting personnel, or staff, "is a study in contrasts between the public institution and the one that belongs to those who work in it, the dramatic facade and the routine tasks behind, and nine justices whose words are law and the workers who produce the words."[76] Yet with less than 400 staff workers and with a budget of less than $15 million, the Court employs far fewer persons and spends far less money than does the Congress or the executive branch. But our focus is on the Court, and it is impossible to fail to notice that the institutional setting in which the Court works today is far more bureaucratic than at any other point in its history. Since midcentury, and especially since the start of the

Burger Court, increasing caseloads have prompted a bureaucratic re-sponse. Compared to earlier eras, the work of the Supreme Court is sup-ported by a greater division of labor among an increasingly professional and specialized staff.

Supporting personnel today include, most importantly, the clerk of the Court, the marshal of the Court, the reporter of decisions, the librar-ian, the public information officer, the administrative assistant to the chief justice, the legal officers, and the law clerks assigned to the justices. Most of these employees and their staffs are appointed by the Court. The law clerks are appointed by the justices whom they serve. Each of these posi-tions has formal tasks to perform, informal roles to play, and a history to be told. Their respective stories could be told in any order, chronological or otherwise, but John Brigham has developed an organizational scheme that allows for the most instructive approach. In his book, *The Cult of the Court,* Brigham distinguishes "institutional support" (provided by the mar-shal, librarian, public information officer, and administrative assistant), "legal support" (provided by the clerk, reporter, and legal officers), and "policy support" (provided largely by the law clerks).[77] We will adopt this scheme to describe in some detail the work of the Court's supporting personnel.

Institutional support, meaning simply the maintenance of the institu-tion, is provided by a relatively large and diverse group of Supreme Court employees, including secretaries, seamstresses, janitors, carpenters, elec-tricians, barbers, cafeteria workers, printers, nurses, chauffeurs, and pol-icy officers. Here we will emphasize the work of four key players. The marshal of the Court has performed a variety of tasks since the creation of the position by Congress in 1867. The marshal supervises nearly 200 employees (such as those mentioned above), oversees building mainte-nance and ensures its security, serves as the Court's business manager and supervises the payment of its expenses, escorts the justices to formal func-tions, arranges the inaugural ceremonies of new justices and memorial services for those who die, and largely controls access to the justices and to the records of the Court. The performance of most of these tasks goes unnoticed by outsiders. More visible is the marshal's role in open court, where the marshal announces the beginning of a session, supervises seat-ing arrangements for the public, and runs the clock and flashing lights that warn the lawyers when their allotted time to speak is near to expiration.[78]

The office of the librarian is an institutional symbol of the Court's tradition and its need for research resources. In the early years the Court had no library of its own. Even after the establishment of the Library of Congress in 1800, the Congress refused to allow the justices to use it. In 1812 Congress reversed its stand, and in 1832 it gave the Court some 2,000 law books. The Court had no librarian at the time, however, so the small collection was cared for by the clerk of the Court until 1884 and by the marshal's office, where a new post of librarian was established in 1887. In 1948 the Congress created the separate office of librarian. The Supreme Court library today, with over 250,000 volumes, is located on the third floor of the Supreme Court Building. This may seem to be a modest collection, but the justices have little need for their own general reference books, given their now easy access to the Library of Congress next door. The justices also have access to a variety of computerized reference tools such as JURIS, LEGIS, LEXIS, SCORIO, and WESTLAW. The Court librarian must be credentialed as a law librarian and supervises a staff of 23, including lawyer-librarians and Ph.D.'s who provide to the justices a variety of useful materials including legislative histories, surveys of state laws, and statistical information.[79] The public information officer, formerly known as the press officer, manages the Court's public image. Created in 1935, the position of public information officer was initially a one-person operation. As the number of reporters covering the Court grew, so did the availability of space in the Court's pressroom. Since 1935 the number of reporters covering the Court full time has grown to about 30, including those from the major network and cable news services, UPI, AP, major national newspapers, and specialized legal periodicals. The principal tasks of the public information officer are to announce those cases on the Court's conference list and those cases scheduled for oral argument, distribute slip opinions on opinion day, and publish the Court's house newsletter. In addition, a bulletin board in the public information office provides the media and other interested parties with information about changes in Court procedure, activities of the justices, and the Court's informal orders. The office also houses and makes available for reading by the public its files of current or pending petitions, briefs, motions, and jurisdictional statements. In short, the public information officer is the Supreme Court's public spokesperson on virtually all matters except its judicial opinions and formal orders, which the justices have long held must speak for themselves.[80] Finally, the position of administrative assistant to the chief justice was created in 1972 at the urging of Chief Justice Burger, though a number of justices and other officers of the Court opposed its creation for fear it would limit their access to the chief. The administrative assistant's staff includes a research associate, several professionals from the Judicial Fellows Program (lawyers and academics chosen to serve in the office for one year), a number of apprentices from undergraduate and law school internship programs, and four secretaries. While the chief justice remains the Court's chief executive officer and chief administrator of the federal judicial system, the administrative assistant does perform a number of crucial tasks. These include the formulation of policy for the research staff at the Federal Judicial Center, the preparation of speeches such as the chief justice's "Year-End Report on the Judiciary" and talks to the ABA, the oversight of both managerial and technological improvements in judicial administration, the preparation of materials for budget hearings, and the handling of liaison with the Congress, the executive branch, and various judicial committees. The administrative assistant's duties are not legislated; the incumbent serves at the pleasure of the chief justice and as his confidential aide. As we learned earlier, Chief Justice Burger's leading legacy will undoubtedly be chronicled as administrative innovation. Unquestionably, the Supreme Court has been the last of the three branches of national government to modernize. The administrative assistant "epitomizes the push toward management science that reflects the foundations of modern political power."[81]

Legal support, meaning simply the maintenance of legal rituals, is provided by a growing number of specialists who sustain the Court by structuring how it handles its legal business, from procuring cases to promulgating their outcomes. Unlike those providing institutional support, the Court clerk, reporter, and legal officers deal principally with legal matters; and unlike those providing policy support, they do not deal directly with the policy implications of the cases they handle. This is not to say, however, that they have no discretion in the performance of their tasks; nor is it to say that they influence only the form and never the substance of the litigation they touch. The Office of the Clerk (not to be confused with the justices's "law clerks," discussed below) is the Court's central administrative office. The Court clerk now has the largest staff at the Court (nearly 50 persons who are career appointees). A recent listing of this staff's diverse duties reads as follows: (1) to manage the Court's docket and argument calendars; (2) to receive and record motions, petitions, briefs, and other formal papers filed with the Court; (3) to distribute the aforementioned papers to the justices; (4) to collect filing fees; (5) to prepare and keep the Court's order list and the *Supreme Court Journal,* which contains the minutes of its sessions and records its formal judgments and mandates; (6) to inform lawyers and lower courts of the Court's formal actions; (7) to supervise the preparation of briefs in *in forma pauperis* cases; (8) to receive and maintain the lower court records after review of a case has been granted; (9) to oversee admission to the Supreme Court Bar and to superintend disbarments; and (10) to serve as the primary liaison with lawyers and litigants before the Court, principally giving them procedural advice.[82] The Office of the Clerk collects the docketing fees ($100 in 1990), and for nearly the first 100 years these fees were used to support the office. At present the filing fees (which total about $200,000 a year) go to the U.S. Treasury, and Congress appropriates the funds necessary to support the office.[83] The early financial independence of the Court clerk often made the incumbent a principal player in the Court's internal politics. In the infamous *Dred Scott* case, for example, the clerk is alleged to have withheld Chief Justice Taney's written opinion from Justice Curtis, thus making the preparation of a dissenting opinion by the furious Curtis most difficult.[84] Even in recent times the clerk's role has been one of some substance. Clerks have been known to telephone lawyers in pending or related cases urging them to bring cases or issues to the Court to expedite the resolution of particular conflicts. The clerk's staff also works with the chief justice's law clerks in processing petitions, thus participating in the crucial, early determination of which cases warrant review by the Court. Thus the clerk is no mere agent of the justices but a transitional figure between the Court and its policy.[85] The position of reporter of decisions had an informal beginning in 1790 and has had a colorful history ever since. During its first quarter century the Court had no official Court reporter charged with disseminating its decisions and opinions to the legal community and the public. The first reporter was Alexander Dallas, who was a lawyer and journalist and, later, a secretary of the treasury. Dallas was self-appointed. He published four volumes of reports between 1790 and 1800. Like the other early reporters who followed him, Dallas worked at his own expense. His reports were then sold to lawyers and other interested parties. His motives were apparently a "mysterious combination of love of law, self-satisfaction, private gain, and public spirit."[86] Dallas was followed by William Cranch, a real estate speculator and district court judge who reported Supreme Court opinions from 1801 to 1815. During Dallas' era Supreme Court opinions were announced only orally in open court primarily to inform the litigants of the Court's decision. Beginning in Cranch's time justices supplemented their oral opinions with written texts; they then supplied the manuscripts to Cranch, who disseminated his reports, highly regarded for their accuracy and clarity, as broadly as possible for personal profit and prestige. In 1816 Congress arranged for the publication of the Court's opinions and Henry Wheaton became the first formally appointed and salaried Court reporter. Wheaton reported for the Court until replaced by Richard Peters in 1827. An interesting and important legal battle then ensued between Wheaton and Peters. When Peters revised all prior reports, leaving out much of Wheaton's material, Wheaton sued on the grounds that his work was his private property protected by copyright. But the Supreme Court ruled that its opinions are public property, a part of the public domain. Peters was followed as Court reporter by Benjamin Howard (1843–60), Jeremiah S. Black (1861–62), and John Wallace (1867–74), who was the last Court reporter to have his name cited with the Court's report. In *Marbury v. Madison*, for example, the citation is 1 Cranch 137 (1803); in *McCulloch v. Maryland*, it is 4 Wheaton 316 (1819); and in *Dred Scott*, it is 19 Howard 393 (1857). Modern reports are published as *United States Reports*, printed by the U.S. Government Printing Office, and sold by the superintendent of documents. The typical citation, to take as example a case mentioned earlier in this chapter, is *Regents v. Bakke*, 438 U.S. 265 (1978). The reporter of decisions today, working with a staff of 11 persons, prepares the reports after the Court's opinions have been delivered. Typographical errors are corrected, all citations are checked, and headnotes or syllabi (summaries of the case) are added by the reporter. These summaries, though helpful to lawyers and particularly to the press, are not considered part of the Court's decision or opinion.[87] The final form of legal support comes from the Legal Office, created in 1973 at the urging of Chief Justice Burger. The three lawyers who make up this office presumably serve to help the Court handle its heavy caseload by dealing with a variety of procedural problems; they also provide a degree of continuity in legal advice to justices, thus compensating for the generally transient nature of the justices' own law clerks. In addition, some would say, they reflect the trend already observed, namely, that which finds the Court increasingly delegating power to specialists.[88] In any event, these officers, known generally as "staff counsel," perform a number of important tasks. They advise the clerk and the justices' law clerks on procedural and jurisdictional questions arising from routine petitions; make recommendations on special motions or other "emergency" applications such as requests for expedited proceedings; assist justices with their circuit duties; make recommendations to the Court on, and assist in the drafting of, revisions of the Court's rules; provide assistance in handling the few original jurisdiction cases that come up; review legislation of possible interest to the Court; and serve as liaison between a justice and the Department of Justice when unhappy persons file nuisance (and normally fruitless) suits against a justice.[89]

Policy support, meaning simply the integration of legal form with policy outputs, is provided mostly by the law clerks to the individual justices. (In a sense, policy support is also provided by legal counsel to the litigants, especially by the Solicitor General's Office when the government is a litigant; these roles have been described earlier in this chapter). In 1850 the justices asked Congress to authorize the hiring of "investigating clerks" to work with them and to copy opinions. When that request was denied, some of the justices began using workers in the Court clerk's office to assist them. The first "law clerk" to an individual justice was hired by Justice Horace Gray at his own expense in 1882. Gray had apparently initiated the practice of using law clerks earlier while he was a state judge in Massachusetts. Finally, in 1886 Congress appropriated $1,600 annually for a "stenographic clerk" for each justice. By Chief Justice Stone's era (1941–46) it was established practice for each justice to have one law clerk and for the chief justice to have two. During the period of the chief justiceship of Fred Vinson (1946–53) and Earl Warren (1953–69), it became increasingly common for each justice to have two clerks. Since 1970 the number of clerks has gradually grown. Today each justice, at his or her discretion, has three or four clerks; and the chief justice, a fifth. Law clerks are hired by the individual justice, normally for one year, though some stay longer. Justices have great discretion in whom they hire, normally selecting top graduates from prestigious law schools. All were white males until Justice Douglas chose the first woman, Lucille Loman, in 1944, and Justice Frankfurter chose the first black, William Coleman, in 1949. The process for selection and the criteria used vary for each justice. Some justices make the selection directly by personal interview; a few allow former clerks to do the interviewing, and, infrequently, selection is based on written application. Some justices rely on recommendations from law school professors. O'Brien writes that four criteria emerge from the scrutiny of actual practice: "the Justice's preference for (1) certain law schools, (2) special geographic regions, (3) prior clerking experience on certain courts or with particular judges, and (4) personal compatibility."[90] Justice Frankfurter had his clerks chosen for him by two professors at Howard Law School. Justice Potter Stewart chose Yale Law School graduates, Justice Frank Murphy chose Michigan Law School graduates, and Justice Tom Clerk preferred graduates of lesser-known institutions. Justice Hugo Black preferred "Southern boys," Justice Powell chose Virginians, and Chief Justice Warren liked Californians. Justice Stevens looks to prior experience, appointing a state supreme court clerk in 1985, for example.[91]

The formal functions of the law clerks are clear. They read, analyze, and prepare memoranda for their justices on the thousands of cases that come to the Court each year. They conduct exhaustive research of precedents, historical information, and legislative records once the writing of an opinion has been assigned to their justice. They also assist in the preparation of the opinion. Other "tasks" expected of them, however, are quite varied, and there remains little agreement on exactly how much political influence they actually have or exert. Their informal tasks vary with the work habits of the justices, ranging from legal work to serving cocktails,[92] from private secretary to a kind of judicial Rasputin.[93] The first law clerk worked for Justice Gray primarily as a servant and a barber. In more recent times Chief Justice Stone wanted his clerks to take walks with him, and Justice Black hoped that his clerks would play tennis with him.[94] Although their formal functions are quite clear, how clerks are actually used depends on their justice's temperament and experience. Justices White, Rehnquist, and Stevens all served earlier in their careers as Supreme Court law clerks. Each has commented on his experiences. Justice White has said: "When I arrived as a clerk, I don't think anything I ever did or said influenced my Justice. I . . . [made] sure that relevant considerations were placed before him, such as opinions from other courts, law journals, ideas of my own—things he wouldn't have time to dig up on his own." Chief Justice Rehnquist once asserted that "the specter of the law clerk as a legal Rasputin, exerting an important influence on the cases actually decided by the Court, may be discarded at once." But Justice Stevens has caught the subtleties perhaps a bit more sharply in writing:

"An interesting loyalty develops between clerks and their Justices. It is much like a lawyer-client relationship, close and confidential. Like a lawyer, a clerk can't tell his client, the Justice, what to do. He can only suggest what can happen if he does or doesn't do something."[95] What we know today about the truth of the matter still resides in various anecdotes. Paul P. Frank, himself a clerk to Justice Black, tells the story of a clerk to Justice Douglas who rewrote substantial portions of a draft opinion by his justice. Douglas said to his clerk: "I can see you've done a lot of work but you are off base here. If and when you get appointed to the Supreme Court, you can write opinions as you choose."[96] Dean Acheson, later secretary of state but also one of Justice Brandeis' clerks, said of his experience: "He wrote the opinion; I wrote the footnotes."[97] There are contrary accounts of the work of the clerks to Justices Butler, Byrnes, and Murphy, who reportedly drafted most of their justices' written work. In fact, within the Court Justice Murphy's clerks were derisively called "Mr. Justice Huddleson" and "Mr. Justice Gressman."[98] On the question of how much substantive influence the memoranda of the clerks have on their justices, two widely known but contrary examples in celebrated cases are frequently cited. On the one hand, clerk Louis Lusky is reported to have literally written important parts of Justice Stone's famous "footnote 4" in *U.S. v. Carolene Products Co.* in 1938.[99] On the other hand, Rehnquist (then clerk to Justice Jackson) utterly failed to convince his justice to sustain the famous "separate but equal" doctrine. Jackson joined a unanimous Court in declaring the doctrine unconstitutional in the celebrated school desegregation case of *Brown v. Board of Education* in 1954.[100] There is somewhat less debate over the role clerks play in the preparation of memos on appeal. That is, although clerks have had only varying success in influencing the substance of what is decided, they do seem to play an indispensable, if not decisive, role in determining what cases should be granted review. With notable exceptions (for example, Justice Frankfurter in the past and Justice Brennan more recently), the justices do give their clerks a major role in the screening process. Justice Stevens, for example, said in 1982 that he "found it necessary to delegate a great deal of responsibility in the review of petitions" to his clerks. "They examine them all and select a smaller minority that they believe I should read myself. As a result, I do not even look at the papers in over 80 percent of the cases that are filed."[101] Indeed, since about 1972 a majority of the justices have "pooled" their clerks. This so-called cert. pool, created by the justices who use it largely in response to the growing caseload of recent years, reviews all of the filings. A clerk's simple memorandum is then circulated to all of the justices participating in the pool. Then, each justice asks one of his or her clerks to read the memo and recommend whether or not to grant review.[102] Court critics, typically those dissatisfied with the substance of Court decisions, have complained that law clerks exert an undue influence on the Court of ever-increasing importance. Some critics, including members of Congress, have called for the creation of minimum qualifications by statute and for Senate confirmation of law clerk appointments.[103] To date such claims of undue influence have not been firmly established, and such calls for congressional involvement in the appointment process have not received much support. Over the years the justices themselves have consistently denied that their law clerks have undue influence. Some justices have insisted that they individually read every petition for review. Further, virtually all the justices have contended that even when various functions are in fact delegated to the clerks, the justices themselves exercise strict supervision and retain final authority. Nevertheless, the law clerks have become increasingly important players in every aspect of the policy process outside the Justices's Conference, from the screening of what cases to hear to the drafting of final opinions. In short, it has become increasingly difficult to sustain the myth of the justices' individuality in an institutional arena of boosted and broadened bureaucratization.[104]

NOTES

[1] Herbert Jacob, *Justice in America* (Boston: Little, Brown, 1984), p. 53.

[2] David M. O'Brien, *Storm Center: The Supreme Court in American Politics* (New York: W. W. Norton, 1986), p. 46.

[3] Ibid., pp. 13–15.

[4] Ibid.

[5] William Rehnquist, "Presidential Appointments to the Supreme Court" (Speech, University of Minnesota, October 19, 1984). Quoted in Laurence H. Tribe, *God Save This Honorable Court* (New York: Random House, 1985), p. x.

[6] Tribe, *God Save This Honorable Court*, pp. x–xi.

[7] O'Brien, *Storm Center*, pp. 13–14.

[8] Henry J. Abraham, "A Bench Happily Filled: Some Historical Reflections on the Supreme Court Appointment Process," 66 *Judicature* (1983), pp. 282, 286. Quote in text taken from O'Brien, *Storm Center*, p. 46.

[9] Tribe, *God Save This Honorable Court*, pp. x–xi, xvi–xix.

[10] John R. Schmidhauser, *Judges and Justices: The Federal Appellate Judiciary* (Boston: Little, Brown, 1979), p. 16.

[11] The foregoing is drawn largely from Schmidhauser, pp. 12–14, 16–18.

[12] William C. Louthan, *The Politics of Justice* (Port Washington, N.Y.: Kennikot Press, 1979), p. 66.

[13] Tribe, *God Save This Honorable Court*, pp. 51–52.

[14] Ibid., pp. 52–53.

[15] Ibid., pp. 55–76.

[16] Ibid., pp. 51, 76.

[17] Elder Witt, ed., *Guide to the United States Supreme Court* (Washington, D.C.: Congressional Quarterly, 1979), p. 655. See also Henry J. Abraham, *Justices and Presidents: A Political History of the Supreme Court* (New York: Oxford University Press, 1974), pp. 109, 118.

[18] Harold W. Stanley and Richard G. Niemi, eds., *Vital Statistics on American Politics* (Washington, D.C., Congressional Quarterly Press, 1988), pp. 243–49.

[19] Alexander Hamilton, *Federalist Paper No. 76*. See Alexander Hamilton, James Madison, and John Jay, *The Federalist Papers* (New York: The New American Library, 1961), p. 457.

[20] Tribe, *God Save This Honorable Court*, pp. 77–92.

[21] Ibid., pp. xv–xix.

[22] Louthan, *The Politics of Justice*, p. 65.

[23] Tribe, pp. viii–xix.

[24] See Witt, *Guide to the United States Supreme Court*, p. 755.

[25] Ibid.

[26] Henry F. Pringle, *The Life and Times of William Howard Taft* (New York: Farrar and Reinhart, 1939), p. 967. Quoted in Laurence Baum, *The Supreme Court* (Washington, D.C.: Congressional Quarterly Press, 1981), p. 60.

[27] Stephen L. Wasby, *The Supreme Court in the Federal Judicial System* (Chicago: Nelson-Hall, 1987), p. 91.

[28] Charles Fairman, "The Retirement of Federal Judges," *Harvard Law Review* (January, 1938), p. 397. Quoted in Witt, *Guide to the United States Supreme Court*, p. 756.

[29] U.S. Congress, House of Representatives, *Congressional Record*, 91st Congress, 2nd session, 1970, 116, pt. 9:11913. Quoted in part in Baum, *The Supreme Court*, p. 61.

[30] Baum, *The Supreme Court*, pp. 61–62.

[31] Wasby, *The Supreme Court*, pp. 93–94.

[32] Linda Greenhouse, "Judicial Impeachment: Is the Process Antiquated?" *New York Times* (May 11, 1988).

[33] Ibid.

[34] Baum, *The Supreme Court*, pp. 68–69.

[35] Louthan, *The Politics of Justice*, pp. 111–13.

[36] Samuel Krislov, *The Supreme Court in the Political Process* (New York: Macmillan, 1965), p. 41.

[37] Jacob, *Justice in America*, p. 89.

[38] Clement E. Vose, *Constitutional Change* (Lexington, Mass.: D. C. Heath, 1972). Summarized in Baum, *The Supreme Court*, p. 70.

[39] Nathan Hakman, "Lobbying the Supreme Court—An Appraisal of 'Political Science Folklore,'" 35 *Fordham Law Review* (1976). Summarized in Baum, *The Supreme Court*, p. 70.

[40] Krislov, *Supreme Court in the Political Process*, p. 42.

[41] Baum, *The Supreme Court*, p. 70.

[42] Stuart Taylor, Jr., "Tuning Out the White House," *New York Times Magazine* (September 11, 1988), p. 98.

[43] The Bakke and O'Hair case studies are drawn in detail from Baum, pp. 70–71.

[44] Krislov, *Supreme Court in the Political Process*, p. 42.

[45] Jacob, *Justice in America*, pp. 149–51.

[46] Louthan, *The Politics of Justice*, pp. 123–29.

[47] Joel F. Handler, "Public Interest Law: Problems and Prospects," in Murray L. Schwartz (ed.), *Law and the American Future* (New York: American Assembly, 1976). See summary in Jacob, *Justice in America*, pp. 150–51.

[48] Louthan, *The Politics of Justice*, pp. 120–21; Jacob, *Justice in America*, p. 42.

[49] Jacob, *Justice in America*, p. 41, citing Karen O'Connor and Lee Epstein, "Amicus Curiae Participation in U.S. Supreme Court Litigation: An Appraisal of Hakam's 'Folklore,'" 16 *Law and Society Review* (1988–82), pp. 311–20.

[50] Henry J. Abraham, *The Judicial Process* (New York: Oxford University Press, 1986), pp. 248–49.

[51] Lee Epstein, *Conservatives in Court* (Knoxville, Tenn.: University of Tennessee Press, 1985).

[52] Wasby, *The Supreme Court*, p. 150.

[53] Karen O'Connor and Lee Epstein, "The Rise of Conservative Interest Group Litigation," 45 *Journal of Politics* (May, 1983), pp. 479–89. Cited in Wasby, *The Supreme Court,* p. 151.

[54] Gregory A. Caldeira and John R. Wright, "Organized Interests and Agenda Setting in the U.S. Supreme Court," 82 *American Political Science Review* 4 (December, 1988), pp. 1109–1127.

[55] Louthan, *The Politics of Justice,* p. 121.

[56] Ibid., pp. 122, 126-27.

[57] Abraham, *The Judicial Process,* pp. 371–72n14.

[58] Wasby, *The Supreme Court,* p. 156. Cited in Deborah L. Rohde, "Class Conflicts in Class Actions," 34 *Stanford Law Review* (July, 1982), pp. 1183-1261.

[59] O'Brien, *Storm Center,* p. 208.

[60] Ibid.

[61] *Jurocracy* is a term used by Donald Horowitz to describe the lawyer who works for the government—"a hybrid species. . . , simultaneously lawyer and bureaucrat." See Donald L. Horowitz, *The Jurocracy: Government Lawyers, Agency Programs, and Judicial Decisions* (Lexington, Mass.: D. C. Heath, 1977).

[62] Francis R. Aumann, *The Instrumentalities of Justice* (Columbus, Ohio: Ohio State University Press, 1956), pp. 96–97.

[63] Louthan, *The Politics of Justice,* p. 83.

[64] Quoted in Witt, *Guide to the United States Supreme Court,* p. 763.

[65] Witt, *Guide to the United States Supreme Court,* p. 763.

[66] Ibid., p. 764.

[67] Krislov, *Supreme Court in the Political Process,* p. 53.

[68] Witt, *Guide to the United States Supreme Court,* p. 764.

[69] John P. Frank, *The Marble Palace: The Supreme Court in American Life* (New York: Knopf, 1958), p. 93. Quoted in Witt, *Guide to the United States Supreme Court,* p. 764.

[70] James Beck, *May It Please the Court* (New York: Macmillan, 1930), p. 20; "Attorney Roles of the Supreme Court in the United States," Microcopy 217, National Archives; Robert L. Stern and Eugene Gressman, *Supreme Court Practice* (Washington, D.C.: Bureau of National Affairs, 1978), pp. 909–910; Krislov, *Supreme Court in the Political Process,* p. 53; Witt, *Guide to the United States Supreme Court,* p. 763.

[71] These percentages are derived from a summary made by Wasby, *The Supreme Court,* p. 147.

[72] Witt, *Guide to the United States Supreme Court,* p. 147.

[73] Jonathan D. Casper, *Lawyers before the Warren Court: Civil Liberties and Civil Rights, 1957–1966* (Urbana, Ill.: University of Illinois Press, 1972).

[74] This description of the roles of the attorney general and solicitor general draws much from Jacob, *Justice in America,* pp. 86, 89–90.

[75] Ibid., pp. 89–91; for a more detailed account of the workings of the solicitor general's office see Horowitz, *The Jurocracy,* pp. 54–60.

[76] John Brigham, *The Cult of the Court* (Philadelphia: Temple University Press, 1987), p. 115.

[77] Ibid., pp. 115–26.

[78] Witt, *Guide to the United States Supreme Court,* pp. 761–62; O'Brien, *Storm Center,* p. 141; Brigham, *The Cult of the Court,* p. 117.

[79] Witt, *Guide to the United States Supreme Court,* pp. 764–65; O'Brien, *Storm Center,* pp. 141–42; Brigham, *The Cult of the Court,* pp. 117–18.

[80] Witt, *Guide to the United States Supreme Court,* p. 764; O'Brien, *Storm Center,* pp. 281–82; Brigham, *The Cult of the Court,* p. 118.

[81] Brigham, *The Cult of the Court,* pp. 118–19; see also O'Brien, *Storm Center,* pp. 144–46.

[82] This list is taken from Witt, *Guide to the United States Supreme Court,* p. 760, and drawn from Stern and Gressman, *Supreme Court Practice,* pp. 17–18.

[83] Brigham, *The Cult of the Court,* p. 119, citing Richard L. Williams, "Supreme Court of the United States: The Staff That Keeps It Operating," 7 *Smithsonian* (Oct.-Nov., 1977), p. 46.

[84] O'Brien, *Storm Center,* p. 137, citing Benjamin Curtis Papers, LC.

[85] Brigham, *The Cult of the Court,* p. 120.

[86] Ibid., p. 119.

[87] Witt, *Guide to the United States Supreme Court,* pp. 762–63; O'Brien, *Storm Center,* pp. 138–41; Brigham, *The Cult of the Court,* pp. 120–22.

[88] Brigham, *The Cult of the Court,* p. 122.

[89] Witt, *Guide to the United States Supreme Court,* p. 764; O'Brien, *Storm Center,* pp. 135–36; Brigham, *The Cult of the Court,* p. 122.

[90] O'Brien, *Storm Center,* p. 125.

[91] Abraham, *The Judicial Process,* pp. 253–54.

[92] O'Brien, *Storm Center,* p. 112.

[93] Abraham, *The Judicial Process,* p. 251.

[94] Witt, *Guide to the United States Supreme Court,* p. 766.

[95] All quotes from ibid.

[96] John P. Frank, "The Supreme Court: The Muckrakers Return," *Journal of the American Bar Association* (February, 1980), p. 164.

[97] Dean Acheson, "Recollections of Service with the Federal Supreme Court," 18 *Alabama Lawyer* (1957), pp. 335, 364; quoted in O'Brien, *Storm Center,* p. 127.

[98] O'Brien, *Storm Center,* p. 127.

[99] Brigham, *The Cult of the Court,* pp. 125–26.

[100] Abraham, *The Judicial Process,* p. 252.

[101] Address to the American Judicature Society, San Francisco, August 8, 1982. Quoted in Abraham, *The Judicial Process,* p. 254.

[102] O'Brien, *Storm Center,* pp. 130–31.

[103] Abraham, *The Judicial Process,* p. 251.

[104] Brigham, *The Cult of the Court,* pp. 124–26.

VI

Supreme Court Decision Making

How and Why the Justices Decide Cases as They Do

INTRODUCTION

Many theories purporting to advance our understanding of Supreme Court decision making have evolved over the years. Rather than a chronological rendering, we will examine these theories as falling into four loosely constructed types: (1) *legalistic-descriptive;* (2) *legalistic-prescriptive;* (3) *behavioral-predictive;* and (4) *behavioral-expositive.* The value of such a typology is twofold. First, the typology embraces all competing claims to the proper methods and principal purposes of political science research: to describe, prescribe, predict, and explain. Second, the typology allows for an understanding of the job of judging that is sufficiently eclectic to embrace nearly all known influences on the justices' decision-making style, influences that are legal, historical, philosophical, economic, sociological, psychological, and political.

LEGALISTIC-DESCRIPTIVE THEORIES

For the most part legalistic-descriptive theories rest on the assumption that the decision-making style of Supreme Court justices is distinct from the decision-making styles of members of Congress and of those working in the executive branch. Those Supreme Court scholars who articulate legalistic-descriptive theories do not necessarily deny that the Court, like the Congress and the president, makes public policy. Indeed, few Supreme Court scholars, including the most traditional among them, still hold to the myth that judges and justices are "above politics" or to the notion that policies emanating from the Court are distinct from policies coming out of the "more political" branches. However, those scholars presenting legalistic-descriptive theories do assume that the characteristic manner in which Supreme Court decisions are arrived at does differ from the decision-making methods of the justices' counterparts in the legislative and executive branches.[1] Indeed, some critics of what we will later examine as the behavioral-predictive and behavioral-expositive theories argue that the existence of "legal" facts and "legal" precedents makes the job of judging idiosyncratic. To them, the judicial process possesses a certain effective uniqueness not amenable to study by social scientists and statisticians but requiring a distinctive legal approach if Supreme Court decision making is to be understood.[2] Our purpose in this chapter is not to prefer, as more enlightening, one set of theories over another. Rather, our purpose is to present clearly all available theories in the hope of producing the most complete understanding.

Supreme Court decision-making theories we are labeling legalistic-descriptive are those that describe legal modes of reasoning and interpretation. Most cases come before the Court require the justices either to construe the U.S. Constitution or to interpret a legislative statute or an administrative regulation. Four modes of reasoning and interpretation are now conventionally assumed to apply to controversies involving the Constitution. Two others apply to controversies in which the issue pertains to a law or administrative regulation. Only rarely does the Court use a single mode in its pure form; more commonly these modes are combined in some fashion. For purposes of clarity, however, we will examine each mode of legal reasoning and interpretation separately. Put simply, the four modes of constitutional construction are (1) decisions based on the "intent of the framers," (2) decisions based on the "meaning of the words," (3) decisions based on "logical analysis," and (4) decisions based on the apparent necessity of "adapting the Constitution to changing times" and circumstances. The two modes of statutory interpretation are (1) decisions based on the "plain-meaning rule" and (2) decisions based on "legislative history."[3]

Reasoning and interpretation based on the *intent of the framers* assumes that Supreme Court justices can determine with some precision what the intentions of the framers were.[4] Some justices have appeared to believe that this is an easy, nearly mechanical task. Justice Owens J. Roberts, for example, once wrote as follows: "When an act of Congress is . . . challenged [as violating the Constitution]. . . , the judicial branch of the Government has only one duty—to lay the article of the Constitution which is invoked beside the statute which is challenged and to decide whether the latter squares with the former."[5] For a variety of reasons, however, Supreme Court decision making based on the interest of the framers is not that simple. First is the question of whose intent we are referring to. Is it the intent of *all* the 55 delegates who were chosen to participate in the Constitutional Convention in 1787, a kind of "collective intent"? Or the intent of only those delegates who were present throughout the convention and who participated at a high rate in its deliberations? Or the intent of only those 39 delegates who signed the newly drafted document? And if it is the intent of any of these groups of delegates, were they all of one view? While the only reliable historical records of the Constitutional Convention are the notes James Madison took in his strange version of shorthand and then edited 20 years later, we do know that at least some of the more active participants had reservations about the document. Further, should the intent of the framers refer to the intent of the delegates to the Constitutional Convention only or also include the intent of the delegates to the state ratifying conventions?[6] Do the *Federalist Papers*, written by Hamilton, Madison, and Jay to encourage New Yorkers to vote for ratification, help clarify intent? Not really, because as well written and tightly reasoned as they are, they were political propaganda. Indeed, that the justices even today nevertheless cite the *Federalist Papers* demonstrates the deficiencies of the historical record.[7] And what if the actual intent of the framers was to write a document sufficiently vague to adapt to changing circumstances over time? The Constitution *is*, at least in parts, vague, ambiguous, and contradictory. Is this because the framers were wise, far-sighted persons who intentionally drafted a document to endure the ages? Or is it the result of the bargaining and political horse-trading required to draft any document they could agree upon, a document of compromise, not a document of consensus? Finally, we have the problem of distinguishing between individual and group intent. Any number of delegates to the Constitutional Convention may have voted the same way on crucial questions but for very different reasons. There is in any context a very real sense in which individuals may have reasons for their votes but the groups of which they are a part do not; and individual reasons, within the context of a group decision, are rarely articulated. In short, there is no reliable mechanism for the final determination of the "intent of the framers."

Nevertheless, contemporary jurists, academics, and politicians continue to rethink and debate the meaning of the Constitution, and how and who should interpret it. In the summer of 1985 U.S. Attorney General Edwin Meese caused quite a stir when he said in a speech that the function of the Supreme Court is to "resurrect the original meaning of Constitutional provisions . . . as the only reliable guide to judgment."[8] In the fall of 1985 Judge Robert Bork of the United States Court of Appeals for the District of Columbia, later to be nominated to the Supreme Court by

President Reagan but rejected by the Senate, asserted that "original intent is the only legitimate basis for institutional decision."[9] The views of Meese and Bork were reinforced by Bruce Fein, a conservative lawyer with close connections to the Justice Department. Said Fein, "Once you unhinge yourself from the intent of the framers, there is no other standard around. . . . "You're basically entrusting to the unelected judiciary the power to do what they want."[10] Such comments led two Supreme Court justices, Stevens and Brennan, to break with the tradition requiring justices not engage in off-the-bench debate with Court critics. For example, in apparent response to Meese and others, Justice Brennan said in a speech in October 1985, "The chorus of lamentations calling for interpretation faithful to 'original intention' . . . must inevitably come from persons who have no familiarity with the historical record."[11] The views expressed by Meese and others, Brennan went on, are "little more than arrogance cloaked as humility." Brennan stressed the need to find "great principles to cope with current problems and current needs," and he concluded that "it is arrogance to pretend that, from our vantage, we can gauge accurately the interest of the framers."[12] In an attempt to set the record straight, John P. Roche, for four decades a respected academic, wrote a letter to the editor of the *New York Times* (on May 18, 1986). Roche wrote:

> The central point is that after . . . 40 years laboring in the primary sources of 18th century American constitutionalism . . . I can sadly testify that not only do I not know the "original intent" of the Framers . . . but I increasingly suspect that much of the time on many of the provisions they didn't either. I know what Madison thought of some things, what Hamilton thought about others, but have no reason to believe their views were the accepted wisdom.[13]

We will return to this debate over "original intent" later in this chapter when we consider legalistic-prescriptive theories. For now suffice it to say that Supreme Court decisions *are* made in a *legal context,* and some scholars as well as some justices would describe the Court's decision-making process largely as an attempt to find and rely on the framers' intent. We will turn now to the second mode of reasoning and interpretation, *the meaning of the words* of the Constitution. Like original intent, this mode emphasizes that decisions are based on continuity with the past. Specifically, the meaning of the Constitution is derived from the meaning of its words at the time they were written. Unlike the determination of intent, which requires reasoning that is historically grounded and a broad base of historical information, the determination of the meaning of the words requires largely lexicographic skills.[14] Although references to the past, whether reasoning via intent or reasoning via the meaning of the words, may seem to make American politics a prisoner of its past, such references need not do so necessarily. For example, Article I, Section 2, Clause 1, states that the

"House of Representatives shall be composed of Members chosen every second Year by the People of the several States." These words were written in 1787. In the mid-twentieth century a variety of unsuccessful attempts were made to get the Supreme Court to rule that the Constitution requires that congressional districts be roughly equal in size. Finally, in 1964 Justice Black used both the "intent" and the "meaning" modes of reasoning and interpretation to rule that the Constitution requires the applications of a "one person, one vote" principle to the drawing of congressional district lines. That principle was shortly thereafter applied to both houses of state legislatures. In short, although a number of problems are associated with the interpretation by intent mode and the interpretation by meaning mode, both have been amenable to innovative use.[15]

Supreme Court decisions based on *logical analysis* are a quite different thing from those based on the framers' intent or on the meaning of the words. This mode is based on the syllogism, and we find its classic usage in Chief Justice Marshall's opinion in the great case of *Marbury v. Madison.* As we learned in Chapter Three, Marshall reasoned in *Marbury* that because of the supremacy clause, a congressional act repugnant to the Constitution is void (major premise). Then Marshall showed how Section 13 of the Judiciary Act of 1789 violated the Constitution (a minor premise stating a fact related to the major premise). It then automatically followed that Section 13 was void. As we also learned in Chapter Three, much of Marshall's argument in *Marbury* was specious. Its logic seemed unassailable because as long as the form of an argument based on logical analysis conforms with the basic rules of inference, the conclusion cannot be criticized as illogical. The argument may, however, be either unjust or absurd or both because it stands apart from factual or empirical analysis; it exists independently of fact or experience, of intent or meaning.[16] A good example of reasoning and interpretation relying on all three modes we have discussed to this point is another of Marshall's famous opinions. In *McCulloch v. Maryland,* as we learned in Chapter Three, Marshall wrote the Court's opinion sustaining the power of Congress to create a national bank. He found that power in the necessary and proper clause (Article I, Section 8, Clause 18), which provides that in addition to the power expressly granted to Congress in the Constitution, the Congress has power to pass any law necessary and proper for implementing its expressed powers. Opponents of this interpretation had argued that the word *necessary* means "indispensable." Marshall argued that in this context the word *necessary* means merely "convenient," "useful," or "calculated to produce an end." Marshall relied on the intent of the framers, the meaning of the word when it was written, and logical analyses to arrive at this conclusion. He reasoned as follows: (1) In other places in the Constitution the phrase *absolutely necessary* is used whereas in the necessary and proper clause there is no prefix such as *absolutely;* thus, the framers could not have used the word *necessary* in one place and the phrase *absolutely necessary* elsewhere in the document and have intended that the meaning be the same. (2) The necessary and proper clause appears in that part of the Constitution in which powers are granted, not in the parts in which limitations on powers are stated; hence, in context the word *necessary* alone cannot have been intended as a limitation on national government power.

Finally, among the legalistic-descriptive theories of constitutional construction, we have the *adaptive mode*. This basis of decision rests on the recognition that however wise and far sighted, the framers could not anticipate precisely the needs of a dynamic society well into the future. Thus, although limited by the Constitution's general framework, justices must sometimes accommodate the document to changing circumstances. As Marshall put it in *McCulloch v. Maryland*, a Constitution intended to endure for ages to come must be "adapted to the various crises of human affairs." The use of the adaptive mode is politically risky, however, because it is likely, at least when used explicitly and in isolation from other modes, to engender opposition from those in society who support the status quo, for such opponents prefer the "political certainty" and "appearance of stability" provided by Constitutional "absolutes." As a consequence, the adaptive mode is used explicitly by justices only rarely, and even then only in combination with one or more of the other modes, or when the other modes are, for some reason, not available to them.[17] Later, when we move from legalistic-descriptive to legalistic-prescriptive theories, we will observe that many of the prescriptive theories are those that take positions ranging from a preference for a little to preference for a lot of adaptation.

When the Supreme Court is confronted with the task of interpreting statutes, as distinct from construing the Constitution, it tends to rely upon two modes of reasoning: the "plain-meaning" mode and the "legislative history" mode. These two approaches, as well as their weaknesses, are classically described by Edward Levi.[18] The Court's interpretation of a statute like its construction of the Constitution is largely constrained, at least theoretically, by our democratic governmental system. Hence, when the Court is asked to interpret a provision of a statute *for the first time*, its job is to "fix the meaning of the words"—that is, to interpret what the statute says based on a literal reading of its text—and to determine its legislative history, which requires the Court to decide what the legislators really meant, as distinct from what they wrote, based on committee reports, floor debate, preamble to the law, if there is one, and so on. Before a statute has been applied and interpreted for the first time, it is an abstraction. No real persons have yet been affected by it; no real parties have yet asked the courts to interpret it within the context of a concrete case and controversy. In short, a statute not yet interpreted by the courts has no flesh and blood; it has met no true proving ground—it is an abstraction. As a result, the Court has a great deal of discretion when deciding what a statute means the first time that statute is interpreted. But once the meaning of its words and the intent of those who wrote it have been established as the result of an initial interpretation, then in all subsequent cases in which the meaning of the statute is raised, judges must decide strictly on the basis that the initial interpretation was correct. This doctrine rests on the supposition that if the initial interpretation was "wrong" in the minds of those who wrote the law, then they would have revised the law to correct the error and to make the law's meaning more precise; their silence after an initial interpretation, on the other hand, must mean that they approve of the interpretation. As a result, the Court has little discretion when deciding what a statute means *after an initial interpretation has been made* and "approved" by the silence of those who wrote the law. In many situations, however, particularly in controversial ones, legislative revision of a misinterpretation cannot be expected. For a variety of reasons, normally political, legislators are frequently either unable or unwilling to revise a statutory interpretation even when a majority thinks it wrong. Hence, legislative silence may not always mean approval, and thus the doctrine requiring courts to rely on the precedent of the initial interpretation is a difficult doctrine that has led to strange results. Levi uses the cases decided following the passage of the Mann Act as an example.

In 1910 Congress passed the Mann Act, making it a federal crime to transport women across state lines "for the purpose of prostitution, or debauchery, or for any other immoral purpose." Nearly any objective study of the Mann Act's legislative history would lead to the conclusion that the law was passed to prevent the systematic enticement and enslavement in prostitution of women by organized crime elements (bands of "white slavers") presumed then to be operating on a broad scale coast to coast. However, in a number of cases arising with the law's implementation, several of which reached the Supreme Court, interpretations of the Mann Act's "purposes" and the "plain meaning" of its words led gradually to an absurd result. Along the way it was decided, among other things, that (1) "debauchery" referred not only to sexual intercourse but also to "any act ultimately leading to sexual activity"; (2) women might in some circumstances be, not the victim of the crime, but the perpetrator of it; and (3) "any other immoral purpose" includes a private and voluntary participation in paid cohabitation totally unconnected to organized vice. Cumulatively, these cases meant that the enforcement of the Mann Act need not be strictly confined to "white slavery" and need not involve organized traffic. The Supreme Court approved. Congress was silent. Finally, on the basis of prior interpretations not revised by Congress, the Supreme Court upheld the conviction of Mormons, who practiced polygamy, for transporting their plural wives across state lines for the purpose of cohabitation. Although dissenters on the Court objected that the meaning of the word *polygamy* is quite different from the meaning of

words like *debauchery* and *prostitution,* the Court's majority felt trapped by
the precedents established in the prior interpretations.[19]

Before moving on to legalistic-prescriptive theories, we should stop
to consider two more elements commonly associated with the legalistic-
descriptive approach: judicial "activism" versus judicial "restraint," and
"strict" versus "loose" constructionism. Activism is difficult to describe
because although it may, in fact, explain more about how justices decide
than does restraint, few justices openly admit to being activists. Activism,
in short, indicates a desire to insert one's policy preferences into Court
decisions in order to achieve policy goals as well as a willingness to overturn the decisions of the "political" branches, that is, the Congress and the
executive, and of state governments to accomplish that objective. Restraint posits that justices should refrain from making public policy. They
should not address policy issues unless it is absolutely necessary to do so to
dispose of a concrete case. If they must address policy issues, they should
frame them as narrowly as possible and never arrive at a rule that is
broader than required to dispose of the case. They should always defer to
the Congress, the executive, and the states on subjective judgments concerning the wisdom or utility of legislation or administrative orders.[20]
Activism and restraint have no natural ideological home. In the 1930s the
activists were the conservatives who struck down much of the early New
Deal legislation; the restraintists were the liberals who fought to sustain
New Deal programs. In the 1960s the activists were the liberals who struck
down both federal and state regulations thought to infringe upon First
Amendment rights; the restraintists were the conservatives who would
have upheld many of these regulations.

The distinction between "strict" and "loose" construction is even
more difficult to describe. The difficulty lies first in the fact that strict
construction has a precise legal meaning but is used rhetorically by politicians to mean something else. In legal circles strict construction means a
literal adherence to the provisions of the Constitution, and thus it is yet
one more way of assuring, at least putatively, judicial objectivity. For example, if the Constitution says that "no law" shall be made abridging
freedom of speech, "no law" means *no* law, period.[21] In the political arena
strict construction often means little more than a politician's characteriza-
tion of the type of justice he or she prefers on the Court. For example,
after the Senate rejected President Nixon's nominations of Haynsworth
and Carswell, a petulant Nixon made the ill-tempered statement that "it is
impossible to get confirmed a nominee from the South who believes like I
do in strict constructionism." The statement was baseless. There were at
the time at least a dozen conservative Southern judges who could have
been confirmed. What Nixon actually meant but could not say publicly
was that he could not pay off Senator Strom Thurmond, who had strongly
supported him in the presidential election, with a nominee the Senate

would approve. As was clear from his campaign speeches in which the Supreme Court was mentioned as an issue, Nixon wanted justices who would be tough on crime. To him at that time strict construction meant particular policy preferences—specifically, a preference for justices who would be ideologically conservative in such policy areas as law enforcement, race relations, and First Amendment rights.[22] The second difficulty in distinguishing strict from loose construction is that loose construction is used by both scholars and justices as a means of justifying very different roles for the Court. Commonly, loose construction is used by those who want the Court to play an activist role on the basis that the language of the Constitution is itself so vague—or loose—that justices must give their own meaning to the document, especially in order to "keep the Constitution in tune with the times." Arguing from the same premise of loose construction can lead also to the opposite result. For example, James Bradley Thayer, an early Supreme Court scholar, wrote that the Constitution is not a specific legal document like a deed or a will, which is, and should be, read closely and interpreted with technical finality. Rather, the Constitution is a grand charter of government, broadly worded, anticipatory of unknown future needs. Hence, the Constitution leaves open such a broad range of choice and judgment that "whatever choice is rational is constitutional." To this point, Thayer's loose construction is the same as that espoused by those who favor a broad role for the Court. But Thayer then turns the loose construction premise to a different purpose. He argues that since reasonable persons will differ about the proper construction of the Constitution, and since any construction that is reasonable is also constitutional, it is nearly impossible for the Congress to make a constitutional error when passing a law. Choice and judgment reside in the Congress, not in the Court. Therefore the Court can properly invalidate a law only when the Congress has made not merely a mistake, but a "mistake" so clear that it is not open to rational question. Thayer's so-called doctrine of the clear mistake is based on a premise of loose construction; but unlike most other loose constructionists, Thayer uses the premise to justify the narrowest of proper policy roles for the Supreme Court.[23]

Generalizing about the legalistic-descriptive theories examined above, we notice that these theories come down to the rather simple notion that Supreme Court justices are guided in their decision making by *intent* (of the framers in constitutional cases and of legislators in statutory interpretations), by *language* (again, of either the framers or the legislators), and by *purpose* (policy objectives of the framers or legislators). However, as we have seen, the claim can often be made either that the authors of a document, whether it be the Constitution or a statute, had no specific intent or that if they had an intent, it is no longer discernable; or that if an intent did exist and is discernable, changing circumstances render it no longer binding. A few noteworthy, concrete cases make the point. In the school prayer cases of the early 1960s, Justice Brennan responded to the argument of those who favored school prayer to the effect that recitations of the Lord's Prayer, Bible reading, and so on, would have been approved by the most vocal of religious freedom advocates among our founding leaders like Jefferson and Madison. Brennan granted that was possible, but he pointed out that both the structure of education and the religious composition of the country had changed dramatically since the founding era. In the time of Jefferson and Madison education was largely private, not public, and we were far more homogeneous in religion (mostly Protestant). Today most persons are educated in public schools and we are religiously far more heterogeneous. Thus, Brennan concluded, "in the face of such profound changes, practices which may have been objectionable to no one in the time of Jefferson and Madison may today be highly offensive to many persons."[24] In a similar vein the Court can alter the meaning of words and purposes. The Constitution guarantees criminal defendants a right to the assistance of an attorney. The original meaning of this right grew out of an ancient common law rule prohibiting criminal defendants from having any attorney at all. The authors of the right to counsel clause merely wanted to prevent the government from prohibiting defendants from bringing attorneys to court with them. It did not occur to the authors that a criminal defendant's financial status may preclude the hiring of an attorney. Yet in a series of cases decided in recent years, the Court has held that the wording of the Constitution not only requires a right to counsel for defendants in criminal cases, federal and state, but also requires that the government must appoint counsel for defendants who cannot afford to pay their own attorneys' fees.[25] Finally, regarding Court decisions altering purposes, we can cite the case of *Home Building and Loan Association v. Blaisdell* (1934),[26] in which the Court upheld, during the Great Depression, an emergency state mortgage moratorium law against the challenge that it violated the Constitutional ban on state action impairing the obligation of contracts (the contract clause). In policy terms the original purpose of the contract clause was to protect creditors from the nasty schemes of state legislatures so common prior to the adoption of the Constitution. More bluntly, from the perspective of the framers the masses contained more debtors than creditors, and they feared that, especially in times of economic difficulty, popularly elected state legislatures would give in to the demands of the masses to ease their debts. The Court said in *Blaisdell* that times of economic emergency do not create governmental power because the Constitution itself was written during a time of emergency and thus its provisions are not altered by emergencies. But, the Court continued, emergency may "furnish the occasion for the exercise of power." With respect to the mortgage moratorium laws, it could be reasoned that laws delaying foreclosures on mortgages served to strengthen the national economy generally, benefiting debtors *and* creditors. This was so because supply-and-demand analysis, available to the Court in 1934 but not to the framers of the Constitution, would predict that the price of property would drop dramatically if massive foreclosures were allowed, adversely affecting creditors. From the viewpoint of the Court's majority in 1934, therefore, the postponement of mortgage foreclosures helped to halt the further decline of the economy. To be sure, these laws did alter the terms of mortgage contracts, and in that sense they violated the specific purposes of the framers. Yet they also accommodated a more general purpose of promoting a healthy economy. Constitutional scholar Lief H. Carter summarizes this case and these events as follows: In *Blaisdell,* "the Court rejected more than constitutional words; it rejected the purpose of the provision. But it did so correctly. . . . [The Court must have] the ability to re-evaluate policies in light of new information . . . , [in this case] based on economic knowledge not fully available to the framers."[27]

LEGALISTIC-PRESCRIPTIVE THEORIES

The essential difference between legalistic-descriptive theories and legalistic-prescriptive theories of Supreme Court decision making is that the latter argue the *ought* of the former. In other words, both types of theories emphasize that Court decisions are made in a legal context yet grant that justices are not strictly bound in all cases to the adherence to intent, meaning, purpose, and precedent. Some amount of discretion exists enabling justices to adapt legal texts (the Constitution, statutes, administrative regulations, prior Court opinions) to changing times and circumstances. The presence of discretion, and hence the opportunity to "make" law as well as to "find" it, is evident in our consideration above of activism versus restraint and of strict versus loose constructionism. Thus legalistic-prescriptive theories are most instructively treated if presented as a continuum ranging from those that prefer a little to those that prefer a lot of adaptation.

Even if we limit our consideration to normative decision-making theories espoused in the twentieth century, we notice that from quite early on there have been those who would restrict the role of justices in adapting legal texts to the times. As we have already learned, James Bradley Thayer argued that justices should invalidate acts of Congress as repugnant to the Constitution only when the Congress has made such a clear mistake that it is not open to rational question. Judge Learned Hand argued that in a government of divided powers (between branches of the national government and between the national government and the states), someone or some institution must keep the Congress, the president, and the states within the spheres of authority that the Constitution created in its two most fundamental principles, federalism and separation of powers. Hand concludes after a lengthy analysis that the Supreme Court is best, but not perfectly, suited to perform this function. However, since the Court has this power only as a matter of necessity, certain restrictions must be observed. Hand's prescription, then, is that the justices be limited in their role to "defining the frontiers of authority." If the president, the Congress, or the states take action that *urgently* threatens the *fixed historical meaning* of federalism and separation of powers, then, and only then, should the justices decide to invalidate the action. In other issue areas (for example, free speech under the Bill of Rights), however, the Court should not act because to do so would be to pass on the "propriety of choices," which is the job of the Congress, the president, and the states. For the Court to act in these areas would be to duplicate the work of the "political" branches and the states. Even in federalism and separation of power cases the justices should decide to strike down actions only reluctantly and sparingly. In practice Hand's prescription of restraint amounts to virtual abstinence.[28] Herbert Wechsler would grant the justices greater leeway than either Thayer or Hand. Indeed, he thinks that the discretion of the justices to decide cases with the effect of undoing legislative, executive, and state policy, as long as the proper procedural and jurisdictional requirements are met, is grounded in the language of the Constitution itself. However, Wechsler insists that Supreme Court decision making must be intellectually coherent and must not be a mere expression of the justices' values or their *ad hoc* views of fairness or convenience. Thus, as a limitation on the discretion of the justices, Wechsler prescribes a doctrine of "neutral principles." In essence, the doctrine of neutral principles is an attempt by Wechsler to fashion a standard of interpretation that permits justices to perform their decision-making task while remaining "disinterested" in the immediate results. How can they do so? By testing not only the application of a principle of law to the case before them but also other, hypothetical applications that the principle implies—preferably cases involving opposing interests. If a justice feels intellectually obligated to apply a principle in both the instant case and in a hypothetical case where applying the principle would serve opposing interests, it is a neutral principle and the decision is a properly principled one. Only in this way can the justices make decisions that transcend the immediate result and avoid both the appearance and the actuality of acting as a "naked power organ."[29]

Thayer, Hand, and Wechsler wrote their prescriptions limiting the discretion of the justices prior to the more recent era when the policy impact of the Warren and Burger Courts' decision making was fully felt and subject to analysis. In the mid-1970s there arose a "neoconservative" critique of the Supreme Court that argued that the Court had become "permanently activist" and intrusive, "undemocratically" expanding rights that neither the people nor the policy-making branches want and insisting on implementations that the executive does not know how to accomplish. This critique characterized the Court as an "imperial judiciary."[30] To the neoconservatives, the imperial judiciary is one that requires the government to do what the legislature has not ordered it to do and what the executive does not feel it wise to do, and one that reaches "into the lives of the people against the will of the people."[31] Specifically, it is a Supreme Court that legitimizes the bussing of children to overcome racial segregation in public schools, that legitimizes government guidelines for employment tests to prevent discriminatory hiring practices, and that extends the protection of due process to students threatened with suspension or expulsion in the public schools. These are just examples of a few of the many Court decisions the neoconservatives criticize. To the neoconservatives, close analysis of the political history of the adoption of the various clauses of the Constitution yields definite answers to many Constitutional questions. To them, the answers provided in cases such as those mentioned above have one or the other of two problems. Either they do not conform to the expressed intent of those who wrote and ratified the Constitution and its amendments, or the questions themselves were never raised, let alone answered, by the Constitution's authors and thus should be left for decision by the people through the political process.[32] The neoconservatives of the mid-1970s expressed particular alarm because they saw in the Burger Court no cyclical return to the conservatism and quietism of the pre-Warren years that their reading of history had taught them to expect. Their fear was that the Supreme Court had become permanently activist. Their preference was for a Court whose justices would base their decision making on the truths that are evident to them in the details of historical records, but they had little hope that such an approach would soon be followed. Thus, their prescription was that the Court be "censured" and that "corrective action" be taken.[33] It was this plan that would by the end of the decade lead to various Court-curbing proposals in Congress, which we will examine in Chapter Nine.

In most of the prescriptions described to this point is the assumption that the Constitution is a legal text containing correct conclusions to litigated cases; that is, there is a discernible law of the Constitution that is objective and constant. Since roughly the early 1980s, approaches based on this assumption have been called *interpretivism*.[34] "Interpretivists" argue that the only correct Constitutional decision is one that "accords binding authority to the text of the Constitution or the intentions of the adopters and is significantly guided by one or more of these sources."[35] As Christopher Wolfe, a leading interpretivist, put it in 1981, "I . . . reject . . . broad relativism . . . , believing that the founders embodied sound political principles in the Constitution, which can be 'interpreted,' and that what the Constitution does not provide rules for should be left to the workings of a democratic process soundly designed by those founders (trusting to amendment to rectify any serious infirmities)."[36] Many of the interpretivists are what Lief Carter calls "legalists"; that is, they "believe the Court must obey the Constitution to preserve the legitimacy of the legal system."[37] Carter is referring here to legal scholars like Wolfe and Gary McDowell[38] and John Agresto.[39] Thus, it should not be surprising that their criticism of noninterpretivist justices leads them to prescriptions for legal solutions. McDowell, for example, would have us adopt an amendment to the Constitution providing that nothing in the Constitution requires the application of the Bill of Rights to the states. Agresto prescribes a constitutional doctrine providing that Supreme Court decisions are binding only on the parties to the case in which the decision is made and on judges. Congress, the president, and the political branches in the states would be free to give their own "meaning" to the "constitutional test." Generally, then, the legally minded interpretivists argue for strict adherence to the Constitution on the grounds that the language of the Constitution itself requires interpretation and democratic theory "illegitimates" noninterpretive ("free-hand lawmaking") decision-making styles.[40] Some interpretists, like Walter Berns,[41] are more philosophical than legal in their approach. They argue, simply, that the framers of the Constitution drafted a valid concrete vision of government that ought not be vacated.

Robert Bork, President Reagan's unsuccessful nominee to the Court, brings us back to the more conventional form of interpretivism. He writes as follows: "[T]he Court's power is legitimate only if it has . . . a valid theory derived from the Constitution. If it does not have such a theory but merely imposes its own value choices, or worse if it pretends to have a theory but actually follows its own predilections, the Court . . . abets the tyranny of the majority or of the minority."[42] Sounding much like Thayer, Bork continues, "Courts must accept any value choice the legislature makes unless it clearly runs contrary to a choice made in the framing of the Constitution."[43] Thus, for Bork, as for most other interpretivists, the framers designed the nearly ideal state. Matters not clearly dealt with in the Constitution are just as clearly outside the purview of the Court and must be considered the business of the political process.[44] This is not an entirely new notion. Nearly 200 years ago Justice James Iredell warned against a Court whose justices made decisions contrary to the choices made by political actors in the legislative and executive branches, federal and state. Although there are limits that the Constitution places on the actions of the political branches, those limits must be found in the Constitution, not in the justices' opinions of what abstract natural rights or justice requires. As Iredell put it, the ideas of natural justice are regulated by no fixed standard; the ablest of justices will differ on the subject; hence, if the Constitution itself imposes no limitations on the political branches and political actors in a given case, there are no limitations.[45]

Supreme Court Justice Antonin Scalia, whom Reagan did succeed in placing on the Court, has written as follows:

> Where do I draw the line [between a policy decision and a legitimate area within which the Supreme Court may operate]? In the area of constitutional rights, I draw the line at the point where the Court plucks out of the air a principle of action. . . . It is very hard to tell you where the line between a proper and an improper decision should be drawn. It would fall short of making fundamental, social determinations that ought to be made through the democratic process, but that the society has not yet made.[46]

There is, of course, a middle ground between the prescriptions of the more avid interpretivists and those of the more avid noninterpretivists (which we examine a bit later). The much-revered scholar of American jurisprudence, Roscoe Pound noticed long before the mid-twentieth century that courts, including the Supreme Court, do not in fact operate with adding-machine accuracy. For better or worse, judges and justices do consider questions of convenience and social interest as well as legal rules. In fact, law itself is not so much *content* as it is *process.* Pound defined the law as "a process of balancing conflicting interests and securing the satisfaction of the maximum of wants with the minimum of friction." It is true that Pound did not believe that judges and justices reached decisions based on abstract ideals like natural law or other value choices; he believed, rather, that they made determinations based on tentative compromises valid only for the present generation as required by particular and contemporary community standards. Still, Pound's studies of judicial decision making led him to find over and over again that law in action is quite commonly different from law in the books.[47] Similarly, the great jurist Oliver Wendell Holmes, even before his appointment to the Supreme Court at the age of 61 in 1902, wrote that "the life of the law has not been logic; it has been experience." By this epigram Holmes meant to express his studied observation that due to a variety of factors (most notably the personal characteristics of the judge, including intuitions and biases), there is great uncertainty and confusion in the law. Hence the law cannot be meaningfully treated through the use of the syllogism as if it were nothing more than a series of axioms in a book of mathematics. Judicial decisions are based instead on "the felt necessities of the time, the prevalent moral and political theories, [and] intuitions of public policy." Thus, for Holmes, when it comes to a *realistic* understanding of judicial decision making, "a page of history is worth a volume of logic."[48] As we will learn later, the work of Holmes and Pound led to the evolution of a school of legal thought called jurisprudential realism, which in turn became the precursor of the "behavioral" types of decision-making theories. For now, it is sufficient to understand that the early work of Holmes and Pound provide a conceptual framework allowing for legalistic-prescriptive theories that plead not for absolutes, constants, and closure (as the interpretivists tend to do) but for indeterminacy, relativism, and acceptance of the notion that the Constitution is always in a state of "becoming."[49]

Although sharing the middle ground, a number of modern writers prescribe differing approaches to Supreme Court decision making. The differing positions taken in two books, both published in 1980 by legal scholars Jesse Choper and John Hart Ely, are illustrative. Choper fashions an argument for restrained Supreme Court decision making when the issues involve federalism or separation of powers, and for a somewhat broader role in civil liberties cases. Unlike Judge Learned Hand, who, as we have learned, thought that the Court could enter the policy arena only to preserve the boundaries of governmental authority as laid out in the Constitution, Choper asserts that Court decisions dealing with the division of power between the branches of government and between the national and state governments are more likely than civil liberties decisions to run contrary to the preferences of democratically elected bodies. Further, Choper argues that the Court may be acting somewhat more appropriately when it makes decisions protecting civil liberties because individual and minority rights are not inevitably protected by the clash of interests within the political process. Protection of the prerogatives of the Congress, the president, and the states, on the other hand, is already adequately provided by the system of countervailing powers. Choper, then, would give the justices some discretion in decision making in civil liberties cases but virtually none in cases involving federalism and separation of powers.[50] John Hart Ely adopts a different approach. He attempts, as others before him have, to develop a theory of Supreme Court decision making that breaks free from the restrictive reliance on the part of the interpretivists but that does not also give the justices discretion to engage in "free-hand lawmaking" by reading their policy preferences into the law. In essence, Ely argues for a "participation-oriented, representation reinforcing" theory of judicial decision making that would allow the Court to invalidate the policy choices of the political branches and the states in order to protect full participation in the political process broadly defined and to guarantee procedural fairness to individuals litigating disputes in the judicial process. In other words, for Ely, policy choices should be made by elected officials in the political branches, not by the justices. If the populace disapproves, it can vote policy makers out of office. Malfunctions in the political process can occur, however, when "the ins are choking off the channels of political change to insure that they will stay in and the outs will stay out."[51] The job of the justices is to protect the integrity of the political process by guaranteeing full participation in it by all. As Carter puts it, Ely would have the justices "interpret neither text nor history but rather what the . . . [Constitution], taken as a whole, would have to mean to be true to itself."[52]

Finally, we will examine several clearly noninterpretivist approaches. The first is presented by Arthur S. Miller in his 1982 book *Toward Increased Judicial Activism*. As the title suggests, Miller defends an activist Court, but his activism is of a particular kind. The important question, Miller says, is not how effectively the justices explain or rationalize their decisions. The real question is, rather, who wins when the Supreme Court decides. Miller's answer is that invariably the monied and propertied win. Even those decisions that appear to assist the disadvantaged merely preserve the status quo by defusing social discontent. The purpose of Miller's book, then, is to recommend a "new normative posture"—used interchangeably in the book with "synthesis" and "theory"—for the Supreme Court. He paves the way for his prescriptions by showing that because the Constitution is always in "a state of becoming," we as a people have already accepted the role of the Court as a "Council of Elders," a national faculty of public theory. From this stance he posits his central argument for judicial activism that furthers the attainment of human dignity. Miller rejects the notion that the intentions of the framers of the Constitution should guide modern decisions. He asserts that each generation of Americans writes its own Constitution, and it is within this context that the Supreme Court, because it is the *only existing governmental organ that can articulate national values,* should pursue an activism of a particular kind, that which enhances basic human dignity. He admits that this involves "openly being a 'superior legislature'" and proceeds to defend his position against activism's many critics—from neoconservatives to the legal profession to those who believe simply that the justices are inadequately prepared or equipped to do what Miller wants. Would the justices have time for a more active role? Yes, if they were to hear cases in panels of three and do away with written opinions. But is it not the case that opinions explain their reasoning process? No, nobody really believes that, and decisions without opinions would, for the better, make lawyers more outwardly result oriented (echoing Lord Mansfield's statement that "our judgments are better than our reasons"[53]). Would it not be the case that Miller's Court would be a less democratic institution? No, because that criterion depends on the validity of that which never was—a true majority rule. But would not Miller's prescription make the Constitution a mere artifact cut adrift from the judiciary? Yes, but that, Miller concludes, is precisely where we are now.[54]

Still, what justification is there for justices making policy and doing so openly? Ronald Dworkin provides a response.[55] Citing many examples, Dworkin concludes that in most cases of Constitutional construction and many cases of statutory interpretation, the intent of the authors is either nonexistent or impossible to determine and thus largely useless as a guide to decision. What, then, should justices do when confronted with competing interpretations of what the law requires? Dworkin says they should choose that interpretation that is "superior" as a matter of "political morality" and that provides a "coherent" justification and "principled" guide to future interpretations. But would not justices disagree about the superior political morality of a given choice? Yes, but as long as justices face the moral decision openly, an informed public will be in a better position to both understand and criticize their decision than it would be if the moral grounds are hidden behind complicated arguments about a nonexistent intent. Would this not make policy makers out of the justices? Yes, but this mere assertion assumes that the framers or the political branches made a clear and knowable policy judgment that the justices are wrong to reverse. Since there is commonly no discoverable intent, there is no knowable policy judgment. Besides, Dworkin concludes, this criticism suggests that the justices do have a method to decide without making a political judgment. And in the real world they do not, except perhaps to flip a coin.

It should be clear by now that many of the legalistic-prescriptive theories of Supreme Court decision making revolve around differing ideas regarding the Supreme Court's proper role in the polity generally. This is a matter of great importance that we will address in Chapter Nine.

BEHAVIORAL-PREDICTIVE THEORIES

The Supreme Court does make its decisions in a legal context, and thus its decision-making *process may be distinctive*. However, Supreme Court justices, like other political actors, are influenced by a *long list of extralegal factors* that interact in intricate ways. This is the premise of behavioral theories of Supreme Court decision making.

As we observed earlier, the works of Roscoe Pound and Oliver Wendell Holmes early in this century led in a school of legal thought called "jurisprudential realism" that led in turn to "judicial behavioralism" in political science. One of the most articulate of the realists was Benjamin Cardozo, who, like Holmes, later became a Supreme Court justice.[56] Holmes had concluded that general propositions do not decide concrete cases. And if general propositions do not decide concrete cases, who does? Judges do! To what extent, then, is the job of judging a science? To what extent is it an art? Does a Supreme Court justice "sit like a kadi under a tree dispensing justice according to considerations of individual expedience"[57] and unlimited discretion? Or does the justice not make law at all but merely find it and objectively apply it to concrete cases? Certainly justices do not always behave as if they are, as Hamilton said they should be, "bound down by strict rules of precedents which serve to define and point out [their] duty in every particular case that comes before [them]."[58]

It is perhaps inevitable, as Bishop Hoadly said, that judges make the law in the process of interpreting it. Hoadly wrote in the eighteenth century that "whoever hath an absolute authority to interpret any written or spoken laws, it is He who is truly the Law Giver to all intents and purposes, and not the Person who first Wrote and spoke them."[59] As long as law remains one of the most familiar means of formalizing public policy, the judicial office in the United States will inevitably involve political, that is, policy-making, power.[60] The value of the scholarship of Pound, Holmes, and Cardozo in stripping the process of the judicial decision of all illusion, however, is sometimes lost in the often accompanying cynicism that assumes that all judges (including justices) desire to bend the law to their individual whims. Such assumptions fail to "depict even dimly the subtleties of the judicial process" and carried to their ultimate conclusion would find every judge "guilty of fraud, hypocrisy, and foolishness."[61] At the very minimum, however, justices must make law in the interstices between precedents. According to the jurisprudential theory of the logical plenitude of the law, judges cannot refuse to decide a case on the ground that there is no precise authority in point.[62] And when there is no precise authority in point, the decisive source of the law is the judge's "inarticulate major premise" or "social picture" of what values and policies lie behind the law. Prior to the findings in research done by modern judicial behavioralists in political science, the best statement of judicial decision making (and laying the groundwork for the behavioralists) was that of Benjamin Cardozo. What do judges do when they decide cases? Cardozo's answer was that they consider precedent, they weigh considerations of social welfare, they ponder common standards of justice and morals, and they seek logical consistency. Where do they get their knowledge? According to Cardozo, judges acquire their knowledge just as legislators do, from experience and study and reflection. There is in all judges a "stream of tendency, whether you choose to call it philosophy or not, which gives coherence and direction to thought and action. . . . All their lives, forces which they do not recognize and cannot name have been tugging at them—inherited instincts, traditional beliefs, acquired convictions; and the result is an outlook on life."[63]

Stemming from Cardozo's writings in jurisprudence, the seminal study of judicial behavioralism by a political scientist is C. Herman Pritchett's *The Roosevelt Court: A Study in Judicial Politics and Values, 1937–1947.*[64] In this 1948 book Pritchett uses the construction of "inter-agreement matrices" and the "scaling of votes" to study bloc activity on the Court and to study the values of its justices. He is able to conclude that justices begin with "different assumptions, that their inarticulate major premises are dissimilar, and that their value systems are differently constructed and weighted." As a result, "their political, economic and social views contrast" and their votes reveal "information about their attitudes and their values."[65] In short, decisions *are* the result of the justices' votes; but what underlies these votes, the justices' attitudes and values, make up the *predictive and expositive* (explanatory) ingredients of the decision.[66] Measuring the motivation of the justices as they decide cases is, of course, quite difficult. Behavioral theories of Supreme Court decision making do assume that justices, like other people, are goal oriented; that is, their decisions depend on their goals.[67] Further, constrained only by the limitations that the American legal and political systems impose, their goal is to maximize their policy preferences.[68] However, identifying the personal policy preferences of the justices may help us understand *what* they decide but very little about *why* they decide as they do.[69] Attempting to *predict* how justices will vote based on extralegal variables can be both difficult and of little significance if the predictions yield no useful explanations. In 1961 Glendon Schubert did a pioneering study of this sort in which he claimed that essentially three observable data are necessary for the study of the behavior of Supreme Court justices: (1) the body movements and facial expressions of the justices during oral argument; (2) the written opinions of the Court; and (3) the votes of the justices for all or a given line of cases.[70] But suppose, for example, that a given study obtains a high correlation between a justice's facial expressions and various groups of his or her decisions. Or suppose that another study finds that if a particular justice pounds a fist while asking a question of counsel during oral argument, it is evidence that the justice will decide against that counsel. Such findings would teach us very little about Supreme Court decision making because the criteria for good prediction are quite different from those for good explanation. In other words, the capacity to predict *what* the justices will decide does not necessarily allow us to explain *why* or *how* they decided.[71] Still, in recent years increasingly sophisticated methods of analysis and increasingly complex conceptualizations have taught us more and more about how judicial decisions are made.

The general thrust of recent and current research identifies and measures the relative weights of the various "determinants" (loosely, "causes") of the judicial decision. These determinants are the "independent variables," and the decision is the "dependent variable." One type of independent variable that has received a great deal of study is the "background attributes" of the judge or justice. In many ways, of course, judges and justices are very similar to each other. They are, in general, far better educated and of higher socioeconomic status than most other people. Further, they share to some degree a common professional socialization experience. Also, they usually have had considerable political experience and come from politically active families.[72] Although it is possible to make these generalizations, there are also significant differences of background among judges and justices. Naturally, then, scholars have attempted to discover relationships between background attributes and judicial decision-making behavior. Background attributes are usually organized for purposes of analysis around four types: (1) *demographic background* (family, immigration, sex, age, race, urban-rural); (2) *sociological background* (class-status, education, work experience, religion, peer groups); (3) *economic background* (income); and (4) *political background* (party affiliation, family politics, political attitudes, ideology, group membership, and so on).[73] For example, prior to the era of behavioral research, it was widely accepted that appellate court judges with the sociological attribute of prior work experience on a lower court, having been schooled in the conservative norms expected of judges, would be more likely than judges without prior experience to adhere to precedent.[74] However, John Schmidhauser found that Supreme Court justices with prior experience are more likely to abandon precedent than justices without prior experience.[75] Apparently they have developed sufficient confidence to disregard precedent in order to achieve their policy objectives.[76] Justices from low socioeconomic status families have also been found more likely to abandon precedent.[77]

Indeed, not just prior experience (or lack thereof) but also party and religious affiliations appear to be significant background attributes. Democratic and Catholic judges are more likely than Republican and Protestant judges to vote for putatively "liberal results," specifically, to vote to protect civil rights and criminal defendants, to favor government regulation of business, and to favor employees over employers.[78] More specifically, Democratic judges are more likely than Republican judges to vote for the administrative agency in business regulation cases, for the government in tax cases, for the tenant in landlord-tenant cases, for the consumer in consumer protection cases, for the claimant in unemployment compensation cases, for the employee in employee-injury cases, and for the defense in criminal cases.[79] In fact, in criminal cases at least three background attributes and one general attitudinal variable are important: Judges with prior experience as prosecutors, judges who are ABA members, and judges who are Protestants are more likely to vote for the prosecution than are judges without prosecutorial experience, who are non-ABA members, and who are Catholics. More generally, liberal judges (those who rank high on "general liberalism" as measured by an attitude questionnaire) vote much more regularly for the defense in criminal cases than those who rank low on liberalism.[80] Although most of the studies coming to these conclusions are studies of state supreme court justices, the general importance of background attributes in the decisional propensities of U.S. Supreme Court justices is undoubtedly similar. The point here is a general one, not the specification of unavoidable determinism. The basic suggestion is that *certain background attributes* are conducive to the formation of *certain attitudes or values* (interrelated sets of attitudes).[81] These in turn affect the decisional behavior of Supreme Court justices; that is, a relationship exists between discrete backgrounds and judicial decision-making tendencies. This is not to say that judges and justices are prisoners of their past but only that the values that determine, in part, their decisions have been shaped by life experiences.[82] The reality probably is that background attributes *influence* and *filter through* the complex interactions between values, role perceptions, and bloc activity to produce a result that is not unassociated with the character of the attributes themselves.[83]

A number of studies have now successfully associated the values of Supreme Court justices with their decision-making tendencies. Three clusters of values have in particular been found in Supreme Court voting behavior for the years 1958–71; these have appropriately been labeled "freedom," "equality," and "New Dealism."[84] By fitting the fifteen justices who served on the Court between 1958 and 1971 into this typology, the value system descriptions shown in Figure 6–1 emerge. Of course, it must be granted that the research technique used to discern these value dimensions cannot be used to prove that values "cause" decisions because there is no way to measure values independent of the votes of the justices; that is, we cannot conclude that values cause votes because we have defined the values in terms of those same votes. To return briefly to background attributes, we must similarly grant that we are not absolutely certain what backgrounds lead to what values. Studying the background attributes of a particular justice may allow for an association of background with decision-making

FIGURE 6-1   Justices and Values Systems

	Freedom	Equality	New Dealism	Value System Description
Douglas	+	+	+	Liberal
Warren	+	+	+	Liberal
Goldberg	+	+	+	Liberal
Fortas	+	+	+	Liberal
Brennan	+	+	+	Liberal
Marshall	+	+	+	Liberal
Black	+	−	+	Populist
White	0	0	0	Moderate
Stewart	0	0	0	Moderate
Clark	−	−	+	New Dealer
Whittaker	−	−	−	Conservative
Frankfurter	−	−	−	Conservative
Harlan	−	−	−	Conservative
Blackmun	−	−	−	Conservative
Burger	−	−	−	Conservative

Legend: + supports the value
          − does not support the value
          0 neutral

Source: Harold J. Spaeth, *An Introduction to Supreme Court Decision Making* (San Francisco: Chandler, 1972), p. 68.

propensities for that justice; but when justices are studied in the aggregate, backgrounds are so discrete, varied, and numerous that the power to predict decisions, let alone explain them, is minimal.[85] However, if the "values-causes-votes" hypothesis were invalid, studies of the sort cited above would not find the repeated issue-oriented voting they have, in fact, found.[86]

BEHAVIORAL-EXPOSITIVE THEORIES

There are many hazards in attempting to synthesize our knowledge of judicial behavior. The general thrust of most of the research we will look at here is to identify and measure the relative weights of the various determinants of the judicial decision. Although this is now the conventional formulation, it leaves a few problems that must be recognized at the outset. First, the very assumption that the decision—treated as a yes, no, or abstain by a judge—is the dependent variable may be misleading. Like other political decision makers, the judge may have options available that go far beyond voting.

> [Their] devices include questioning counsel during argument; making formal presentations at official conferences; sending memoranda to one, several, or all of their colleagues; having private conversations with fellow members of the court. . . . Thus if we restrict ourselves to votes as measures of commitment to values . . . we ignore a sizable portion of decisional choices actually open to judges. . . . The range is considerably broader than yes, abstain, no.[87]

Further, judges may be playing games with their votes. They may vote opposite to their primary predilection, waiting for a better or more opportune time to press their views. They may also do this as a bargaining technique or as part of an image-building tactic to make more effective their future move in another direction.[88] Obviously, the simple correlation of a judge's attitudes or values with his or her formal decision in such circumstances would not produce meaningful results. Second, although inherent in the exercise of the judicial decision is a significant element of discretion that can be utilized by the judge to secure policy objectives, a number of important limitations are also present, and it has been nearly impossible for social scientists to pinpoint the discretion-fixity breaking point. These limitations include: (1) the need to experiment, which sometimes causes personal predilections to give way to the demands of original situations; (2) legal training, common to all judges, which results in a tendency never to ignore the value of legal reasoning and often produces a psychological desire for certainty, which can easily be found in the form of "binding authority" or logical argument from legal principles; (3) the occasional need to escape the agony of decision by relying on established rules; and (4) competing perceptions and strategies between judges and between the court and its constituents.[89] We can describe these limitations but have found it extremely difficult to measure them. Third, even if we could assume that judicial decisions and opinion were unaffected by the gamesmanship and limitations suggested above, decisions reached and opinions written would still at least occasionally produce the mistaken impression they were based on personal predilection rather than precedent and legal reasoning. One reason for this appears to be the necessity of advocacy; that is, the need to persuade colleagues often turns the simplicity of opinion writing into special pleading. Stimulated by the inevitability of personal antagonisms, such a tendency leads to simplistic and overstated conclusions. Another reason is that heavy workload and frequent demands for speedy decisions sometimes lead to the use of standard arguments to support conclusions reached, not on the basis of predilection as they therefore appear, but on the basis of a complex calculus of legal reasoning.[90]

However, when all is said and done, the judicial decision-making process is not even that simple. The role perception of the judge as either an activist or restraintist (or something else) may be a significant intervening variable. Activism, as we learned earlier, is difficult to describe because although it may, in fact, explain more judicial decisions than does restraint, few judges will publicly admit to being activists. Activism, in short, indicates a desire to insert one's policy preferences into judicial decisions in order to achieve policy goals as well as a willingness to overturn the decisions of the political branches to accomplish that objective. For some judges in some cases, though, role demands may be stronger than policy preferences; or to put it differently, playing the proper role may be the highest of competing values. Judicial restraint, as described earlier, posits that judges should refrain from making public policy. They should not address policy issues unless absolutely necessary to do so to dispose of a concrete case. If they must address policy issues, they should frame them as narrowly as possible and never arrive at a rule that is broader than required to dispose of the case. They should always defer to the political branches of government (legislatures and executives) on subjective judgments concerning the wisdom or utility of legislation and administrative orders. They should, in short, stay out of the political thicket. It is true that restraint is practiced not only by those judges who are truly guided by the restraintist role demand and apply it generally and across the board but also by those who are guided by policy preferences and apply it selectively in particular instances to promote their policy goals. But clearly the often conflicting demands of policy preference and role have a lot to do with how judges decide, as the following account of Justice Wiley Rutledge's decision in *Colegrove v. Green*[91] illustrates.

Colegrove involved a suit to restrain Illinois from electing congressmen from grossly unequal districts. The Court's majority followed Justice Frankfurter's argument that the issue in question was one "of a peculiarly political nature and therefore not meet for judicial determination." In the majority's view, legislative apportionment was a "political question" to be dealt with by legislative bodies or administrative commissions. The Court, the majority reasoned, should remain aloof from political entanglements; it should not allow itself to be perceived by the public as a policy maker, or else it would lose the one source of power it has—sustained public confidence in its antiseptic impartiality. In 1946 the Court was short handed. Justice Jackson was in Nuremberg and Justice Stone, recently deceased, had not yet been replaced. Of the remaining seven justices, three (Black, Douglas, and Murphy) clearly favored intervention in the apportionment controversy. Three others (Frankfurter, Reed, and Burton) wanted to stay out of the political thicket. Rutledge held the swing vote and an examination of his past decision-making behavior would have indicated a high value accorded to equality and hence a prediction that he would join those who wished to intervene in the apportionment controversy here. Rutledge changed his mind twice in the matter. At first he agreed with Frankfurter that the Court should remain aloof, especially since it could provide no remedy. The best it could do would be to invalidate the presently malapportioned system, leaving Illinois with no choice but to elect congressmen at large across the state unless the state legislature or governor were to act before the next election. But then the high place Rutledge accorded to the value of equality prevailed. He decided that in an electoral system where one district had eight times the population of another, the resulting discrimination necessarily deprives citizens of equal protection of the laws. Finally, however, Rutledge's role demand prevailed. He valued equality, but he also exhibited remarkable restraint when he felt restraint necessary in order to achieve a firm result; to preserve the image of symmetry, continuity, and certainty in the law; or to protect the Court's standing with the public. In *Colegrove* he did not want to see a seven-judge Court make such an important decision as to intervene in an apportionment controversy for the first time. He feared that a nine-judge Court, once restored, might well order a reargument and reverse the decision. Such a turnabout, he felt, would damage the Court. So in the end he joined with the restraintists, Frankfurter, Reed, and Burton, to form a 4-3 majority against intervention. In the complex calculus of decision, role had prevailed over policy preference in this instance.[92]

 In addition to values and role demands must be considered the impact of bloc activity on the judicial decision. A "bloc," according to Schubert, "consists of three or more judges who manifest a relatively high degree of interagreement in their voting, whether in the majority or in dissent, over a period of at least a term."[93] Schubert identified and analyzed a "certiorari bloc" of Murphy, Rutledge, Black, and Douglas operating in the Supreme Court from 1943 to 1949, a bloc which successfully pursued an objective of supporting claimants in Federal Employer's Liability Act cases. Schubert postulated that these four justices created a bloc with the deliberate objective of forcing upon the rest of the Court the consideration of an issue the bloc wanted decided in a particular way. Assuming that

> the objective of the bloc was to maximize the number of decisions favorable to workmen's claims, game theory can prescribe how the bloc should behave rationally in order to accomplish this objective. Four Justices are adequate to grant certiorari, but not (normally) to decide cases on the merits. It is assumed that, during this period, the remaining five Justices had no fixed predisposition either toward or against the claimants. The only question in these cases is whether the trial court correctly evaluated evidence; the cases turn, in other words, on questions of fact rather than law. Typically, they fall into two categories: (a) the trial court directs a judgment for the defendant railroad on the ground that the evidence is insufficient for the case to go to a jury, or else the court directs a judgment for the defendant notwithstanding a jury verdict for the plaintiff; or (b) the trial judge enters a judgment for the plaintiff on the basis of a jury verdict. In either event, the decision of the trial court has been affirmed or reversed by a court of appeals, and either the plaintiff workman or the defendant railroad has petitioned the Supreme Court for certiorari.[94]

Now, the bloc of Murphy, Rutledge, Black, and Douglas needed only to pick up one additional favorable vote on the merits; and assuming there is an equal chance that any of the five uncommitted justices will vote either for or against a claimant if the court of appeals has disagreed with the trial court, the chances of the bloc picking up that vote should be 31:32 because the only permutation of the five uncommitted members on which the bloc could lose would be for all five to vote against the claimant. Thus, according to game theory, the bloc's pure strategy would be never to vote in favor of petitions filed by railroads, always to vote to grant certiorari in cases in which review is sought by workers and in which appellate court has reversed a judgment in favor of the plaintiff, and always to vote for the petitioner on the merits. If the bloc plays the game rationally, always following its pure strategy, the Court should decide 97 percent of the cases in favor of the claimants. Schubert found that, as a matter of fact, the payoff to the certiorari bloc on FELA (Federal Employer's Liability Act) cases from 1943 to 1949 was 92 percent in cases in which the bloc adhered to its pure strategy.[95]

The construction of interagreement matrices to study bloc activity was, in fact, begun before Schubert's study of the certiorari bloc by C. Herman Pritchett in his seminal works *The Roosevelt Court* and *Civil Liberties and the Vinson Court.*[96] Pritchett discovered a "libertarian activist bloc" consisting of the same four justices as Schubert's certiorari bloc and operating during the same period. The libertarian activist bloc, perhaps the best-known bloc within recent years, demonstrated an extremely high rate of interagreement in support of civil liberties issues. Pritchett found that while the average rate of support of the Court for these issues was 35 percent during the period, only five of the eleven different justices serving on the Court in the 1940s had averages above this mean. Specifically, the following individual rates of support were found: Murphy, 100 percent; Rutledge, 96 percent; Douglas, 89 percent; Black, 87 percent; and Frankfurter, 61 percent. Pritchett's hypothesis was that decisions involving civil liberties issues are primarily influenced by the interaction of two factors: (1) "the direction and intensity of a Justice's libertarian sympathies, which will vary according to his weighing of the relative claims of liberty and order"; and (2) "the conception which the Justice holds of his judicial role and the obligations imposed on him by his judicial function."[97] Thus, he concludes, Murphy, Rutledge, Black, and Douglas were both libertarian and activist, while Frankfurter was libertarian in personal sympathies but a self-restraintist in judicial role. The other six justices, Pritchett labeled simply "less Libertarian."[98]

The pioneering bloc analyses of Schubert and Pritchett help suggest both the complexity of the judicial decision and the "gaming" that often transpires in the formation of a majority vote. More recent studies using even more advanced techniques suggest that the making of judicial decisions may be more complex than even Schubert and Pritchett supposed. The cost model of David Atkinson and Dale Neuman is illustrative.[99] Regarding the bloc variable as well as others we have discussed, hypotheses for testing are today commonly generated from the careful examination of the private papers of judges. Atkinson and Neuman used such private papers to generate three plausible hypotheses of judicial behavior: (H_1) Supreme Court justices vote so as to protect the institutional stability of the Court; (H_2) Supreme Court justices vote so as to avoid isolation; and (H_3) Supreme Court justices vote so as to protect the integrity of their doctrinal commitments.[100] Using vote data collected for individual justices during four Court terms (1949–52), Atkinson and Neuman developed a "cost index" revealing the cost in terms of personal isolation and/or lost institutional stability for any justice dissenting or concurring. They found a good deal of consistency in voting behavior over the four terms and identified a "Truman bloc" (of Justices Vinson, Clark, Burton, and Minton, all Truman appointees) that voted almost invariably in accordance with the first hypothesis.

Although this approach has its shortcomings,[101] it is useful in helping to determine empirically which of various plausible hypotheses is most supported by the data for a given judge. As such, it not only helps to explain bloc voting but also dramatizes the complex interplay of the at once conflicting and complementing variables of values, role perceptions, and bloc activity.

We must also make a brief comment about the mode of reasoning a judge uses in arriving at a decision. Although there are as yet no aggregate data on the matter of intellectual method, studies of individual judges and justices suggest the hypothesis that it varies with the value content of the case before the judge. The intellectual method of Wiley Rutledge is again illustrative. For Rutledge the premises of democracy logically entailed the expansion of the welfare state. At the same time, he insisted that for democracy to survive, the fundamental moral standards of human rights and freedoms had to be maintained. As he saw it, nothing in the Constitution precluded the use of far-reaching public power; but that same Constitution, he believed, absolutely prohibited governmental intrusions into the private provinces of personal rights. In his mind the apparently competing values of security and freedom were not, however, incompatible. To support his views on socioeconomic issues, his intellectual method was pragmatic and based on a fundamental realism. On issues of personal freedom, though, his mode of reasoning was largely a priori and reflected an ethic and a humanism characteristic of natural law jurisprudence. We referred earlier to Cardozo's "complex brew," the judicial decision. We now understand that the ingredients, namely, values, role perceptions, and bloc activity, must be stirred with differing ladles of intellectual method.

Finally, today few social scientists would disagree that the values of judges are among the crucial determinants of their decisions. But clearly the facts presented by a concrete case and the legal precedents related to those facts are also important determinants. Indeed, some studies show that as many as eight of ten decisions in unanimous cases can be predicted accurately using precedent alone as the independent variable; whereas values alone can predict no more than one of three decisions in unanimous cases.[102] It is true, of course, that the percentages of accurate predictions using values alone increases in nonunanimous cases, and generally nonunanimous cases are recognized as providing a better clue to judicial motivation because the unanimous decision is one in which either (1) the legal precedent is so clear that any exercise of judicial discretion is completely foreclosed or (2) discretion was available, but because the respective values of the judges were all so similar, they all came to the same answer. Hence, nonunanimous decisions are usually used for decision-making analyses because judges working with an identical set of facts are coming to different conclusions; thus, there is some assurance that the result was influenced at least in part by values. Still, a central problem remains: how to measure the relative weights of values and facts as they combine to produce the judicial decision.

Until recently, it was widely assumed that values and facts were dichotomous variables. That is, some studies emphasized the importance of facts and concluded that facts determined values; others emphasized values and concluded that values determined facts. Today, although it is difficult to generalize from one study, Werner Grumbaum's computer-based content analysis of *Williams v. Rhodes*[103] has led to a wholly different set of conclusions. Both value and fact variables are significant in the judicial decision-making process. However, they are not dichotomous variables; they are complementary and associative. That is, there is no evidence indicating either that facts determine values or that values determine facts. Rather, the relation between fact and value variables is one in which facts influence values and values influence the perception of facts. In other words, the two variables are associated and neither variable alone accounts for the voting outcome. The finding noted above helps to explain why facts alone frequently appear to predict decisions. The facts of a case fix its position on the justice's value scale, and it is this position that determines the justice's vote. Facts alone appear to predict outcome because when a justice's values remain stable over a long period of time, he or she will decide cases of similar factual content similarly. But it is not the facts alone that determine the outcome; it is the association of facts with the justice's previous typical values.[104]

The determinants of Supreme Court decision making as described in this chapter are outlined in Figure 6–2.

NOTES

[1] Charles H. Sheldon, *The American Judicial Process: Models and Approaches* (New York: Dodd, Mead, 1974), p. 1.

[2] See, for example, Theodor L. Becker, "Inquiry into a School of Thought in the Judicial Behavior Movement," 7 *Midwest Journal of Political Science* (August, 1963), pp. 254–66.

[3] See Harold J. Spaeth, *An Introduction to Supreme Court Decision Making* (San Francisco: Chandler, 1972), pp. 47–56; and David W. Rohde and Harold J. Spaeth, *Supreme Court Decision Making* (San Francisco: W. H. Freeman, 1976), pp. 40–46.

[4] Harold J. Spaeth, *Supreme Court Policy Making: Explanation and Prediction* (San Francisco: W. H. Freeman, 1979), p. 65.

[5] From Justice Robert's opinion for the Court in *U.S. v. Butler*, 297 U.S. 1 (1936).

[6] Spaeth, *Supreme Court Policy Making*, p. 65.

[7] Ibid.

[8] Philip Shenon, "Meese and His New Vision of the Constitution," *New York Times* (October 17, 1985).

[9] Stuart Taylor, Jr., "Federal Appellate Judge Assails Judicial Activism on Constitution," *New York Times* (November 19, 1985).

[10] Shenon, "Meese and His New Vision of the Constitution."

[11] Stuart Taylor, Jr., "Administration Trolling for Constitutional Debate," *New York Times* (October 28, 1985).

[12] Shenon, "Meese and His New Vision of the Constitution."

[13] John P. Roche, letter to the editor, *New York Times* (May 18, 1986).

[14] Spaeth, *An Introduction to Supreme Court Decision Making*, p. 48; and Rohde and Spaeth, *Supreme Court Decision Making*, p. 41.

[15] Spaeth, *Supreme Court Policy Making*, pp. 66–67.

[16] Ibid., pp. 67–69.

[17] Spaeth, *An Introduction to Supreme Court Decision Making*, pp. 52–53.

FIGURE 6-2 Determinants of Supreme Court Decision Making

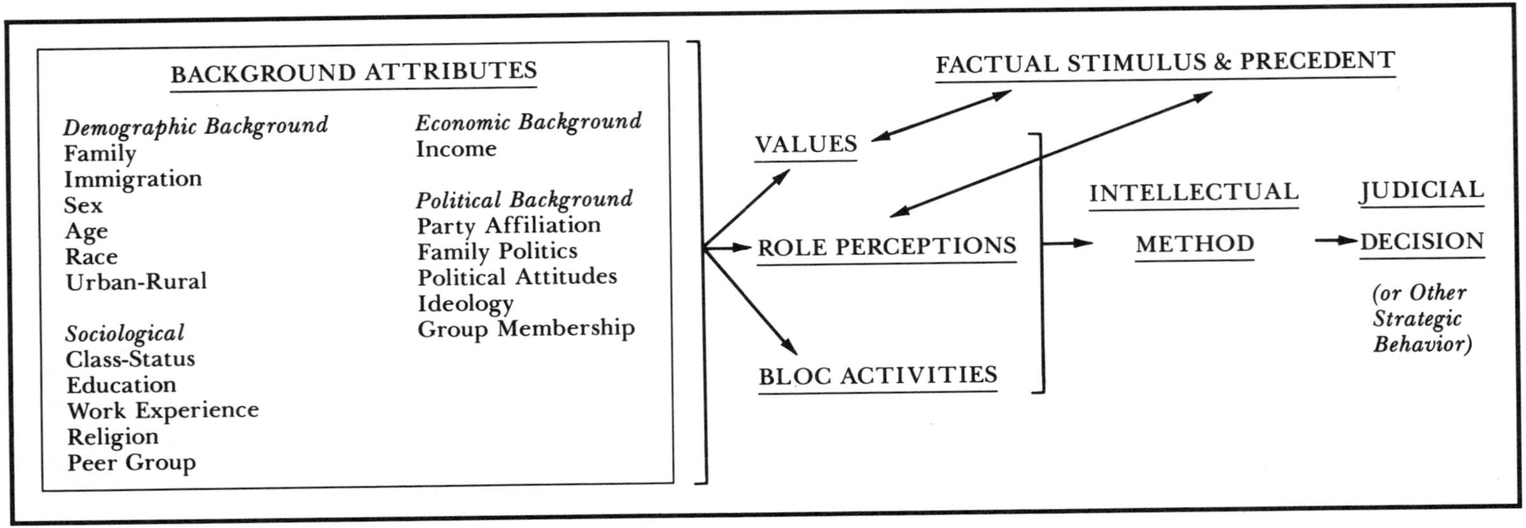

BACKGROUND ATTRIBUTES

Demographic Background
Family
Immigration
Sex
Age
Race
Urban-Rural

Sociological
Class-Status
Education
Work Experience
Religion
Peer Group

Economic Background
Income

Political Background
Party Affiliation
Family Politics
Political Attitudes
Ideology
Group Membership

VALUES

ROLE PERCEPTIONS

BLOC ACTIVITIES

FACTUAL STIMULUS & PRECEDENT

INTELLECTUAL METHOD

JUDICIAL DECISION

(or Other Strategic Behavior)

[18] Edward Levi, *An Introduction to Legal Reasoning* (Chicago: University of Chicago Press, 1949).

[19] Ibid.

[20] William C. Louthan, *The Politics of Justice* (Port Washington, N.Y.: Kennikot Press, 1979), pp. 73–74.

[21] Spaeth, *An Introduction to Supreme Court Decision Making*, pp. 59–60; Spaeth, *Supreme Court Policy Making*, p. 81.

[22] Ibid.

[23] James Bradley Thayer, "The Origin and Scope of the American Doctrine of Constitutional Law," 7 *Harvard Law Review* 129 (1893). Printed also in James Bradley Thayer, *Legal Essays* (Boston: Boston Book Co., 1908), p. 1. See analysis of Thayer's doctrine in Alexander M. Bickel, *The Least Dangerous Branch* (Indianapolis: Bobbs-Merrill, 1962), pp. 35–39.

[24] *Abington Township v. Schempp*, 374 U.S. 203 (1963). See analysis in Lief H. Carter, *Reason in Law* (Boston: Little, Brown, 1984), pp. 238–39.

[25] *Gideon v. Wainwright*, 372 U.S. 335 (1963). See the analysis in Carter, *Reason in Law*, pp. 239–40.

[26] 290 U.S. 398 (1934).

[27] Carter, *Reason in Law*, pp. 236–37, 240–41.

[28] Learned Hand, *The Bill of Rights* (Cambridge: Harvard University Press, 1958).

[29] Herbert Wechsler, *Principles, Politics and Fundamental Law* (Cambridge: Harvard University Press, 1961).

[30] See, for example, Nathan Glazer, "Toward an Imperial Judiciary?" in Noltron Glazer and Irving Kristol (eds.), *The American Commonwealth—1976* (New York: Basic Books, 1976), pp. 104–123; Wallace Mendelson, "Mr. Justice Douglas and Government by the Judiciary," 38 *Journal of Politics* 4 (November, 1976), pp. 918–37; and Lino Groglia, "Judicial Imperialism: The School Busing Decisions" (Paper delivered at the annual convention of the American Political Science Association, Washington, D.C., September, 1977).

[31] Glazer, "Towards an Imperial Judiciary?" pp. 106, 109.

[32] Raoul Berger, *Government by Judiciary* (Cambridge: Harvard University Press, 1977).

[33] Glazer, "Towards an Imperial Judiciary?" p. 122; Mendelson, "Mr. Justice Douglas," p. 918; Groglia, "Judicial Imperialism," p. 15.

[34] An excellent summary and critique of leading "interpretivists" can be found in Lief H. Carter, *Contemporary Constitutional Lawmaking* (New York: Pergamon Press, 1985), pp. 40–70. The present analysis follows Carter closely.

[35] Paul Brest and Sanford Levinson, *Process of Constitutional Decisionmaking* (Boston: Little, Brown, 1983), p. 395.

[36] Christopher Wolfe, "A Theory of U.S. Constitutional History," 42 *Journal of Politics* 292 (1981), p. 325. See also Wolfe's complete exposition of his thesis in *The Rise of Modern Judicial Review: From Constitutional Interpretation to Judge-Made Law* (New York: Basic Books, 1986).

[37] Carter, *Contemporary Constitutional Lawmaking*, p. 45.

[38] Gary McDowell, *Equity and the Constitution* (Chicago: University of Chicago Press, 1982).

[39] John Agresto, "The Limits of Judicial Supremacy: A Proposal for 'Checked' Activism," 14 *Georgia Law Review* 471 (1980).

[40] Carter, *Contemporary Constitutional Lawmaking*, p. 45.

[41] Walter Berns, *The First Amendment and the Future of American Democracy* (New York: Basic Books, 1976).

[42] Robert Bork, "Neutral Principles and Some First Amendment Problems," 47 *Indiana Law Journal* 1 (1971).

[43] Ibid.

[44] Carter, *Contemporary Constitutional Lawmaking*, p. 48.

[45] Justice Iredell, concurring in *Calder v. Bull*, 3 U.S. (3 Dall.) 386 (1798).

[46] Antonin Scalia, *An Imperial Judiciary: Fact or Myth* 35 (1979) (American Enterprise Institute Forum).

[47] Pound's leading works are *An Introduction to the Philosophy of Law* (New Haven: Yale University Press, 1922), *Law and Morals* (Chapel Hill: University of North Carolina Press, 1924), and *Social Control through Law* (New Haven: Yale University Press, 1942).

[48] Holmes's leading works are *The Common Law* (Boston: Little, Brown, 1938; published originally in 1881) and "The Path of the Law," 10 *Harvard Law Review* (1897).

[49] Arthur Selwyn Miller, *Toward Increased Judicial Activism* (Westport, Conn.: Greenwood Press, 1982), p. xi.

[50] Jesse Choper, *Judicial Review and the National Political Process: A Functional Reconsideration of the Role of the Supreme Court* (Chicago: University of Chicago Press, 1980).

[51] John Hart Ely, *Democracy and Distrust: A Theory of Judicial Review* (Cambridge: Harvard University Press, 1980), p. 109.

[52] Carter, *Contemporary Constitutional Lawmaking*, p. 87.

[53] Quoted in ibid., p. 33.

[54] William C. Louthan, review of Miller, *Toward Increased Judicial Activism*, in *The Annals of the American Academy of Political and Social Science* (January, 1984), pp. 179–80.

[55] See Ronald Dworkin, *Taking Rights Seriously* (Cambridge: Harvard University Press, 1977); "How to Read the Civil Rights Act," *New York Review of Books* (September, 1979); *A Matter of Principle* (Cambridge: Harvard University Press, 1985); and *Law's Empire* (Cambridge: Harvard University Press, 1986).

[56] See Benjamin N. Cardozo, *The Nature of the Judicial Process* (New Haven: Yale University Press, 1921); and Cardozo, *The Paradoxes of Legal Science* (New York: Columbia University Press, 1928).

[57] Justice Felix Frankfurter in *Terminellio v. Chicago*, 337 U.S. 1 (1949).

[58] Alexander Hamilton, James Madison, and John Jay, *The Federalist Papers*, No. 78, (New York: The New American Library, 1961), p. 471.

[59] Bishop Hoadly's Sermon, preached before the King, 1717. Quoted in Lockhart, et al. *Constitutional Law* (St. Paul: West Publishing Co., 1986), p. 1.

[60] Walter F. Murphy, *Elements of Judicial Strategy* (Chicago: University of Chicago Press, 1964), p. 1.

[61] Wallace Mendelson, "The Neo-Behavioral Approach to the Judicial Decision: A Critique," 57 *American Political Science Review* (1963), p. 603.

[62] George Whitecross Paton, *Jurisprudence* (London: Oxford University Press, 1951), p. 150.

[63] Cardozo, *The Nature of the Judicial Process*, pp. 9–10, 112–15, 170–72.

[64] (New York: Macmillan, 1948).

[65] Ibid., p. xii.

[66] Sheldon, *The American Judicial Process*, p. 25.

[67] Spaeth, *Supreme Court Policy Making*, p. 109.

[68] Murphy, *Elements of Judicial Strategy*, p. vii.

[69] Spaeth, *Supreme Court Policy Making*, p. 118.

[70] Glendon Schubert, "A Psychometric Model of the Supreme Court," V *American Behavioral Scientist* (November, 1961), pp. 14–18.

[71] This criticism is more fully developed in Becker, "Inquiry into a School of Thought."

[72] Walter F. Murphy and Joseph Tannenhaus, *The Study of Public Law* (New York: Random House, 1972), p. 99.

[73] See Sheldon, *The American Judicial Process*, pp. 18–23.

[74] Herbert Jacob, *Justice in America* (Boston: Little, Brown, 1984), pp. 132–33.

[75] John Schmidhauser, *Constitutional Law in the Political Process* (Chicago: Rand McNally, 1963), pp. 511–12.

[76] Jacob, *Justice in America*, p. 133.

[77] Schmidhauser, *Constitutional Law in the Political Process*, pp. 512–13.

[78] Stuart Nagel, "Political Party Affiliation and Judges' Decisions," 55 *American Political Science Review* (1961), p. 843; and Nagel, "Testing Relations between Judicial Characteristics and Judicial Decision Making," 15 *Western Political Quarterly* (1962), p. 425.

[79] See summary in Jacob, *Justice in America*, p. 133.

[80] Stuart Nagel, "Judicial Backgrounds and Criminal Cases," 53 *Journal of Criminal Law, Criminology, and Police Science* (1962), p. 355.

[81] Spaeth, *Supreme Court Policy Making*, p. 125.

[82] Sheldon Goldman, "Voting Behavior on the United States Courts of Appeals, 1961–1964," 60 *American Political Science Review* (1966), p. 374.

[83] Louthan, *The Politics of Justice*, p. 72.

[84] Spaeth, *An Introduction to Supreme Court Decision Making*, pp. 64–66.

[85] Sheldon, *The American Judicial Process*, pp. 37–38.

[86] Sheldon Goldman and Thomas P. Jahnige, *The Federal Courts as a Political System* (New York: Harper & Row, 1976), p. 160.

[87] Murphy and Tannenhaus, *The Study of Public Law*, pp. 110–11.

[88] Murphy, *Elements of Judicial Strategy*, pp. 1–11.

[89] William C. Louthan, *Mr. Justice Wiley Rutledge and Questions of Public Policy: A Study of Discretion and Objectivity in Judicial Decision-Making* (Unpublished Ph.D. dissertation, Ohio State University, 1970), pp. 181–82.

[90] J. Woodford Howard, *Mr. Justice Murphy: A Political Biography* (Princeton, N.J.: Princeton University Press, 1968), pp. 346, 481–88.

[91] 328 U.S. 549 (1946).

[92] Louthan, *Mr. Justice Wiley Rutledge*, pp. 162–63.

[93] Glendon Schubert, *Constitutional Politics* (New York: Holt, Rinehart & Winston, 1960), p. 155.

[94] Ibid., p. 109.

[95] Ibid., pp. 108–110.

[96] (Chicago: University of Chicago Press, 1954).

[97] *Vinson Court*, p. 191.

[98] *Roosevelt Court*, pp. 41–43, 240–53; *Vinson Court*, pp. 190–92.

[99] David N. Atkinson and Dale A. Neuman, "Toward a Cost Theory of Judicial Alignments: The Case of the Truman Bloc," 13 *Midwest Journal of Political Science* (1969), pp. 271–83.

[100] Ibid., p. 275.

[101] See David W. Rohde, "Comments on a Cost Theory of Judicial Alignments," 14 *Midwest Journal of Political Science* (1970), pp. 331–36.

[102] Werner F. Grumbaum, "Analytical and Simulation Models for Explaining Judicial Decision-Making," in Joel B. Grossman and Joseph Tannenhaus (eds.), *Frontiers of Judicial Research* (New York: Wiley, 1969), pp. 315–16.

[103] 393 U.S. 23 (1968).

[104] Grumbaum, "A Quantitative Analysis of the 'Presidential Ballot' Case," 4 *Journal of Politics* (1972), pp. 221–43.

VII

Supreme Court Policy Making
The Allocation of Power

JUDICIAL POWER: THE JUSTICES SHAPE THEIR OWN ROLE

In Chapter Three we undertook a brief overview of American constitutional development from late nineteenth century beginnings through the end of the Burger Court era in 1986. In Chapters Seven and Eight we will approach the Supreme Court's constitutional policy making from an analytical, rather than a developmental (historical or chronological), perspective. In this chapter our topics are the contours of judicial power, the doctrine of separation of powers, the powers of Congress, and the powers of the president. The result should be a basic understanding of the constitutional allocation of powers in American national government, at least as that allocation has been described and decreed by the Supreme Court. Then in Chapter Eight we will examine the flip side of the constitutional coin—the limitations on governmental powers, federal and state. As elsewhere in this book Chapters Seven and Eight treat the Supreme Court as a political institution, its justices as both political practitioners and political philosophers, and their opinions as the closest thing we have to an original American political theory other than *The Federalist Papers*.

According to Article III, Section 2, Clause 1, the federal "judicial power" extends to all cases "in law and equity, arising under the Constitution, the laws of the United States, and treaties . . . made under their authority . . . , cases of admiralty and maritime jurisdiction . . . , controversies between two or more states . . . , [controversies] between a state and citizens of another state . . . , [and] controversies to which the United States . . . [is] a party." The only major amendment to this clause was adopted in 1798 in response to the Court's decision in *Chisholm v. Georgia* (1793).[1] As we learned in Chapter Three, the Court held in *Chisholm* that states of the Union (in this case, Georgia) are amenable to the jurisdiction of the national judiciary and suable by a citizen of another state in the federal courts. The best historical evidence is that the framers of the Constitution never intended such an interpretation of the federal judicial power. Thus, in 1798 the Eleventh Amendment was added to the Constitution providing that "the judicial power of the United States shall not be construed to extend to any suit in law or equity, commenced or prosecuted against one of the United States by citizens of another state."

While the statement of the federal "judicial power" in the Constitution is relatively clear, the various statements contained in the Constitution about the "jurisdiction" of the federal courts are, in some instances at least, relatively ambiguous. As we learned earlier, the "original jurisdiction" of the Supreme Court is explicit and clear, subject to change only by Constitutional amendment; that is, it cannot be altered by an act of Congress alone. However, the Supreme Court's "appellate jurisdiction" is anything but clear and, as we will learn in Chapter Nine in our examination of current "Court-curbing" tactics, still a matter of debate and controversy. In Article III, Section 2, Clause 2, the Constitution provides that the Supreme Court shall have "appellate jurisdiction" over *all* cases—other than those for which its jurisdiction is "original"—but "with such exceptions and under such regulations as the *Congress* shall make" [emphasis added]. The actual extent of congressional power to control the Supreme Court's appellate jurisdiction, given under the so-called exceptions and regulations clause, has long been a matter of both intellectual debate and political intrigue. May the Congress, for example, entirely or in part cut off the Supreme Court's capacity to hear and decide cases on appeal any time it sees fit? Did the Congress act properly in 1869 when, fearing that the Court would invalidate the Reconstruction Acts, it prevented the Court from determining their validity by withdrawing the Court's jurisdiction established under the Habeas Corpus Act of 1867? Clearly in that instance the Congress used its control over the Court's appellate jurisdiction for policy purposes, and the Court seemingly acquiesced in the result in *Ex Parte McCardle* (1869).[2] Would the *McCardle* case be decided the same way today absent the rather extraordinary circumstances of the Civil War and Reconstruction? It is largely because such questions remain without a firm answer that in recent years Congress has indirectly tried to reverse Supreme Court policy making with which it has been unhappy by directly curtailing the Court's appellate jurisdiction to hear and decide particular classes of cases. (Again, we will return to both the law and the politics of the controversy in Chapter Nine.) It must be granted, of course, that most of the limits placed on the Supreme Court's judicial power have been imposed by the Court itself; especially after the establishment of judicial review in *Marbury,* the justices have acted to shape their own role by fashioning various doctrines of restraint and other rules limiting their jurisdiction. Such self-limitations form the core of this chapter. However, before leaving the *distinction* between "judicial power" and "appellate jurisdiction" and the efforts of Congress to use the latter to regulate the former, we should examine in some detail one of the more interesting and controversial cases dividing the Congress and the Court, to wit, *Yakus v. U.S.* (1944).[3]

The *Yakus* case arose under the Emergency Price Control Act of 1942, which was designed essentially to prevent during World War II the rise in prices and wartime profiteering that had cost the people and the government dearly during World War I.[4] The act established the United States Emergency Court of Appeals and conferred upon it "exclusive jurisdiction to determine the validity of any regulation or order of the Price Administrator"; it further declared that "no Court, Federal, State or Territorial shall have jurisdiction or power to restrain, enjoin or set aside any provision of this Act." In *Yakus* certain merchants were indicted and convicted for selling beef at prices above the maximum prices fixed by the administrator. In accordance with the exclusive jurisdiction mandate of the act, Yakus was refused the opportunity in the criminal court of contending that the regulation was invalid. In other words, Yakus allegedly abrogated a rule set by the price administrator under the terms of the Price Control Act. The validity of any such rule could be challenged only in the United States Emergency Court of Appeals, but the regular federal district courts, in their criminal jurisdiction, were charged with implementing, or enforcing, the law and the administrator's rules. When in the federal district court, Yakus attempted to defend his actions, not by denying them, but by arguing the invalidity of the rule, he was told that the question of the rule's validity could be treated only in the United States Emergency Court of Appeals. Yakus then appealed to the Supreme Court, arguing that the statute as interpreted and applied in the orders of the price administrator deprived him of his property without due process of law. The Supreme Court's majority disagreed. It held that the terms of the statute were "broad enough to deprive the district court of power to consider the validity of the administrative regulation or order as a defense to a criminal prosecution for its violation," and that this did not deny the defendant his constitutional rights, since prior to his conviction he might, following a protest to the administrator, have brought a suit for injunction in the United States Emergency Court of Appeals.

Justices Rutledge and Roberts dissented strongly. Rutledge wrote that Congress had conferred jurisdiction on the regular federal courts in enforcement proceedings but at the same time denied them jurisdiction to consider the validity of the regulations for which the enforcement was sought. This, Rutledge argued, was for all practical purposes *a limitation not of jurisdiction but a limitation on and an "unwarranted abridgement" of judicial power!* In Rutledge's view, the Emergency Price Control Act afforded too little recourse to the regular federal courts for individuals allegedly violating its regulations. He condemned the mingling of civil and criminal proceedings. He noted that the means of enforcing the act included both criminal proceedings and suits for the recovery of civil penalties. Thus what was in essence a single trial was divided into "separate segments, with some of the issues essential to guilt triable in another court in a highly summary civil proceeding held elsewhere." He excoriated the entire procedure as "piecemeal," "chopped up," and "disruptive of constitutional guarantees in relation to trials for crime."

Nevertheless, the Court's majority acquiesced in one of Congress's most bold attempts to limit the Court's judicial power. Certainly, important questions remained. First was the question whether a decision that a regulation was invalid would constitute a defense to enforcement proceedings arising out of violations occurring before the final decision of invalidity. In oral argument for the government in *Yakus,* the solicitor general had contended that the statute imposed an unqualified obligation to obey until the regulation was finally held invalid, and consequently that a conviction for such violation would stand, regardless of invalidity.[5] The majority avoided this question. Second was the question regarding the nature of the "judicial power" and of the power of Congress to "control" it. As Edwin S. Corwin pointed out, the Emergency Price Control Act as construed in the *Yakus* case "broke over what has always been thought to be the fundamental distinction between the 'judicial power' which the Constitution itself confers on the national courts and their 'jurisdiction' which for the most part it leaves with Congress to assign."[6]

We have addressed the *Yakus* case in some detail because it illustrates two very important points about the relationship between the Court and the Congress. First, and obviously from the above, *Yakus* is one of the most glaring examples of how Congress may, in fact if not in law, strike at judicial power through control over jurisdiction. Second, it illustrates how a Supreme Court justice may secure positive action from Congress through persuasion on the merits, even in a minority opinion.[7] A dissenting opinion can be not only an appeal to history or to future judges but also an appeal to contemporaries—to members of Congress, to the president, to lower court judges, to interest groups—to change the decision of the majority.[8] Rutledge's dissent in *Yakus* exemplifies an appeal that succeeded in securing positive action at least partially meeting his objectives. Just at the time the *Yakus* case was decided, the Banking and Currency Committees of both houses of Congress were considering the renewal of price control legislation. Rutledge's dissent in *Yakus* focused congressional attention on the procedural provisions of the statute and moved a number of members of Congress to press for substantial procedural revisions. As finally rewritten and enacted, the law (1) permitted a defendant in either criminal or civil proceedings to file a complaint in the United States Emergency Court of Appeals challenging the validity of the regulations he or she was charged with violating, (2) authorized the regular courts charged with enforcement (normally a federal district court) to stay the execution of judgment in its proceedings until the validity question was settled, and (3) flatly provided that a determination of invalidity would be a defense to charges of prior violations.[9] Thus, while the revised Price Control Act preserved the essential features of exclusive jurisdiction in the United States Emergency Court of Appeals, it also met some of Justice Rutledge's objections to the 1942 act.

For the most part, as indicated earlier, limitations on the exercise of judicial power by the Supreme Court have been self-imposed. The Court formally established its power to invalidate acts of Congress in *Marbury* (1803), its power to invalidate state legislative acts in *Fletcher v. Peck* (1810),[10] and its supremacy on matters of federal law over state supreme courts in *Martin v. Hunter's Lessee* (1816).[11] Subsequently, the Court has imposed a variety of limitations on its exercise of these powers. These limitations are not only numerous but often highly technical, and it is not our purpose here to examine all of them, nor even some of them in intricate detail. It may, however, be helpful to survey the major limitations with an example or two of each. Generally, the Court has insisted that it will not act when there is no real "case or controversy"; this can mean that there is no true "*adverse relationship*" between the parties to the case or that the issue presented for adjudication either is not yet "ripe" for consideration or is "moot"; when the issue presented is a "political question"; and when the party bringing the suit lacks "standing to sue."

We will begin with the necessity of a true adverse relationship between the parties. An early twentieth-century case provides, with its references to history, an excellent example. This is the case of *Muskrat v. U.S.* (1911).[12] In 1902 Congress made what it called a final allotment of lands to certain Cherokee Indians and then passed a law allowing four of the allottees to bring suits against the United States challenging the validity of any subsequent allotments. When, in fact, Congress passed subsequent legislation increasing the number of allottees, Muskrat (one of the original allottees, and one of the four designated to challenge subsequent allotments) brought just such a suit. The Supreme Court ruled that the "judicial power" extends only to "concrete cases and controversies," that is, cases in which there is an "actual antagonistic assertion of rights" by one party against another, a "real," "earnest," "vital" controversy. According to the Court, such did not exist in this case. Why not? Certainly the subsequent congressional legislation did change the terms of the original allotment, so why could Muskrat not challenge it? The Court's answer was that even though the United States was made a party defendant in the case, the government did not necessarily have an interest adverse to the claimants; the government *might* have an adverse interest in some hypothetical circumstances, but *not* in this case. The Court also determined that it is obvious that the purpose of the law granting the four named, original allottees authority to sue was to give the Court an opportunity to determine the validity of acts of Congress, that is, in effect to render an "advisory opinion" in cases that *might* arise, and this the Court cannot do. To clarify, suppose that Muskrat had sued not the government but one of the subsequent allottees. Would this be a concrete case and controversy? Yes, because there would then be a real, antagonistic controversy between Muskrat and the subsequent allottee, and the rights of the two parties *would* depend on the validity of the law making the subsequent allotment. In other words, if and when such a real, vital controversy *did* arise, the Court would have to decide it, and in doing so the Court could not be bound by any prior mere "advisory" opinion rendered in circumstances such as those of *Muskrat v. U.S.* Indeed, the Court's opinion cited a variety of precedents against the rendering of advisory opinions dating back to 1793, when the Court refused to grant advice to President Washington and Secretary of State Jefferson on the proper legal construction of certain treaties.

Scholarly literature abounds with commentary on and criticism of advisory opinions. Felix Frankfurter opposed advisory opinions largely on the ground that they would force the Court to make its judgment in the abstract, without the relevant "facts" that are at the core of any real case. Others, though, have argued that the Court should render advisory opinions because without them a potentially invalid law may, until challenged and upheld, persuade people to refrain from engaging in legitimate activity or, conversely, may, until challenged and invalidated, injure people who have engaged in activities on the assumption that the law was valid.[13] Of course, not every alleged violation of the Constitution can be challenged in Court. Chief Justice John Marshall made this clear long before the *Muskrat* case. As Marshall pointed out in 1821,[14] there just may be some instances of a constitutional violation that simply cannot be brought within the jurisdiction of the Supreme Court. He provided a hypothetical example. The Constitution prohibits both the national government and the states from granting "titles of nobility." But if a state nevertheless did so, the Supreme Court could not render a decision invalidating it. Why not? Because the state, having granted a title of nobility to a person, would have no interest adverse to that person. Nor would the person have an interest adverse to the state. Nor would there be any other person or party with an interest adverse to either the state or the person granted the title. So, although the state law granting the title is theoretically unconstitutional no party exists to challenge its validity. Thus, the Supreme Court could render no decision on the matter that was not purely hypothetical and merely "advisory." In these circumstances the Court would have no power to annul the grant.

Two other judicially created doctrines relating to whether there is a "case or controversy" are the doctrines of "mootness" and "ripeness." In law a "moot case" is one that seeks to determine an abstract question that does not arise upon existing facts or rights.[15] More specifically, a moot case seeks a judgment "on some matter which, when rendered, for any reason, cannot have any practical legal effect upon a then existing controversy."[16] At the United States Supreme Court level the most celebrated case declared moot in recent years is *DeFunis v. Odegaard* (1974).[17] This case involved a preferential admissions policy for blacks, Chicanos, American Indians, and Filipinos used by the University of Washington Law School. Mr. DeFunis, a white male, applied for admission. The law school's admissions practice under the policy in effect was to use a LSAT cut-off point for nonminority applicants but not for those minorities covered by the preferential admissions policy. DeFunis made the first cut but was later denied admission when the remaining applications of nonminority applicants were more closely scrutinized. Some of the minority applicants who were admitted were better qualified than DeFunis when measured by the traditional standards of test scores and undergraduate grade point average, and not all minority applicants were admitted. However, 37 of the minority applicants who were admitted were less qualified, again by traditional standards, than was DeFunis. DeFunis then brought suit in a state trial court arguing that the law school's admissions policy was a violation of equal protection. The trial court agreed with DeFunis and ordered that he be admitted, which he was. The law school then appealed to the state supreme court, which reversed the trial court decision but ruled that its decision be stayed until a final decision could be reached by the Supreme Court upon appeal by DeFunis. During the lengthy process of appeals, DeFunis remained in law school. The law school stipulated that if it ultimately won the case, DeFunis would be asked to leave school, but that it would allow him to finish any term for which he was then registered. As things turned out, DeFunis was in his last term of law school by the time his case finally reached the Supreme Court. The Court, 5–4, held the case moot: "There is a line of decisions in this Court standing for the proposition that the 'voluntary cessation of allegedly illegal conduct does not deprive the tribunal of power to hear and determine the case, i.e., does not make the case moot . . . ,'" the majority wrote. "Otherwise, 'the defendant is free to return to his old ways.' . . . But, mootness in the present case depends not at all upon a 'voluntary cessation' of the admissions practices that were the subject of this litigation. It depends, instead, upon the simple fact that DeFunis is now in the final quarter of the final year of his course of study, and the settled and unchallenged policy of the

Law School to permit him to complete the term for which he is now enrolled." In short, a Supreme Court decision would have no practical legal effect on DeFunis's status.

The dissent raised a particular and a general objection. First, they complained that "any number of unexpected events—illness, economic necessity, even academic failure—might prevent .. . . [DeFunis's] graduation at the end of the term. Were that misfortune to befall, and were . . . [he] required to register for yet another term, the prospect that he would again face the hurdle of the admissions policy is real." The majority dismissed this argument as mere "speculative contingencies" not requiring a decision on the merits of the case. Second, the dissent pointed out more generally that "few constitutional questions in recent history have stirred as much debate, and they will not disappear." In other words, the dissent was raising one of a number of common criticisms of mootness decisions, namely, that they encourage unnecessary repetitious litigation, especially when rendered in cases involving important constitutional issues that are nearly certain to arise again. This was almost certainly true in *DeFunis*. Most interested parties in society expected a decision on the merits in the case. Because of its direct connection to affirmative action concepts generally, the issue in this case had prompted the submission of many amicus curiae briefs. Law school deans, civil rights groups, and labor organizations were among the many "friends of the court." The Court had at its disposal all the legal materials it needed to make a decision on an issue that would almost certainly not just go away. (Indeed, as we have seen, the issue did arise again, as predicted by the dissent, just four short years later in the *Bakke* case.)

The doctrine of mootness, as a self-imposed limitation on judicial power, works at its best when used as a tool of judicial economy or as an exercise in self-restraint, a kind of specific application of the rule against advisory opinions. However, there are examples of abuse. In 1922, when child labor laws were particularly controversial, the Court was called upon to determine the validity of a law regulating the labor of persons between the ages of 14 and 16. To steer clear of a controversial matter, the Court held off decision until more than two years after the oral arguments. Then, since the plaintiff was over 16, the Court held the case moot because the plaintiff was no longer subject to the law and no decision would have a practical legal effect on him.[18] There are as well some judicially created exceptions to the mootness doctrine. For example, the Court has ruled that a case may not be moot if the issue it presents is "capable of repetition, yet evading review."[19] Suppose that a person brings a suit arguing that a state law has denied him or her the right to vote, but the next election is held before the case is decided. Further suppose that that person argues that even if another suit is brought immediately the judicial process is so slow that a decision in the second suit is unlikely before the next election is held.

In such a situation the Court might hold that the case cannot be mooted by the occurrence of an election because the plaintiff's issue is "capable of repetition" but under the circumstances likely to evade review.[20] The Court has also held that a case may not be moot if it involves "adverse collateral legal consequences." For example, in *Sebron v. New York*[21] a convicted criminal defendant sought to challenge the constitutionality of his conviction after he had served his sentence. Reversing prior rulings of mootness in such circumstances, the Court granted "the obvious fact of life that most criminal convictions do in fact entail collateral legal consequences. The mere 'possibility' that this will be the case is enough to preserve a criminal case from ending "ignominiously in the limbo of mootness.'"[22]

The doctrine of ripeness, like the doctrine of mootness, has to do with *when* a claim or right may be suitably asserted. Ripeness, though, relates specifically to whether judgment may be rendered *now* or only at some future time when other events have occurred.[23] In other words, may the Court render a decision *in advance* about a right or some other claim *before* that right or claim has actually been contested? The cases revolving around the issue of the constitutionality of the Connecticut birth control laws provide an example.[24] In the early 1960s Connecticut state law still prohibited the use of birth control medicines and instruments and punished as accessories any persons who counseled their use or disseminated birth control information or devices. In 1961 a physician, one Dr. Buxton, brought suit alleging that the Connecticut law prevented the conscientious exercise of his profession. Although the state's attorney admitted his intent to prosecute violations of the law, the fact was that no prosecution for the use or sale of birth control devices had occurred in recent years. In other words, the law *was* on the books but it was *not* then being enforced. Dr. Buxton's position was that he was being deterred as a prudent citizen from acting in a conscientiously professional manner whether the likelihood of enforcement was very great or merely possible or even improbable. Clearly, the legality of antibirth control laws was by 1961 a matter of great public concern. Just as clearly, Dr. Buxton had brought to court not a feigned but a real controversy. His "standing" to sue (we will discuss "standing" later) was not in question. And, certainly, the constitutional ground upon which antibirth control laws might be invalidated was a major matter of interest to the legal community. The Supreme Court, however, refused to decide the case essentially on the ground that although the issue was "worthy," it was not "ripe" for consideration.[25] The Court's rationale proceeded more or less as follows: (1) There is a law in fact but not enforced; (2) this political equilibrium exists because those forces that favor the law were strong enough to have it passed but not now strong enough to have it enforced, whereas those forces that oppose the law are strong enough to discourage enforcement but not now strong enough to have the law repealed; (3) the state should demonstrate to the Court either that it no longer wants the law by repealing it or that it does want the law by enforcing it; and (4) if and when the law is enforced, the constitutional issue, still worthy but now also "ripe," will be addressed by the Court. In short, the Court was saying that the enforcement or nonenforcement of a law is a reflection of political pressures. In this case, the legal issue was one over which the political process was in deadlock. The doctrine requiring "ripeness" as applied to these circumstances prescribes that the Court should not tamper with the political equilibrium; rather, the Court is wiser to wait until the deadlock is broken and an enforcement decision is made; it should then render judgment.[26] Four years later the Court did exactly that. In *Griswold v. Connecticut* the Court held that a state unconstitutionally interferes with personal privacy rights when it prohibits the use of contraceptives.[27]

A somewhat different category of self-imposed limitations on judicial power is described by the "political questions" doctrine. In brief, this doctrine asserts that some types of issues are not appropriate for determination by the Court (and the Court should thus stay out of the political thicket in which such issues reside), and, in particular, the Court should not interfere with the discretionary authority of the other branches and agencies of government. There has been some confusion, however, over exactly what types of issues are "inherently political" and thus nonjusticiable. Some questions once considered political and therefore not answered by the Court have since received judicial treatment and are thus no longer considered political (as we will soon observe, an example of such a switch and a source of some of the current confusion is the legislative apportionment issue). Some justices have seemed truly to believe in the doctrine generally and have applied it across the board; other Justices have seemed to invoke the doctrine only in particular instances to advance personal policy goals. It should not be surprising, then, that one commentator has written that political questions "are those which judges choose not to decide, and a question becomes political by the judge's refusal to decide it."[28] Although worth noting, the cynicism captured by that definition oversimplifies the matter.

John Marshall wrote in *Marbury v. Madison* that the Court is obligated to decide all issues properly before it unless the Constitution expressly commits the determination of the issue to the autonomous decision of another branch or agency of government. In Marshall's formulation, then, the category of "political questions" is rigidly defined and limited. Laurence Tribe labels Marshall's formulation as the "classical" view. A "political" view would hold that the category of political questions also comprises cases in which a Supreme Court decision on the merits of the issue presented would inevitably lead the Court to compromise an important principle or undermine its own authority in the long run. A "functional" view would prevent the Court from deciding cases whenever it lacks access to relevant information or senses the need for uniformity of decision, especially as with the other branches of government that have a wider range of responsibilities than does the judiciary.[29] While these definitions and categories appear vague, even evasive, the actual cases are a bit clearer. For example, the Court held in 1849 that although the Constitution requires expressly that the national government must guarantee to each of the states a "republican form of government" (the so-called guaranty clause, Article IV, Section 4), the question of whether or not the government of a particular state is "republican" is a political question that must be decided by the political branches, not by the Court.[30] On the one hand, the Congress might make the determination—as in this case, in which the charter government of a state and an insurgent government contested the power to govern—by accepting or rejecting competing delegations sent to sit in Congress. On the other hand, the president might make the determination by responding to selected requests for assistance in putting down domestic violence. The Court's decision in this case appears to be based on the actual unambiguous action of the president in recognizing the lawful authority of the charter government, the need for finality in the president's decision, and, in any event, the lack of any criteria or machinery for the Supreme Court to use in determining which of the two competing governments was republican. Similarly, the Court has held that the question of whether or not a state has ratified a constitutional amendment is a "political question."[31] Questions bearing on the conduct of foreign relations have often been regarded as political because discretion in this area is constitutionally committed to the Congress or the president, because the statement of foreign policy requires a single voice, and because the Supreme Court is usually without any standards of application in this area. This does not necessarily mean that the conduct of foreign relations is always beyond judicial cognizance; but the Court has held, for example, that the political branches alone must decide when or whether a war has ended[32] and that the Court cannot decide a dispute between the president and Congress over the power to terminate treaties.[33] Finally, before 1962 the Court had held that the question of legislative apportionment (typically cases involving the allegation that a legislative body was malapportioned) constituted a political question.[34] The Court's decision to enter the political thicket of malapportionment in *Baker v. Carr*[35] in 1962, and its rationale for doing so, is a further instruction in the contours of the political questions doctrine.

    Baker v. Carr involved the allegation that a state legislature, which had not been reapportioned since 1901, was malapportioned, thus denying voters in the state "equal protection" under the equal protection clause of the Constitution. The counterargument was, essentially, that whatever the wording of the allegation, the issue was nonjusticiable because the only rights asserted were those resting on the guaranty clause, which the Court had long held to be within the definition of a political question. The Court disagreed. It laid down six factors that shape the contours of the political questions doctrine. Reordering the Court's list of the six factors to fit Tribe's three "views" of the doctrine, we find the "classical" view in "a textually demonstrable constitutional commitment to a coordinate political department"; the "political" view in "the impossibility of a court's undertaking independent resolution without expressing lack of respect due coordinate branches of government," in "an unusual need for unquestioning adherence to a political decision already made," and in "the potentiality of embarrassment from multifarious pronouncements by various departments on one question"; and the "functional" view in "a lack of judicially discoverable and manageable standards for resolving [the issue]" and in "the impossibility of deciding without an initial policy determination of a kind clearly for nonjudicial discretion."[36] The Court concluded that none of these "threads catches this case." It is true, the Court said, that this *is* a "political case"; that is, it involves the allocation of political power within a state. Yet that does not necessarily make the issue of legislative apportionment a political question. Each of the six factors defining the contours of a political question, though varying slightly according to setting and circumstance, has one or more elements relating to separation of powers. That is why, the Court continued, guaranty clause cases are generally considered to constitute political questions; they deal with the relationship between the Supreme Court and the coordinate branches of the national government. However, it is not the guaranty clause but the equal protection clause that is invoked in this case. Accordingly, the Court decided in *Baker v. Carr* that the question of legislative apportionment is not a political question (the only obstacle to it being case or controversy) and is justiciable by the Supreme Court.

It may be possible to glean a clearer understanding of the doctrines of mootness, ripeness, and political questions by examining some hypothetical questions that could have arisen around the controversy over the failed attempt to secure ratification of the Equal Rights Amendment (ERA). The Constitution provides that amendments may be made to the document whenever *initiated* by a two-thirds vote in both houses of Congress followed by a vote in three-quarters of the states to *ratify* the initiated amendment. The ERA was in fact initiated by congressional vote. But the difficult and drawn-out process of ratification raised several constitutional questions. We will examine one of them. Today ratification requires the agreement of 38 states. In fact, that number was never achieved in the fight over the ERA. However, while the ratification battle was raging, some states that had previously voted to ratify subsequently voted to rescind their ratification votes. The question is, Are ratification votes rescindable? To put the question in concrete and practical terms, Do we count those states that ratify and then rescind among those that have ratified or among those that have not? Hypothetically, now, if we suppose the number of states that have voted to ratify, including those that have subsequently rescinded, does not reach 38, the Court might hold that the issue is not "ripe" for consideration. This would be because no decision *at that time* would have a practical legal effect. Even *with* the rescinded votes, the ERA would be short of the 38 required for ratification. Suppose, however, that the number of states voting to ratify exceeds the 38 required by *more than* the number of rescinded votes. The Court might hold that the issue is "moot"; that is, it need not decide whether rescinded votes are allowable because under the circumstances described the ERA would have passed even if rescinded votes were disallowed. In both hypotheticals the ground for using the doctrine of ripeness or mootness could be that no decision would have the "impact of actuality"; in other words, no decree would in fact affect the rights of the parties. But now suppose a more difficult scenario: Thirty-eight states have voted to ratify, but one or more of those have rescinded—or suppose any other combination that would leave us short of 38, for example, 39 with two or more rescinded votes, 40 with three or more rescinded votes, and so on. In that circumstance, neither the doctrine of ripeness nor the doctrine of mootness could be invoked by the Court to limit its own power or to otherwise avoid rendering a decision in a highly controversial matter. However, the Court might well declare, at least if precedent were to prevail, that the issue of whether or not a state has ratified an amendment is a political question, constitutionally committed to the Congress to resolve and therefore not appropriate for Supreme Court determination.[37]

Lastly, the doctrine of "standing to sue" relates to *who* may bring a case making certain assertions. Normally, assuming that a case is otherwise justiciable, the question is whether the party wishing to bring the case "has a sufficient *stake* in . . . [the] controversy to obtain [a] judicial resolution of [it]."[38] As we will learn in greater detail, "standing" questions differ from other questions of justiciability in that they emphasize "the *party* seeking to get his complaint before" the Court rather than "the *issues* he wishes to have adjudicated."[39] As we might expect, standing requirements were relaxed during the Warren Court years and then tightened up by the Burger Court. The general parameters of standing can be gleaned from a consideration of two cases, one coming toward the end of the Warren years and the other coming near the end of the Burger years. In *Flast v. Cohen* (1968) the plaintiffs were federal taxpayers who sought to enjoin federal expenditures under the Education Act of 1965 on the ground that they violated the establishment clause of the First Amendment. The lower federal court had held that the plaintiff lacked standing because, as established in *Frothingham v. Mellon* (1923),[40] there is an absolute bar against taxpayer suits challenging the spending powers of Congress. Writing for the majority in *Flast,* however, Chief Justice Warren pointed out that there is some confusion over the meaning and significance of the *Frothingham* case. There is at least some reason to believe that the decision in that case rested largely on policy considerations, specifically a fear that the Court would be inundated with thousands of similar taxpayer suits that might follow a favorable ruling on standing. If that is so, Warren reasoned, the Court might wish to rethink the *Frothingham* case in light of the availability of the devices of "class actions" and "joinder" (generally, making it possible to hear many contests at one time) adopted subsequent to the decision in *Frothingham*. In *Flast* the government's position was that the principle of separation of powers and the deference owed under that principle by the Court to the Congress and the president make it utterly impossible for the Court to entertain a suit by a taxpayer against federal spending programs. Warren answered this argument in a footnote:

> The logic of the Government's argument would compel it to concede that a taxpayer would lack standing even if Congress engaged in such palpably unconstitutional conduct as providing funds for the construction of churches for particular sects. The Government contends there might be individuals in society other than taxpayers who could invoke federal judicial power to challenge such unconstitutional appropriations. However, if as we conclude *there are circumstances under which a taxpayer will be a proper and appropriate party to seek judicial review of federal statutes* [emphasis added], the taxpayer's access to federal courts should not be barred because there might be at large in society a hypothetical plaintiff who might possibly bring such a suit.

Warren then laid down the circumstances in which a taxpayer would have standing to challenge federal laws. First, there must be a "nexus" or "logical link" between the status of the party (in this case, "taxpayer") and the type of federal law being challenged (in this case, the expenditure of tax-raised funds). In *Flast* that logical link does exist. Second, there must be a similar nexus between the status of the party and the claim made (in this case, "taxpayer" challenging a "spending" program) and a precise constitutional limitation (in this case, the establishment clause). In *Flast* that logical link also exists. Both "nexuses" being satisfied, the taxpayer in this case *was* granted standing. *Frothingham's* absolute bar to taxpayer suits was gone, and in a concurring opinion Justice Douglas urged taxpayers to become "vigilant private attorneys general" with standing to raise important constitutional questions and to protect personal liberty.

By 1984, however, both the focus and the gist of Warren's treatment of standing in *Flast v. Cohen* would be discarded. In addition, Douglas's invitation to taxpayers to become private attorneys general, though it never was an invitation issued by a majority of the Court, would clearly be withdrawn. In *Allen v. Wright* (1984)[41] the Court asserted that the doctrine of standing is "built on a single basic idea—the idea of separation of powers." More specifically, the doctrine of standing is intended, and should be used, to deter litigants from drawing the Court into needless discord with the Congress or the president. In *Allen v. Wright* parents of black public school children in school districts in the process of desegregating brought a nationwide class action suit seeking (1) a ruling that IRS guidelines and procedures were insufficient to "fulfill its obligation to deny tax-exempt status to racially discriminatory private schools" and (2) injunctive relief requiring the IRS to deny the exemptions to a greater number of private schools. The Supreme Court held in *Allen* that the black parents had no standing to bring the suit. The parents had argued that the IRS had harmed them by failing to enforce fully its policy of refusing tax exemptions to racially discriminatory private schools. Justice O'Connor wrote in her opinion for the Court that the parents' complaint "alleges no connection between the asserted desegregation injury and the challenged IRS conduct direct enough to overcome the substantial separation-of-powers barriers to a suit seeking an injunction to reform administrative procedures." It is "uncertain," O'Connor wrote, how many racially discriminatory private schools *are* receiving tax-exempt status. It is "speculative," in any event, whether the withdrawal of tax exemption would lead any particular school to change its policies. Since the black parents did not claim that they or their children had personally been denied equal treatment, they could not establish standing based on the "generalized grievance" of an "abstract stigmatic injury." Justice Brennan, in dissent, held out for the older but now discarded approach of the *Flast* case. He wrote that the black parents had "alleged a direct causal relationship between the government action they challenge and the injury they suffer: their inability to receive an education in a racially integrated school is directly and adversely affected by the tax-exempt status granted by the IRS to racially discriminatory schools in their respective school districts. Common sense alone would recognize that the elimination of tax-exempt status for racially discriminatory private schools would serve to lessen the impact those institutions have in defeating efforts to desegregate the public schools." Brennan clearly saw in this dispute over standing and separation of powers a different role for the Supreme Court than did the Court's majority. He criticized the majority for ignoring "the important historical role that the courts have played in the nation's efforts to eliminate racial discrimination from our schools." He castigated the majority for "improperly requiring the . . . [parents] to prove their case on the merits in order to defeat a motion to dismiss" for lack of standing. And he demonstrated his desire to keep the doors of access to the Court open to litigants when he observed in a footnote to his dissent, "Even if the Court were correct in its conclusion that there is an insufficient factual basis alleged in the complaint, the proper disposition would be to remand in order to afford the . . . [parents] an opportunity to amend their complaint." But the pendulum of political power inside the Supreme Court had already swung away from the remaining defenders of the *Flast* rationale. The Burger Court had changed the focus and force of debates over standing: In the future such debates would be grounded on the "basic" and the "single" idea of separation of powers.[42]

THE SEPARATION OF POWERS: THE POWERS OF CONGRESS

The doctrine of "separation of powers" as understood by students in a basic course in American government is a relatively simple idea. There we are taught that most of the framers of the Constitution believed that the accumulation of all governmental powers (legislative, executive, and judicial) in the same hands inevitably amounts to tyranny. Accordingly, in Articles I, II, and III the framers allocated separate powers to each of three branches and attempted to guarantee that the branches would remain separate over time by giving to them different constituencies; that is, participants in each branch would not only have different functions but would also be selected differently so that their contrasting constituencies, or power bases, would keep each branch independent of the other. Of course, absolute separation might provide not just a deterrent to tyrannical government but also an obstacle to any effective government at all. Thus, although philosophically attuned to the teachings of Locke and Montesquieu, the framers were sufficiently practical to provide for linkages between the branches. *All* legislative power is not in fact allocated to Congress because the president has, among other things, a duty to make legislative recommendations to Congress and a power to disapprove, or "veto," laws the Congress passes. *All* executive power is not allocated to the president because the Congress is empowered to approve, or give its "advice and consent" to, many presidential appointees and the treaties the executive branch negotiates. Indeed, further, the president's administration or implementation of the laws is dependent upon the power of Congress to control expenditures, the so-called power of the purse. In most basic courses in American government, then, we are taught that our constitutional system is one of "separation of powers" but with certain "checks and balances" that serve both to limit what government can do in the name of protecting individual liberty and to induce each branch, when necessary, to cooperate with the other branches.

For a number of reasons, however, though in the general case correct, these easy formulations can be a bit misleading. First, these formulations often fail to distinguish the Constitution itself from American constitutional law. The provision of separation of powers in the Constitution itself requires serious attention from a practical perspective. For example, if it is true that the provision of separation of powers succeeds in protecting individual liberties but only at the cost of confusion and inefficiency in government, is the doctrine of separation working? Some recent books address and examine the doctrine from the perspective of its provision in the Constitution itself as their primary focus, the Supreme Court's treatment of the doctrine in the evolution of constitutional law being treated secondarily. Robert Goldwin and Art Kaufman's *Separation of Powers—Does It Still Work?* is an excellent example.[43] Here, in contrast, our focus is on the Court and what it has had to say about the doctrine. Second, basic formulations frequently underestimate, or at least underemphasize, the potential for conflict among the branches. Abuses of power are commonly ignored. An excellent corrective is offered by Louis Fisher's *Constitutional Conflicts between Congress and the President.* We will follow Fisher's lead in this book by examining "the central legal and constitutional conflicts between the President and Congress."[44] Finally, in some basic formulations it is asserted that in our governmental system there is a separation both "functionally," between the branches of the national government, and "territorially," between the national and state governments. This formulation confuses the two basic but quite different principles of American government. The Constitution's first principle is *federalism,* or the division of the authority to govern between the national government and the states. Its second principle is *separation of powers,* which is the division of governmental powers or, better, functions between the branches of the national government. To be sure, it is sometimes difficult to distinguish between the two in concrete cases. When in Chapter Three we discussed *McCulloch v. Maryland* (the power to create a national bank), *Gibbons v. Ogden* (the power to regulate commerce), and *Helvering v. Davis* (the power to tax and spend for social programs), we were looking at the expansion of national governing authority at the expense of state power within the context of federalism. We were at the same time, however, dealing with the constitutional sources and scope of the legislative powers of Congress. Similarly, in Chapter Eight we will deal with the Supreme Court's gradual application of the Bill of Rights to the states. Our purpose there will be to show how the Supreme Court has placed limitations on governmental power to protect individual rights and liberties. Since the authors of the Bill of Rights did not intend to limit state power, but only national power, by adding those amendments to the Constitution the Supreme Court's decisions in this area deal directly with the principle of federalism. The point is that federalism is nearly always implicit and frequently explicit in Supreme Court decisions of all kinds. Thus, in this chapter as well as elsewhere in this book, we do not address federalism directly or in isolation from other issues. Here in our consideration of congressional and presidential powers it is subsumed under the doctrine of separation of powers.

The Constitution contains no explicit declaration of the doctrine of separation of powers. Rather, the doctrine is derived from the organization of Articles I, II, and III, which conveys the theory that certain powers and functions of government are properly performed by only one branch and that these powers and functions cannot, therefore, be deleted to another branch or interfered with by another branch. However, the separation of powers is not absolute, and the lines of demarcation have been loosened, the boundaries of power relaxed, by Supreme Court interpretations. In the area of congressional delegation of authority to the executive branch, for example, the Court has long granted that administrators need discretion in implementing the laws. In *The Brig Aurora v. U.S.* (1813)[45] the Court upheld congressional legislation authorizing the president to revive the Non-Intercourse Act (a trade embargo) upon the president's finding of specified facts concerning the conduct of foreign nations. In *Hampton & Co. v. U.S.* (1928)[46] the Court upheld a provision of the Tariff Act of 1921 that authorized the president to calculate and to alter from time to time the amount of the tariff according to a formula specified in the act to keep it in line with the original purposes of the legislation. The Court wrote in *Hampton & Co.* that it is true that Congress may not transfer its legislative power to the president, but that a distinction must be made between its "purely legislative power," which cannot be delegated, and the "simple conferring of discretion" as to the execution of a law. A conferring of discretion, such as the fixing of customs duties in this case, is constitutionally permissible as long as the Congress sets down by legislation an "intelligible principle" (in this case, the formula) according to which the validity of the president's actions can be judged.

Indeed, prior to 1935 the Supreme Court had never invalidated an act of Congress on the grounds that it was an unconstitutional delegation of legislative authority to the president. Then came the famous "Hot Oil" case, *Panama Refining Co. v. Ryan* (1935).[47] In this case a provision of the National Industrial Recovery Act was challenged. That provision authorized the president to prohibit the interstate shipment of oil produced or taken out of storage in violation of state laws. The president then issued such an executive order under that authority. The Court held that the Congress had impermissibly granted the president an absolute and uncontrollable discretion because it had not, as required by *Hampton Co.*, set down an "intelligible principle" by which the validity of the president's order could be judged. Briefly thereafter the Court continued to insist that any delegation of power to the president or to an administrative agency must be accompanied by clear standards of implementation.[48] Strict limitations on what powers the Congress may delegate, however, did not last long. In 1939 the Court upheld a provision of the Agricultural Marketing Agreement Act authorizing the secretary of agriculture, in stipulated circumstances, to create "milk marketing areas" and to fix milk prices within those areas.[49] To take a more recent example, in 1976 the Court upheld a delegation of authority to the president to adjust the importation of oil, including the imposition of license fees on imported oil, whenever the president found that the quantities of oil imported threatened national security.[50] Obviously, the Congress cannot delegate away powers it does not have, in short, powers not granted to it and powers prohibited to it by the Constitution itself. Just as obviously, Congress cannot delegate away powers the Constitution intended only for Congress; for example, the Senate could not delegate away its authority to ratify treaties. Beyond such obvious limitations, though, the Court has been very reluctant in recent years to invalidate on separation of powers grounds congressional delegation of authority to the president.[51] This reluctance has come in for some criticism. At least one highly respected scholar has argued that the Court should return to a position of demanding that the Congress provide clear guidance to the executive whenever power is delegated and that when such guidance is absent or lacking in specificity, the delegation should be invalidated. This argument is packaged as a plea not for judicial activism but for judicial restraint. The idea is that the Court, reluctant to invalidate congressional acts, ends up "legislating" in the name of "construction" in order to make the meaning of a statute delegating authority constitutionally acceptable. If the Congress were ordered to provide the appropriate guidance, the clear standards of implementations, the "intelligible principle" as previously required, the Congress, in effect, would be forced to do its own work, thus constricting rather than expanding the Court's role in the long run.[52] As we will soon learn, the Court has quite recently made a number of important decisions in cases litigated under the general rubric of separation of powers. But the problem of congressional delegation of authority has received relatively little attention.

Congressional action affecting presidential powers, in contrast, has received a great deal of attention in recent years. The most important decisions have dealt with the so-called legislative veto and with the powers of appointment and removal.

The "legislative veto" is a device both Republicans and Democrats in both the House and the Senate used frequently over the years prior to 1983 to assert control over bureaucratic agencies that issued regulations Congress did not intend to authorize in original legislation. In this sense the legislative veto was a kind of one-house check on delegation of authority to the executive branch. Until quite recently it was a device particularly favored by Republicans. The Republican party platform in 1980 supported use of the legislative veto; and in a 1980 campaign speech Ronald Reagan argued for even "greater [legislative] authority to veto regulations approved by the executive branch." It was ironic, then, when the Reagan administration became the challenger of the legislative veto in the landmark case of *INS v. Chadha* in 1983.[53] An adequate appreciation of the great policy importance of this case requires a brief digression.

Historically, under the legislative veto either or both houses of Congress could, by simple majority vote, block particular actions taken by the president or an executive branch agency or official to implement authority Congress had delegated. The practice dates to 1932 when Congress wrote a legislative veto provision into a law authorizing President Hoover to reorganize the executive branch. From this first instance in 1932 to the appearance of the *Chadha* case a half century later, legislative veto provisions were written into more than 200 congressional statutes. During most of this period Republicans in the legislative and executive branches tended to support the practice as a means of controlling the executive branch and restricting presidential power. Toward the end of this period public interest groups tended to oppose legislative vetoes because the practice encouraged special interests to persuade one or both houses of Congress to gut laws protecting consumers and the environment by vetoing administrative regulations. In the *Chadha* case, interestingly, public interest groups joined a Republican administration in opposing the legislative veto.

INS v. Chadha began as a relatively minor immigration case; it ended as a landmark ruling outlawing the legislative veto. The Immigration and Naturalization Act of 1952 authorized the U.S. attorney general to suspend the deportation of a deportable alien, under specified conditions, if the deportation would produce "extreme hardship," but it also gave to each house of Congress the power to veto the attorney general's decision to suspend a particular deportation. In this case, the attorney general suspended the deportation of an Asian-born student from Kenya (Jagish Rai Chadha) who had overstayed his visa. The House of Representatives, disagreeing with the attorney general's finding of hardship, vetoed the attorney general's decision with a simple majority vote resolution. Chadha challenged the veto in the Ninth Circuit Court of Appeals, which ruled in his favor. The Ninth Circuit Court held that the legislative veto violated the constitutional principle of separation of powers because it is "a prohibited legislative intrusion upon the executive and judicial branches." Lawyers for the House of Representatives then appealed to the Supreme Court. In their arguments the House lawyers asserted that the legislative veto is an intended and necessary check on executive branch agencies. Lawyers for the Reagan Justice Department argued, to the contrary, that the legislative veto strips the executive branch of the independence intended by the framers and intrudes upon the president's power to manage the executive branch. In practical terms a Supreme Court ruling against the legislative veto in this case would sustain the attorney general's suspension of Chadha's deportation. He could stay, which was probably all that mattered to him. But in policy terms the issue framed by this case presented a classic conflict and confrontation over separation of powers.

In the end the breadth of the Supreme Court's decision was surprising to most Court-watchers.

Although it granted that Congress is given the power to legislate in the area of immigration and naturalization (Article I, Section 8, Clause 4), the Court pointed out that the exercise of that power requires the enactment of a law, that is, the passage of a bill by both houses of Congress and presentment to the president for his signature. Not everything the Congress does requires bicameralism and presentment to the president. One house on its own may pass a resolution of praise or a resolution to alter its committee system; but whenever a matter is "regarded as legislative in character and effect," a law is required. The Congress could have achieved its objective in this case of overruling the suspension of deportation in either of two ways. It could have passed legislation requiring deportation, or it could have passed legislation repealing from the 1952 act that portion authorizing the Justice Department to suspend deportation. However, it could do neither of these without the passage of a regular law, that is, without a majority vote in both houses plus presentment to the president for his signature, or a two-thirds vote in both houses if the president vetoed the measure. In essence the Court's ruling in *Chadha* ran as follows: (1) Matters regarding naturalization and deportation are *legislative* in character and effect; (2) Some part of the legislative power in this area may be delegated to the *executive* branch (for example, the power to suspend deportation) as long as an "intelligible principle" accompanies the delegation—which in this case it did; (3) For the Congress to subsequently undo what the executive has done (for example, to overrule the decision to suspend deportation) requires a law, not a mere legislative veto. It would not have mattered, the Court added, whether this had been a "two-house" rather than a "one-house" veto. Congress may disapprove executive branch action only if a bill to that effect passes both houses and receives the president's signature. If the president vetoes that bill, Congress may then block the executive branch's actions only by a two-thirds vote to override the president's veto. In short, the Court's opinion in *Chadha* appears to have invalidated every use of the legislative veto. And subsequent decisions have extended the ban to legislative vetoes of rules made by independent regulatory agencies.[54]

A quite different subject of Supreme Court policy making in the area of separation of powers is the law and politics of appointing and removing government officials. This subject has received close Supreme Court attention, especially in the twentieth century, with some of the most recent results being of large significance. The Constitution allocates to the president the power "by and with the Advice and Consent of the Senate . . . [to] appoint ambassadors . . . , Judges of the Supreme Court, and *all other Officers of the United States,* whose appointments are not herein otherwise provided for, and which shall be established by Law; but the Congress may by Law vest the Appointment of such inferior officers, as they think proper, in the President alone, in the Courts of Law, or in the Heads of Departments" (Article II, Section 2, Clause 2; emphasis added). There is no expressed provision in the Constitution for the removal of government officials appointed under that clause, but the power of removal has generally been treated as a power necessarily derived from the power to appoint. Following a Supreme Court decision reached in 1926, it was widely assumed that the Congress could not limit the president's power to remove officials he had appointed. This decision came in *Myers v. U.S.* [55] in which the removal of Myers, a first-class postmaster, was contested. An act of Congress passed in 1876 provided that such postmasters be appointed and removed by the president with the advice and consent of the Senate. The Senate in this case refused to consent to the president's decision to remove Myers from his position. The issue the Supreme Court chose to treat was whether the president's power of removal of executive officers he had appointed only with Senate consent is full and complete without Senate consent. The Court's answer was yes and its rationale was broad. The president is charged by the Constitution with executing the laws. Since the president cannot do this alone, he selects persons to work with him and act under him. The president's selection of subordinates is essential to the performance of his duty to execute the laws. Similarly, the Court concluded, the president's power to remove those for whom he feels he can no longer be responsible is essential to the performance of the president's duties. Did this mean the president's power of removal is entirely unencumbered by congressional limitations? For a while it seemed so. But the broad rule of *Myers v. U.S.* was cut back in 1935 in *Humphrey's Executor v. U.S.* [56] This case involved the president's removal of a federal trade commissioner. The Federal Trade Commission Act allowed the president to remove a commissioner for "inefficiency, neglect of duty, or malfeasance in office." In 1933 President Roosevelt asked William E. Humphrey, who had been appointed to the Federal Trade Commission (FTC) in 1931 by President Hoover, to resign. Roosevelt believed that Humphrey's views on the policies and the administration of the FTC differed from his own and those of his administration and said that "the work of the Commission can be carried out most effectively with personnel of my own selection." [57] Humphrey refused to resign. Roosevelt then removed him for policy reasons rather than for the reasons stated in the FTC Act. The Supreme Court held unanimously that the president did not have the authority to so remove the commissioner. The Court reasoned that in establishing the FTC the Congress intended to create a body of experts who would gain experience with length of service and who would be independent of the executive. To hold that FTC commissioners remain in office merely at the will of the president would thwart the purposes Congress envisioned. The Court then distinguished *Humphrey's Executor* from *Myers* by pointing out that *Myers* involved a position in a traditional executive department for which the president assumes primary responsibility while *Humphrey's Executor* involved an agency created by Congress to implement legislative policy largely free from executive influence. This distinction was sustained in 1958 in *Wiener v. U.S.*[58]

Several more recent cases serve to refine the relationship between the appointment power and the doctrine of separation. If *Humphrey's Executor* and *Wiener* seem to be examples of the Court allowing the Congress to flex its muscles, then the case of *Buckley v. Valeo* in 1976 is an example of the Court erecting a barrier to congressional domination of the executive.[59] This case involved, among other things, a provision of the Federal Elections Campaign Act authorizing Congress to appoint four of the six members of the Federal Elections Commission (FEC). The FEC's powers extended not only to the determination of eligibility for federal campaign funds and to traditional administrative rule making but also to an enforcement function exemplified by the discretionary power to seek judicial relief. The Court held that the provision of the law allowing congressional appointment of some of the commission's members was invalid. It violated the doctrine of separation because it ran afoul of the president's power under the appointments clause of the Constitution. The FEC commissioners are "Officers of the United States"; they exercise significant authority pursuant to laws of the United States and must, therefore, be appointed by the executive as prescribed in the Constitution. Even if the FEC's functions were considered to be predominantly "quasi-legislative" or "quasi-judicial" in nature and its members were considered independent of the executive in their day-to-day operations, the executive could not be excluded from selecting the commissioners. Although *Humphrey's Executor* was correct in ruling that the president may not insist that such commissioners be removable at his will, nothing in that case allows the Congress to appoint officials who perform administrative functions. In short, the Court concluded, the Congress may not both legislate and enforce. Thus, the contested procedure by which Congress named four of six FEC commissioners violated the separation of powers doctrine.

In 1988 the appointments power was further refined. The refinement came in a case presenting a challenge to the "independent counsel" (formerly "special prosecutor") provisions of the Ethics in Government Act of 1978.[60] The Supreme Court's decision, one of its most politically significant decisions in many years, rejected the Reagan administration's insistence that "only a completely unfettered executive branch could function with sufficient vigor to satisfy the constitutional imperative of separation of powers."[61] In the end this case brought the Supreme Court into a struggle involving an important structural change in the government, a debate concerning the limits of the separation doctrine, and a fight over the implementation of the first-ever, governmentwide ethics law imposing uniform ethics rules on all three branches of the federal government. Among recent cases this case, perhaps better than any other, exhibits the Court as school-master of the Republic. It thus deserves our close attention.

The Ethics in Government Act of 1978 requires, among other things, public financial disclosures from roughly the top 14,000 federal government officials, including the president and vice president, members of the Congress, and justices of the Supreme Court. It also attempts to discourage the "revolving door" practice by which executive officials leaving government take high-paying jobs as lobbyists for the very industries they had regulated, using their insider's knowledge and friendships with former government colleagues to obtain favors for their new employers. To get at this problem the law prohibits former officials from having any kind of business contact with their former agency for one year after leaving government, and it permanently bars former officials from representing private interests in specific matters on which they had worked as government officials. The law also establishes a permanent authorization for a "special prosecutor's" office to look into allegations of misconduct by top government officials. The law was passed in 1978 for five years, extended in 1982 (when the name "special prosecutor" was changed to "independent counsel" to avoid the implication that an investigation inevitably leads to a prosecution), and extended again for five years in December 1987. In the current system if a serious allegation regarding a top government official is made, the Justice Department asks a panel of three federal judges, the "Special Division," to (1) *appoint* an independent counsel, normally a prominent attorney in private practice, and (2) *define* the scope of the investigation. The independent counsel can be removed from office upon the recommendation of the attorney general, but only for specified reasons and only with the approval of the special court that appointed him or her.[62]

The independent counsel provision of the 1978 act is a post-Watergate reform intended to protect criminal investigations of top government officials from political influence in the White House and the Justice Department. An adequate appreciation of the more recent controversy requires a brief reference to the investigation of the Watergate scandal. That investigation foundered briefly after President Nixon in 1973 fired the investigator of that era, Archibold Cox, for insisting on access to the White House tapes (actually a series of infamous firings now known as the "Saturday night massacre"). The immediate result was the creation of a "special prosecutor" position *within* the Justice Department. That special prosecutor (who turned out to be Leon Jaworski) was given complete authority to control the course of the investigation and possible subsequent litigation, as well as the greatest degree of independence possible. He could be fired by the president for extraordinary improprieties, but only if the president first gained consensus support for the firing from the majority and minority leaders of both Houses of Congress and from the chairperson and ranking minority member of the Judiciary Committees of the two houses. Obviously, such consensus would be unlikely if the firing was politically motivated. As Peter Rodino, chairperson of the House Judiciary Committee, has said, "One of the things Watergate and the 'Saturday night massacre' taught us was that having high officials investigated by those who work for them or are closely allied with them is not a good idea."[63] The "Jaworski style" special prosecutor approach did insulate the investigation from interference from those in the executive branch who might be the subject of the investigation. And since it was housed in the Justice Department, the special prosecutor's work was, technically at least, done by the executive branch. This approach was acceptable as long as the prosecutor was vigorous, as Jaworski was in Watergate, and so long as the only concern was to insulate the prosecutor from the unwarranted influence of higher-ups in the Justice Department or others in the executive branch being investigated or with an interest in protecting their friends. Still, if a given prosecutor were not to proceed vigorously, work hard, push, and uncover any wrongdoing that had occurred, a problem would linger. In response to the Watergate experience, the 1978 act and its independent counsel provision were adopted.

Although President Reagan had signed the bill extending the act in 1983, he and the Justice Department supported the challenge to the independent counsel provision in the case we are about to consider. The challenge was avowedly based on the assertion that the provision violated the doctrine of separation of powers. There were those commentators, however, who wondered whether the challenge was politically motivated. This was understandable because at the time a half-dozen incumbent or former Reagan administration officials were targets of investigations by independent counsels. John C. McKay was investigating former presidential aide Lyn C. Nofziger and incumbent attorney general Edwin Meese, possibly leading to conflict-of-interest charges in the Wedtech military contracting scandal. Lawrence E. Walsh was investigating Oliver North's involvement in the Iran-Contra scandal. Whitney North Seymour was investigating the possibly illegal lobbying activities of former Reagan aide Michael K. Deaver. And, in the case in which the challenge to the independent counsel finally came, Alexia Morrison was investigating former assistant attorney general Theodore Olson regarding possibly perjured congressional testimony about the EPA and alleged political manipulation of the toxic waste cleanup program. Joined by the Justice Department, attorneys for the suspects tended to argue that in essence criminal prosecutions are a function of the executive branch. Thus, that provision of the 1978 act that places the independent counsel under the supervision of judges infringes upon the powers of the executive branch in violation of the doctrine of separation of powers. In other words, the power of the executive branch to conduct criminal prosecution cannot be taken away by Congress or the judiciary. The rebuttal tended to be that the framers did not intend to create a complete division or strict separation of authority or function among the three branches. Rather, they intended a pragmatic approach to separation of powers that would prevent one branch from unduly disrupting another, and the independent counsel system constitutes no such undue disruption. Clearly, even if the Reagan administration's opposition to the independent counsel provision was politically motivated, the issue of separation the provision raised deserved debate and required a response from the Court.[64] That response came in 1988 in the case of *Morrison v. Olson.*

In January 1988 the United States Court of Appeals for the District of Columbia ruled, 2–1, that the independent counsel provision of the 1978 act was unconstitutional because Congress had transferred to itself and to the judiciary significant law enforcement functions belonging to the president and the Justice Department. The provision was found to violate the separation doctrine by invading the president's power to appoint and remove top government officials and to control federal criminal investigations and prosecutions. Further, persons under investigation may suffer unfair treatment because independent counsels are commonly under great public pressure to indict. Judge Laurence H. Silberman, writing for the two-person majority, concluded, "The Act as a whole, taking into account its appointment, removal, and supervisory provisions, so deeply invades the President's executive prerogatives and responsibilities and so jeopardizes individual liberty as to be unconstitutional." Judge Ruth Bader Ginsburg, alone in dissent, wrote that

> the Ethics in Government Act is a carefully considered Congressional journey into the sometimes arcane realm of the separation of powers doctrine, more particularly into areas the framers left undefined. . . . There is an irony in the majority's holding . . . , for the measure strives to maintain the structural design that is the genius of our Constitution—the system of mutual checks and balances; the Act's sole purpose is to curb abuses of executive branch power.

Immediately following the decision, independent counsel Morrison stated her continuing belief in the provision's constitutionality and her intent to appeal to the Supreme Court.[65]

In June 1988 the Supreme Court, 7–1, overturned the decision of the U.S. court of appeals. Only Justice Scalia dissented. Chief Justice Rehnquist delivered the Court's opinion upholding the independent counsel law. Rehnquist rejected various arguments for invalidating the law point by point. He said the law violated no specific constitutional provision, nor did it violate the general doctrine of separation of powers. The appointment of independent counsels by courts was valid, Rehnquist wrote, under that clause of the Constitution authorizing Congress to vest the appointment of "inferior officers" in courts of law. Further, Rehnquist found nothing in the appointments and supervisory functions of the

Special Division (court) inconsistent with the duties of judges as spelled out in the Constitution. The law amounted to no usurpation of executive powers by the Congress because it gave Congress no control over the independent counsels. Finally, with respect to the general doctrine of separation of powers, Rehnquist wrote that the law "gives the executive branch sufficient control over the independent counsel to insure that the President is able to perform his constitutionally assigned duties." This decision was a staggering rebuff to the Reagan administration and its conservative supporters who saw the independent counsel law as just one more in an array of restraints placed on the executive branch by a liberal Congress.[66]

Finally, we have the case of *Bowsher v. Synar* (1986)[67] involving the budget-balancing Gramm-Rudman Act of 1985. Here the question was not, as in *Morrison*, how congressional action can affect presidential powers of appointment and supervision of executive branch functions but how congressional control can be used over executive branch action through the removal power. Certainly we should be able to learn something about the Supreme Court's treatment of the doctrine of separation of powers in a case such as this one in which the dissent asserts the majority's "efforts to police separation of powers" is "misguided," resting on "untenable constitutional propositions" and "leading to regrettable results."

The Gramm-Rudman Act of 1985 was a novel attempt to deal with the massive federal deficit that in recent years had been running in the range of $200 billion annually. The purpose of the act was to eliminate the federal budget deficit by fiscal year 1991. To achieve that goal the act set a "maximum deficit amount" for federal spending for each of fiscal years 1986 through 1991, the size of the deficit reducing to zero in 1991 (the targeted deficits were $171.9 billion in 1986, $144 billion in 1987, $108 billion in 1988, $72 billion in 1989, $36 billion in 1990, and zero deficit in 1991). Further, the act stipulated that if the deficit were to exceed the maximum by more than a specified amount in any fiscal year, "automatic" and "across-the-board" cuts would be required to reach the targeted deficit level, with half the cuts made to defense programs and half made to nondefense programs. These "automatic" cuts were to be made through a rather complicated process in which the directors of the Office of Management and Budget (the OMB in the executive branch) and the Congressional Budget Office (the CBO in the legislative branch) would independently estimate the amount of the deficit for each upcoming fiscal year. These two directors were then independently to calculate the budget reductions necessary if their estimates exceeded the targeted deficit amount. The directors were to report jointly their estimates and calculated reductions to the comptroller general of the United States. The comptroller general (Charles A. Bowsher in this case) heads the Government Accounting Office (GAO), which is a staff arm of the Congress. (According to an act of

Congress passed in 1921, the comptroller general is to be appointed to a 15-year term by the president but removable only at the initiative of the Congress, either by impeachment or by an ordinary joint resolution on the broad grounds of "inefficiency," "neglect of duty," "malfeasance," and so forth.) After reviewing the directors' reports, the comptroller general, would report to the president his conclusions regarding estimates, allocations, and spending cuts required to meet the deficit targets. The president *must* then issue a "sequestration" order mandating the spending cuts specified by the comptroller general. In passing the Gramm-Rudman Act Congress anticipated that the courts might declare unconstitutional a procedure vesting "executive" authority in a government official subject to removal by Congress alone. Accordingly, the Congress provided in the act a "fallback" deficit reduction plan in which the reports of the directors of OMB and CBO would be submitted to a specially created, temporary joint committee of Congress, which would in turn present a resolution to Congress based on the directors' reports. That resolution would be voted on under special rules not allowing amendments and if passed would serve as the basis for the president's sequestration order.

The actual history of the early implementation of Gramm-Rudman suggests the perhaps inevitable conflict between the president and the Congress that any budget-balancing law would produce. In the very first year the Congress and the president could not agree on taxing and spending measures necessary to bring the deficit below the target of $171.9 billion for fiscal year 1986. In March 1986 an automatic spending cut of $11.7 billion was made, under the procedure described in the law, to meet the mandated goal. President Reagan's proposed budget for fiscal year 1987 of $994 billion did not reduce the deficit by the targeted amount of $144 billion. But conflict with Congress was inevitable because Reagan's proposed budget eliminated or cut nearly every domestic program while providing for an 8 percent increase in defense programs. Obviously, the president would in these circumstances prefer to avoid the implementation of automatic, across-the-board spending cuts that would take a large chunk out of the Pentagon's budget. At the same time Congress was unlikely to approve the cuts contained in the president's budget. However, under the Gramm-Rudman law, if the president and Congress could not agree on a budget containing cuts sufficient to keep the deficit below the target of $144 billion, the comptroller general would in effect be authorized to order spending cuts according to the formula and process prescribed in the law.

Not all members of Congress supported the Gramm-Rudman Act. Oklahoma congressman Mike Synar, for example, believed the automatic cuts provision was a "gimmick," a "trick," an "easy answer" to a problem Congress itself should handle. Congress ought not give its responsibility away. At the same time, though he had signed the law, President Reagan expressed concern about "constitutionally suspect provisions" in it. Thus, when Congressman Synar and 11 other members of Congress brought suit challenging the constitutionality of Gramm-Rudman, though the federal government was the nominal defendant, the Justice Department joined the plaintiffs, arguing that the law put too much power in the hands of the comptroller general and, indeed, in effect made the president subservient to him. The federal district court held that the Congress could delegate authority over the budget to the president or persons answerable to him, but not to the comptroller general or others removable by Congress alone through ordinary legislation. On appeal to the Supreme Court the law was defended by lawyers for the comptroller general, the Senate, and the bipartisan leadership of the House. Those opposing the law and seeking to sustain the district court's ruling were lawyers for Congressman Synar and his colleagues, and lawyers for the Justice Department.

Chief Justice Burger wrote the Supreme Court's majority opinion invalidating the automatic mechanism for spending cuts at the heart of the Gramm-Rudman Act. Burger wrote that Congress cannot both make and execute the laws: "The structure of the Constitution does not permit Congress to execute the laws; it follows that Congress cannot grant to an officer under its control what it does not possess." The duties assigned by the act to the comptroller general are not merely "ministerial" or "mechanical"; they are "plainly" executive functions in constitutional terms because they require the comptroller general to interpret a law enacted by Congress to implement the legislative mandate. There is also no escaping the conclusion that Congress retains removal authority over the comptroller general. The Congress created the position of comptroller general because it believed it needed an officer responsible to it alone to check upon the application of public funds in accordance with appropriations. "We conclude," Burger wrote, "that Congress cannot reserve for itself the power of removal of an officer charged with the execution of the laws except by impeachment." Further, since Congress has retained to itself that very removal authority, it may not entrust the comptroller general with executive powers. Burger and the majority did not rule on Solicitor General Fried's argument that the powers that the act delegated to the comptroller general could be constitutionally exercised *only* by an official serving at the pleasure of the president. Nor did the majority deal with the more extreme assertion made in public addresses by Attorney General Meese, that it is unconstitutional for *any* regulatory agency to be independent of the president. Rather, the spending cuts mechanism was invalidated on the narrower ground that the removal power made the comptroller general subservient to Congress and that Congress had thus, in effect, intruded upon executive branch powers by retaining control over the execution of the law.

After the decision, could the Congress correct the "flaw" in the law by repeating its own authority to remove the comptroller general and then revive the automatic mechanism? Or could the Congress now pass a law assigning the budget-cutting function to a different government official not removable by Congress, such as the director of OMB? It was unnecessary for the Court to decide these issues, and it did not. Some supporters of the law vowed to fix it along the lines suggested above, but there were also members of Congress in both parties who opposed these remedies. The Congress was left with the "fallback" provision of using the ordinary legislative process to enact spending cuts leading step by step to the elimination of the deficit. Of course, it was difficult to know what the Congress would do under the circumstances. Although the Court's decision put pressure on Congress to produce the cuts through ordinary legislation, the Congress and the president cannot be required to agree. Indeed, it was specifically because the Congress and the president had not been able to agree on controversial spending cuts and tax increases that the automatic mechanism had been built into the budget-balancing law, an attempt by a nearly paralyzed Congress and a disgruntled executive branch to craft a compromise to reduce the deficit. Perhaps this is the reason Justice White and Blackmun argued in dissent that the majority opinion took a "distressingly formalistic view of separation of powers" to invalidate "one of the most novel and far-reaching responses to a national crisis [the huge deficit] since the New Deal." White and Blackmun pointed out that the 1921 provision giving Congress power to remove the comptroller general had *never* been used and therefore was of "minimal political significance" and "should be regarded as a triviality." However, Burger, emphasizing the "dangers of Congressional usurpation of executive branch functions," asserted that "the Framers recognized that . . . structural protections against abuse of power were critical to preserving liberty."[68]

What do cases like these tell us about the doctrine of separation of powers and the Supreme Court's role as a policy maker in this area? First, that although Congress will be given some leeway in putting limitations on the executive power (*Morrison*), the Court will not allow Congress to appoint officials who perform executive functions (*Buckley*) or to participate in the administration of the laws itself (*Chadha*) or through its agents (*Bowsher*). Second, judges and justices by training and temperament often tend to undervalue the importance of political compromise and consensus, and the conventional distinction between "liberal activists" and "conservative strict constructionists" often fails to explain the policies they make. It should be pointed out, for example, that in *Bowsher v. Synar,* the three-judge panel of the federal district court that first and unanimously invalidated the spending cuts mechanism was made up of one Johnson, one Carter, and one Reagan appointee. Together they fashioned a decision sound in its logic but unsophisticated in its understanding of the old-fashioned politics of compromise that had produced the Gramm-Rudman Act.[69] The Supreme Court's majority seemed similarly oblivious to the political convenience of the law. If we were to argue in the Court's defense that the Court is not supposed to consider matters of political compromise and convenience, then we would be stating one of the Supreme Court's shortcomings as a policy maker.

THE SEPARATION OF POWERS: POWERS OF THE PRESIDENT

Presidential action affecting congressional powers, like congressional action affecting presidential powers, has drawn the Supreme Court into a policy-making role, particularly in the last half century. The most important decisions have dealt with the issue of "inherent" power in the presidency and with the doctrine of executive privileges.

One of the more perplexing questions of American constitutional law has always been, What are the limits on the president's powers, especially in times of emergency? This question has been difficult to answer because the ambiguity of Article II allows for contrasting theories. This ambiguity is evident in the differences between Articles I and II. Article I vests the legislative power in the Congress and proceeds to grant a long list of legislative powers to the Congress (Article I, Section 8, Clauses 1–18). Although Supreme Court interpretations have expanded congressional powers over the years well beyond those powers expressly granted in the Constitution, the list of "expressed powers" given to Congress in Article I could have been fairly seen in 1789 as a reasonably complete list. By contrast, although Article II vests the executive power in the president, it contains no comparable lists of executive powers. Like William Howard Taft, some presidents have nevertheless asserted and behaved in accordance with the theory that the chief executive can do only those things expressly granted in Article II—a most restrictive view that would hardly comport with the actual behavior of many presidents and with the actual behavior of no modern presidents. Others like Theodore Roosevelt have asserted and acted on the theory that the president can do whatever he thinks the needs of the nation require so long as those actions are not expressly prohibited by the Constitution. This theory probably explains and justifies the actual behavior of most of our presidents from Washington to the present. Finally, some presidents, as for example, Lincoln and Franklin Roosevelt, have endorsed and acted in accordance with the theory that, at least in times of emergency, the president can take whatever actions the times and circumstances require even if those actions are expressly prohibited by the Constitution. Normally actions of this sort are justified on the grounds of an asserted "compelling" or "commanding" public interest. Perhaps the classic example is Lincoln's assertion during the Civil War that had he refused to take certain actions he deemed necessary but others deemed constitutionally suspect, he would "save the Constitution" but "lose the nation." For the most part, the Supreme Court has been reluctant to enter the debate over whether there resides in the office of the presidency such "inherent," "implied," "aggregate," "residual," or "emergency" powers. Two twentieth-century cases are generally regarded as framing the boundaries of presidential powers. *U.S. v. Curtiss-Wright Co.* (1936)[70] is probably the most expansive treatment given by the Supreme Court to the nature of presidential powers, many of the dicta in the case seeming to justify "inherent" power, at least in foreign policy making. *Youngstown Sheet & Tube Co. v. Sawyer* (1952),[71] however, suggests that the assertion of "inherent" power in the presidency, even in times of emergency, is a highly dubious rationale for presidential action in the domestic policy making sphere.

Curtiss-Wright arose in circumstances in which congressional policy avowed to limit a war then going on between Bolivia and Paraguay and a consequent congressional delegation of authority to the president prohibited the sale of arms to these warring nations. After the president issued such an order, the defendant corporation was charged with conspiring to sell machine guns to Bolivia. Curtiss-Wright Company asserted in defense that the president's order was invalid because it was based on an unconstitutional delegation of authority from the Congress to the president and because there is no inherent power in the presidency alone to issue such an order. In simple terms the Court ruled that the delegation of authority was valid but unnecessary because in international affairs the president has an exclusive power not requiring an act of Congress as a basis for its exercise. The president's order was thus valid and would have been valid even without the congressional delegation of authority. The breadth of the Court's ruling in *Curtiss-Wright* and the great historical significance assigned to the case, however, reside not in the simplicity of the Court's ruling but in the sweeping endorsement of presidential power in foreign affairs contained in Justice Sutherland's opinion.

Sutherland argues that the foreign policy-making power derives from "sovereignty." Thus, it never resides in the states separately. Rather, it passed from "the Crown" to the "united colonies" (in the Declaration of Independence) to the "Union" (in the Articles of Confederation) to the "more perfect Union" (in the Constitution). Consequently, when the framers divided up powers between the national government and the states, they divided domestic powers only, not foreign policy making powers. Some critics have contended that Sutherland's reading of history was wrong. They assert that the states did have foreign policy-making power prior to the adoption of the Constitution and that when that document was drafted, the domestic powers were expressly divided up and the foreign policy powers tacitly transferred from the states to the new national government. The critics' contention, however, has no practical effect on Sutherland's conclusion. Whether the foreign policy-making powers reside in sovereignty or were tacitly transferred, the conclusion is that they are exercised by the national government only. More important is Sutherland's argument that the foreign policy-making power is different from the domestic policy-making power not only in its origin but also in its character. Participation in the making of foreign policy "is limited." The president alone speaks and listens for the nation. The president alone negotiates treaties. The Senate must ratify treaties, but it cannot intrude upon the negotiations process. The president is the eyes, the ears, the mouthpiece of the nation in the international field. And, Sutherland says, this is as it should be, because the president has superior information and there is often the need to act quickly. Sutherland's essay in *Curtiss-Wright* is mostly dicta (not binding law because it goes well beyond the rationale required to settle the legal issue). But it is powerful dicta. To this day Sutherland's opinion in *Curtiss-Wright* is the broadest endorsement ever made by the Supreme Court of an inherent power in the presidency.

The possibility that such a broad endorsement would be made applicable to domestic politics greatly diminished as a result of the Court's decision in *Youngstown Sheet & Tube Co. v. Sawyer,* the famous "Steel Seizure" case of 1952. Here, President Truman issued an executive order in 1952 authorizing Secretary of Commerce Sawyer to seize and operate most of the nation's steel mills. The order was based not on congressional authorization but rather on the grounds that a prevailing labor dispute and scheduled strikes in the steel industry, which was engaged in defense production, created a national emergency. The applicable labor relations law of the time, the Taft-Hartley Act of 1947, contained provisions for dealing with labor disputes of the sort presented. It also contained a provision whereby strikes could be enjoined pending review by a board of inquiry, but that provision also allowed the strike to continue after 80 days if the employees rejected the employer's last offer of settlement. The president believed, however, that the impending strike created a danger of great urgency and that he could not wait for the dispute to be settled under the time-consuming terms of the Taft-Hartley Act. Truman took his action without claiming that it was based on congressional authorization. Nor could anything in the Taft-Hartley Act be construed as implicitly granting the president the seizure power to prevent work stoppage because an amendment to that effect was debated when the bill was under consideration and was explicitly rejected. Thus, Truman grounded his authority on the "aggregate" of his powers in Article II.

At first glance it appears that the "Steel Seizure" case and *Curtiss-Wright* can be contrasted in two ways. Although both cases involved the controversial exercise of presidential power in a time of emergency, the action taken in *Curtiss-Wright* dealt with foreign affairs and was based on congressional authorization, while the action taken in "Steel Seizure" dealt with domestic affairs and was not based on congressional authorization.

However, Sutherland said in *Curtiss-Wright* that the president's order would have been valid even without congressional authorization. This allows us to compare the outcomes of two cases in which the essential difference is that one dealt with the extent of presidential power in a time of "international emergency" while the other dealt with the extent of presidential power in a time of "domestic crisis." As it turns out, Truman's order was invalidated, leaving us with the conclusion that if there is an "inherent" power in the presidency to exercise extraordinary power to meet an emergency, that power is limited to the sphere of international affairs.

When the "Steel Seizure" case was before the federal trial court, the judge in the case asked Truman's lawyers on what authority they based the president's order. Their response was, in short, "Sections One, Two, and Three of Article II and whatever other powers may flow therefrom." When the judge then asked whether they meant the president's powers are unlimited in times of emergency, their response was that in times of emergency the president may take whatever action is necessary to address the emergency, limited only by "the ballot box and impeachment." Apparently, Truman's lawyers were of the view that when a president is confronted with an emergency the only limits on his power are political, not legal. The trial court disagreed, as did the Supreme Court upon appeal. The Court held that the aggregate of the president's constitutional powers as chief executive and as commander-in-chief do not justify an order such as the one issued by Truman. As chief executive, the president is to see to it that "the laws be faithfully executed." This clause refutes the very idea that the president is a lawmaker. There is no question, the Court said, that the Congress could adopt policies such as the seizure order or that Congress could authorize the president to issue such an order. But the Congress has taken no such action. "The President's order does not direct that a congressional policy be executed in a manner prescribed by Congress—it directs that a presidential power be executed in a manner prescribed by the President." This the president, as chief executive, cannot do. Nor can he issue the order in his capacity as commander-in-chief. The power to take possession of private property in order to keep labor disputes from stopping production is a power vested by our constitutional system in the lawmakers in Congress, not in military authorities. And the existence of an emergency does not alter the constitutional scheme. "The Founders of this Nation entrusted the lawmaking power to the Congress alone in both good and bad times."

It is important to observe here that even the three dissenting justices, who would have upheld Truman's order, did not base their reasoning on the existence of an "inherent power" in the presidency. Rather, they argued that Truman was simply attempting to "faithfully execute" two congressional policies. He seized the steel mills to execute the policy of procuring military equipment. Although the strike may have been averted by granting the price concessions requested by the steel companies, such concessions would serve to defeat the separate congressional policy of price stabilization. Thus, in the view of the dissenters, "rather than fail to execute either legislative program, the President acted to execute both." Indeed, only Truman appointee Justice Tom Clark seemed to endorse the notion of "inherent" power. Concurring with the majority, Clark wrote:

> The Constitution does grant to the President extensive authority in times of grave and imperative national emergency. . . . I conclude that where the Congress has laid down specific procedures to deal with the type of crisis confronting the President, he must follow those procedures in meeting the crisis [and, for Clark, the Taft-Hartley Act laid down such procedures]; but that in the absence of such action by Congress, the President's independent power to act depends upon the gravity of the situation confronting the nation.

Clark's opinion is perhaps the most sweeping endorsement we have from a Supreme Court justice of nearly unlimited presidential power in times of domestic crisis. But we must emphasize that Clark's view is that of only one justice and, even then, written in an opinion concurring with a decision invalidating an exercise of presidential power.

Finally, we have the doctrine of "executive privilege," which provides, generally, that presidents may withhold information or materials in their possession from Congress and the courts if in the president's view disclosure would somehow endanger the national interest. Most presidents from Washington to the present have employed the doctrine, and while executive privilege has been used only infrequently to deny information to courts, privilege has been asserted often to deny documents or testimony to Congress, indeed, some 50 times between 1952 and 1974, more than 20 times by the Nixon administration alone.[72] Many years of conflict between presidents and Congresses over the doctrine have yet to produce a definitive resolution by the Supreme Court.[73] The Watergate scandal of the early 1970s, with its famous "White House Tapes" case, did, however, give the Supreme Court an opportunity to rule on the doctrine of executive privilege at least as it pertains to the rather extraordinary circumstances of that case.

United States v. Nixon (1974)[74] arose in the course of investigations and litigation, referred to earlier in this chapter in a different context, relating to the Watergate scandal by Special Prosecutor Leon Jaworski. After securing an indictment against seven Nixon staff members and political associates for Watergate-related offenses, Jaworski secured from a federal district court a subpoena to the president to produce specified White House tapes of conversations containing evidence relevant to the pending criminal cases. Nixon's lawyers moved to quash the subpoena, asserting an absolute executive privilege based on two grounds: (1) the importance of protecting the confidentiality of communications between high government officials and those who serve and advise them; and (2) the independence of the executive branch, under the doctrine of separation of powers, which insulates the President from a judicial subpoena in an ongoing criminal prosecution. The district court denied the motion to quash, and upon review the Supreme Court upheld the subpoena on July 24, 1974. In his opinion for a unanimous Court, Chief Justice Burger wrote, "[N]either the doctrine of separation of powers, nor the need for confidentiality of high level communications, without more, can sustain an absolute, unqualified presidential privilege of immunity from judicial process under all circumstances."

Regarding the point on separation of powers, the Court said the framers did not intend the separate, coequal branches "to operate with absolute independence." The president's Article II powers do include executive privilege, but that immunity is not absolute. If the president could claim an absolute privilege against a subpoena essential to the enforcement of criminal states, the "constitutional balance" of a "workable government" as intended by the framers would be upset, and the role of the federal courts under their Article III powers would be "gravely impair[ed]."

Regarding the point on confidentiality the Court agreed that the "President's need for complete candor and objectivity from advisers calls for great deference from the courts. . . . Human experience teaches that those who expect public dissemination of their remarks may well temper candor with a concern for appearances and for their own interests to the detriment of the decision-making process." Yet the presidential privilege to protect confidential communications must be weighed against the legitimate needs of the judicial process in the fair administration of criminal justice. In criminal cases, our adversary system of justice is utterly dependent upon the production of all relevant facts, and "it is imperative to the function of courts that compulsory process be available for the production of evidence needed either by the prosecution or by the defense." It is the "manifest duty of the courts to vindicate" the guarantees of criminal justice rights as provided for in the Fifth and Sixth Amendments to the Constitution. "[T]o accomplish that it is essential that all relevant and admissible evidence be produced." Weighing the need for relevant evidence in criminal litigation against the president's general claim of privilege based on the need for confidentiality, the Court concluded as follows: "A President's acknowledged need for confidentiality in the communications of his office is general in nature, whereas the constitutional need for production of relevant evidence in a criminal proceeding is specific and central to the fair adjudication of a particular criminal case in the administration of justice." Hence, absent a more specific claim by the president to the effect that the subpoenaed communications contain state secrets (sensitive military or diplomatic discussions), the subpoena must be sustained.

We should notice that the Court was not asked to rule, nor did it rule, on the balance between the president's *generalized* interest in confidentiality and the need for evidence in *civil* litigation, or on the balance between the need for evidence in *criminal* litigation and the president's *specific* interest in protecting military or diplomatic secrets. Further, this case had nothing to do with, and thus sheds no light on, the age-old battle between the president and the Congress over executive privilege. Thus, *U.S. v. Nixon* teaches us just one narrow point about the doctrine: Presidents may not invoke the doctrine of executive privilege based upon a generalized need to protect the confidentiality of executive branch communications when the materials sought are needed in the prosecution and defense of a criminal case. As Laurence Tribe has written, even this may go too far.

> The Court's decision makes more sense when its proclamations are put in the context of the peculiar facts of the *Nixon* case. Although the opinion carefully avoided the issue of possible wrongdoing on the part of the President, that possibility was of course perceived and may have affected the Court's conclusion. And, although the language of the opinion gives no hint of it, the *Nixon* decision may eventually be construed as dealing only with the scope of presidential privilege when the President may have a conflict of interest, hence posing no threat to privilege in a more traditional setting.[75]

Whatever the truth may be on this matter, the fact is that a unanimous Court, including four Nixon appointees, ruled against the president's claim of executive privilege. And while the logic of the Court's opinion may not bear close scrutiny in future years, the Supreme Court's centrality to power politics in America is evident in Richard Nixon's resignation from office just two weeks after the Court's decision was announced.

In our system of separation of powers and checks and balances among coequal branches of the national government, conflicts are chronic and balance is impermanent. It is inevitable that each branch will from time to time flex its muscles. When it is the Congress or the president doing the flexing, they will occasionally encounter barriers erected by the Supreme Court. Congress will not always win. Nor will the president. Most of the time the Supreme Court has insisted that the framers did not intend the doctrine of separation of powers to deal with the trivial. For the most part, the Court has acted in a pragmatic fashion to guarantee that while the branches remain "independent," the system remains "workable."

NOTES

[1] 2 Doll. 419 (1793).
[2] 7 Wall. 506 (1869).
[3] 321 U.S. 414 (1944).
[4] See the account by Carl Brent Swisher, *American Constitutional Development* (New York: Houghton Mifflin, 1954), pp. 1002–1003.

[5] Harvey Mansfield, *A Short History of OPA* (Washington, D.C.: Office of Price Administration, 1948), p. 277.

[6] Edward S. Corwin, *Total War and the Constitution* (New York: Knopf, 1947), p. 130.

[7] Walter F. Murphy, *Elements of Judicial Strategy* (Chicago: University of Chicago Press, 1964), p. 124.

[8] Benjamin N. Cardozo, "Law and Literature," 14 *Yale Review* (1925), pp. 699, 715–16. The same point is made by Charles Evans Hughes, *The Supreme Court of the United States* (New York: Columbia University Press, 1928), p. 68. See also Murphy, p. 60n60.

[9] Mansfield, *A Short History of OPA*, pp. 277–78.

[10] 6 *Cranch* 87 (1810).

[11] 1 *Wheat.* 304 (1816).

[12] 219 U.S. 346 (1911).

[13] Note "Advisory Opinions on the Constitutionality of Statutes," 69 *Harvard Law Review* (1956); "The Case for an Advisory Function in the Federal Judiciary," 50 *Georgia Law Review* (1962); Felix Frankfurter, "A Note on Advisory Opinions," 37 *Harvard Law Review* (1924). See the summary "Pro's and Con's of Advisory Opinions" in William B. Lockhart et al., *Constitutional Law* (St. Paul: West Publishing Co., 1986), pp. 1521–25.

[14] *Cohens v. Virginia*, 6 Wheat. 264 (1821).

[15] *Adams v. Union R. Co.*, 21 R.I. 134.

[16] *Smith v. Smith*, 245 N.W. 644.

[17] 416 U.S. 312 (1974).

[18] *Atherton Mills v. Johnson*, 259 U.S. 13 (1922).

[19] *Moore v. Ogilvie*, 394 U.S. 814 (1969).

[20] Lockhart et al., *Constitutional Law*, p. 1525.

[21] 392 U.S. 40 (1968).

[22] See Lockhart et al., *Constitutional Law*, pp. 1526–27.

[23] Ibid., p. 1527.

[24] See Alexander Bickel, *The Least Dangerous Branch* (Indianapolis: Bobbs-Merrill, 1962), pp. 143–56.

[25] *Poe v. Ullman*, 367 U.S. 497 (1961).

[26] Bickel, *The Least Dangerous Branch*, pp. 146, 166.

[27] *Griswold v. Connecticut*, 381 U.S. 479 (1965).

[28] Jack W. Peltason, *Federal Courts in the Political Process* (Garden City, N.Y.: Doubleday, 1955), p. 10.

[29] Laurence H. Tribe, *American Constitutional Law* (Mineola, N.Y.: Foundation Press, 1988), pp. 96–97.

[30] *Luther v. Borden*, 7 How. 1 (1849).

[31] *Coleman v. Miller*, 307 U.S. 433 (1939).

[32] *Martin v. Mott*, 12 Wheat. 19 (1827).

[33] *Goldwater v. Carter*, 444 U.S. 996 (1979).

[34] *Colegove v. Green*, 328 U.S. 549 (1946).

[35] 369 U.S. 186 (1962).

[36] Tribe, *American Constitutional Law*, pp. 965–97n6.

[37] For contrasting views on the proper judicial role in the amendment process, see Walter Dellinger, "The Legitimacy of Constitutional Change: Rethinking the Amendment Process," 97 *Harvard Law Review* 386 (1983); Laurence Tribe, "A Constitution We Are Amending: In Defense of a Restrained Judicial Role," 97 *Harvard Law Review* 433 (1983); and Dellinger, "Constitutional Politics: A Rejoinder," 97 *Harvard Law Review* 446 (1983).

[38] *Sierra Club v. Morton*, 405 U.S. 727 (1972).

[39] *Flast v. Cohen*, 392 U.S. 83 (1968) (emphasis added).

[40] 262 U.S. 447 (1923).

[41] *Allen v. Wright,* 468 U.S. 737 (1984).

[42] See analyses in Tribe, *American Constitutional Law,* pp. 107–110, and Lockhart et al., *Constitutional Law,* pp. 1535–37, 1559–60.

[43] Robert A. Goldwin and Art Kaufman, eds., *Separation of Powers—Does It Still Work?* (Washington, D.C.: American Enterprise Institute, 1986), pp. ix–xi.

[44] Louis Fisher, *Constitutional Conflicts between Congress and the President* (Princeton, N.J.: Princeton University Press, 1985), p. xiii.

[45] 7 Cranch 382 (1813).

[46] 276 U.S. 394 (1928).

[47] 293 U.S. 388 (1928).

[48] See, for example, *Schechter Poultry Corp. v. U.S.,* 295 U.S. 495 (1935).

[49] *U.S. v. Rock Royal Co-op., Inc.,* 307 U.S. 533 (1939).

[50] *FEA v. Algonquin SNG, Inc.,* 426 U.S. 548 (1976); See Tribe, *American Constitutional Law,* pp. 362–63, especially 362n4.

[51] Ibid.

[52] Theodore J. Lowi, *The End of Liberalism* (New York: W. W. Norton, 1969), pp. 287–99.

[53] 462 U.S. 919 (1983).

[54] *Process Gas Consumers Group v. Federal Energy Regulatory Commission,* 463 U.S. 1216 (1983).

[55] *Myers v. U.S.,* 272 U.S. 52 (1926).

[56] *Humphrey's Executor v. U.S.,* 295 U.S. 602 (1935).

[57] Quoted in Fisher, *Constitutional Conflicts,* p. 78.

[58] 357 U.S. 349 (1958).

[59] 424 U.S. 1 (1976).

[60] *Morrison v. Olson,* 485 U.S. 714 (1988).

[61] Linda Greenhouse, "Fetters on the Executive: By Finding No Threat in Prosecutor Law, the Court Rejects a Constitutional Vision," *New York Times* (June 30, 1988).

[62] Clifford D. May, "A Case against Special Prosecutors?" *New York Times* (June 21, 1987).

[63] Quoted in ibid.

[64] Ibid.

[65] Stuart Taylor, Jr., "U.S. Court Upsets Law on Appointing Key Prosecutors," *New York Times* (January 23, 1988).

[66] Stuart Taylor, Jr., "Supreme Court Vote Upholds Law on Special Prosecutors; 7–1 Ruling Is Rebuff to Reagan," *New York Times* (June 30, 1988).

[67] 478 U.S. 714 (1986).

[68] "As Backer's Vow to Fix Law, Others Say Job Is Congress's," *New York Times* (July 8, 1986); Stuart Taylor, Jr., "High Court Voids Major Step in Law That Cuts Deficit," *New York Times* (July 8, 1986).

[69] See Kenneth R. Feinberg, "Gramm-Rudman Is Not Court Material," *New York Times* (January 15, 1986).

[70] 299 U.S. 304 (1936).

[71] 343 U.S. 579 (1952).

[72] Dorsen and Shattuck, "Executive Privilege, the Congress, and the Courts," 35 *Ohio State Law Journal* 1–3 (1974); See Lockhart et al., *Constitutional Law,* p. 226.

[73] Lockhart et al., *Constitutional Law,* p. 226.

[74] 418 U.S. 683 (1974).

[75] Tribe, *American Constitutional Law,* pp. 281–82.

VIII

Supreme Court Policy Making

Limitations on Governmental Powers

THE NATIONALIZATION OF THE BILL OF RIGHTS

For most of its history prior to World War I, the Supreme Court was preoccupied with cases enabling it to define the doctrines of federalism and separation of powers. The original Constitution of seven articles deals in the main with the allocation of governing power between the national government and the states, and with the separation of powers between the branches of the national government. It is a "document of limitations" largely in the sense that the governing authority created is limited. It speaks only briefly to limitations that revolve around civil rights and liberties. Most of the constitutional protections of civil rights and liberties are found in the Bill of Rights (Amendments I–IX, added to the Constitution in 1791), but the Bill of Rights operated only as a limitation on national government action until gradually applied to the states by the Supreme Court in the twentieth century. It is true that the due process and equal protection clauses of the Fourteenth Amendment (limiting state action) were added to the Constitution immediately following the Civil War in 1868, but their purposes were not to be fulfilled by Supreme Court interpretation until well into the twentieth century. The process by which most of the Bill of Rights has been "nationalized," that is, "absorbed" or "incorporated" into the Fourteenth Amendment and thus made applicable to the states, did not even *begin* until the 1920s. It is still going on. The doctrine of "preferred freedoms," according to which some rights are more important to the preservation of democracy than are others and thus deserve a preferred position and special protection in our constitutional scheme, did not *first* appear until the 1930s. Its evolution is still going on. The application of the equal protection clause to women did not even begin until the 1970s, and it is still going on. The idea that "justice for all" might require preference for some—affirmative action—and the idea that "nontextual rights" such as "privacy," "autonomy," and "personhood" afford individuals added protections are ideas elucidated by the Supreme Court largely in the 1980s. Obviously, that elucidation too is still going on. The simple point is that, except for property rights, the Supreme Court did not begin, in any significant way at least, to fulfill its responsibilities as the guardian of individual rights and liberties until the twentieth century. Since roughly the 1920s, however, the Supreme Court as schoolmaster of the Republic has initiated three major developments in American constitutional law: (1) the nationalization of the Bill of Rights; (2) the articulation of the doctrine of preferred freedoms; and (3) the pronouncement of new rights dealing with affirmative action, gender, and privacy. These three developments will be the topics of this chapter.

The original Constitution of 1787, before the addition of the Bill of Rights in 1791, created a new national government without tampering in any significant way with the patterns of government in the original states. The document of 1787 did place some limitations on the powers of the states as well as limitations on the powers of the national government, but most such limitations were designed, not to protect individual rights, but to protect the integrity of the federal system. For example, the states are prohibited by the original document from printing or coining money and from entering into treaties or alliances with other nations or other states of the Union. Similarly, the national government is prohibited in the exercise of its commerce and taxing powers from showing preference for the seaports of one state over those of another. Again, this limitation relates to the maintenance of the federal system. Indeed, the original document lists only four limitations that revolve around civil rights and liberties, and they are limitations on the powers of both the national government and the states. Neither the national government nor the states may suspend the writ of habeas corpus, pass bills of attainder, pass *ex post facto* laws, or grant titles of nobility. With these exceptions, there are no precise limitations on state powers listed in the original document, and for the reasons stated below, it would be difficult to conclude that those who wrote and ratified the Bill of Rights intended them to apply to the states. First, the original states already had their own constitutions, and these documents contained their own bills of rights limiting state governmental action. These state bills of rights were neither identical to each other nor to the national Bill of Rights, but, customarily, they contained many of the rights written into the Bill of Rights in 1791. It would seem surprising, even unnecessary, to add to the United States Constitution a list of rights protecting individuals from state government action. Second, the cry heard around the state ratifying conventions between 1787 and 1789 demanding the addition of a list of rights to the original document derived from a widespread fear of the power of the proposed new national government, not from a fear or mistrust of the already existing state governments. Third, only one of the seventeen amendments debated by the authors of the Bill of Rights contained the phrase "no state shall." Simple logic permits the inference (though there are counterarguments) that the omission of any reference to the states in the other sixteen proposed amendments means they were not intended to apply to the states.[1] In any event, although virtually all scholars agree that the Bill of Rights as added to the Constitution in 1791 was intended to apply only to the national government, it took a Supreme Court decision to settle the matter dispositively. That decision came in 1833 in the case of *Barron v. Baltimore.*[2]

In *Barron* a city road-paving program necessitating the diversion of streams from their normal course resulted in large deposits of sand and gravel building up around Barron's wharf. The consequential damage to Barron's wharf prevented the access of vessels and made the wharf unfit for shipping. Barron claimed that for all practical purposes the city's program had taken his private property for public use without just compensation. At that time some state constitutions contained provisions for just compensation. However, unfortunately for Barron, Maryland's constitution did not. Thus, if he were to be protected at all, it would have to be under the Fifth Amendment's guarantee that "private property [shall not] be taken for public use without just compensation." However, the Supreme Court, relying on the logic and historical analysis presented above, ruled that the provisions of the Bill of Rights do not apply to the states. The law on this matter remained unchanged until after the Civil War.

One of the three postwar amendments, the Fourteenth, contained a most important provision that eventually would lead to the application of the Bill of Rights to the states. This, however, did not happen immediately. The due process clause of the Fourteenth Amendment provides that *no state* shall "deprive any person of life, *liberty,* or property, without *due process* of law" (emphasis added). Eventually the question would become whether or not the word *liberty* in the Fourteenth Amendment was intended to "incorporate" or "absorb" the provisions of the Bill of Rights, hence making them applicable to the states. As we will see, some justices such as Hugo Black have held to the view that such an incorporation was indeed the intent of those who wrote and ratified the Fourteenth Amendment. In a dissenting opinion crafted in 1947,[3] Justice Black wrote, "I . . . follow what I believe was the original purpose of the Fourteenth Amendment—to extend to all the people of the nation the complete protection of the Bill of Rights." Historical research has produced both support and skepticism for this "theory of incorporation," and scholars remain divided on the actual history of the amendment. Charles Fairman, after extensive research and in direct response to Black's assertion, has written that "the record of history is against him"; the evidence against his view is "a high mountain" while the evidence in support of his view is "a few pebbles and stone."[4] Elder Witt, on the other hand, quotes Representative John A. Bingham, who authored the due process clause, as saying that the provisions of the Bill of Rights "were never limitations upon the power of the states until made so by the Fourteenth Amendment."[5]

Supreme Court justices have been as divided as have scholars on the original purpose and proper application of the Fourteenth Amendment, although today Justice Black's view has largely triumphed for all practical purposes. The possibility of applying provisions of the Bill of Rights to the states through the Fourteenth Amendment first came to the Supreme Court in 1908 in the case of *Twining v. New Jersey.*[6] Here, the directors of a New Jersey bank were indicted for intentionally exhibiting false papers to a state bank examiner. The defendants called no witnesses and did not testify in their own behalf at their trial. In his charge to the jury the trial court judge made adverse comments about the refusal of the defendants to take the stand to refute the accusations against them. In the view of the defendants, these adverse comments violated their right against self-incrimination. At that time the constitutions of some other states included a right against self-incrimination. Unfortunately, the constitution of New Jersey did not. Thus, if the defendants were to be protected, it would have to be under the Fifth Amendment's guarantee against self-incrimination. However, the Supreme Court ruled in *Twining* that neither the general historical meaning of due process nor the prior decisions of the Court made the guarantee against self-incrimination an inalienable right of every citizen of a free government. In short, the Bill of Rights was not written to protect citizens against state action (*Barron*), and the addition of the Fourteenth Amendment did not alter that fact (*Twining*).

Fifteen years later, however, the Supreme Court suggested for the first time that the word *liberty* may mean more than "property rights," thus opening the door to one of the most spectacular developments in American constitutional law. This came in *Meyer v. Nebraska* (1923)[7] involving a state law prohibiting the teaching of foreign languages to any student who had not yet passed the eighth grade. The law applied to teachers in private and parochial as well as public schools. The Supreme Court granted that the states have a broad leeway in making reasonable regulations for all schools. But, the Court said, this law deprives teachers of the liberty secured to them by the due process of the Fourteenth Amendment. In doing so, the Supreme Court proclaimed a meaning of liberty broader than the right to acquire and enjoy property that henceforth could not be denied without due process of law.

Relatively rapidly thereafter the Court made all the First Amendment rights applicable to the states through "incorporation" or "absorption" into the Fourteenth Amendment. Freedom of speech was incorporated in *Gitlow v. New York* (1925),[8] freedom of press in *Near v. Minnesota* (1931),[9] freedom of assembly in *DeJonge v. Oregon* (1937),[10] and freedom of religion in *Cantwell v. Connecticut* (1940).[11] In *Cantwell* a unanimous Court spoke as follows:

> We hold that the statute [a breach-of-the-peace ordinance used against Jehovah Witness adherents seeking converts on the city streets], as construed and applied to the appellants, deprives them of their liberty without due process of law in contravention of the Fourteenth Amendment. *The fundamental concept of liberty embodied in that Amendment embraces the liberties guaranteed by the First Amendment.* The First Amendment declares that Congress shall make no law respecting an establishment of religion or prohibiting the free exercise thereof. The Fourteenth Amendment has rendered the legislature of the states as incompetent as Congress to enact such laws. [Emphasis added.]

The process of incorporation has proceeded by fits and starts since 1940 with the result that today most but not all of the provisions of the Bill of Rights have been made applicable to the states. This process has advanced case by case with individual justices adopting differing approaches to incorporation. Three distinct approaches have emerged: "selective" incorporation, "simple" or "straight" incorporation, and "incorporation plus." The first of these, "selective" incorporation, has commended itself to most of the justices sitting on the Court since the incorporation process began. It has been articulated most notably by Justices Cardozo and Frankfurter. In *Palko v. Connecticut* (1937)[12] the Court was asked to consider whether the right against double jeopardy contained in the Fifth Amendment was applicable to the states through the Fourteenth Amendment. Adopting the "selective" incorporation approach and relying on what has come to be called the fundamental rights test, the Court ruled that it was not. Justice Cardozo wrote in *Palko* that the "ordered liberty" and "fundamental fairness" required of the states by the due process clause of the Fourteenth Amendment do not make all of the Bill of Rights ipso facto applicable to the states. Rather, in each case, to be protected against state action the right asserted must be "of a very essence of a scheme of ordered liberty" and so deeply "rooted in the traditions and conscience of our people as to be ranked as fundamental." By an 8–1 vote the Supreme Court concluded in *Palko* that the right against double jeopardy was not such a fundamental right. (This decision was overturned in 1969 in *Benton v. Maryland.*[13]) In *Adamson v. California* (1947)[14] the Court was asked to reconsider its ruling in *Twining* regarding the issue of self-incrimination, specifically whether a judge's or, in this case, prosecutor's adverse comments about a defendant's failure to take the stand in his or her own defense violate the Fourteenth Amendment. Writing for a five-justice majority, Justice Frankfurter said that they do not. The Fourteenth Amendment, he said, is *not* a "shorthand summary" of the Bill of Rights. Rather, its application to the states is limited to violations of "accepted notions of justice" only. In Justice Black's dissent in *Adamson*, in contrast, we see the classic statement of the "strict" or "straight" incorporation approach. Black had at least two reasons for arguing that *all* of the Bill of Rights, no less and no more, was applicable to the states. First, as we have learned, was his reading of the history of the Fourteenth Amendment. Second was his fear that the "selective" approach gives too much power to judges to use "natural law" concepts and personal judgment to determine what rights are in and what rights are out. Black wrote:

> I fear to see the consequences of the Court's practice of substituting its own concepts of decency and fundamental justice for the language of the Bill of Rights as its point of departure in interpreting and enforcing that Bill of Rights. If the choice must be between the selective process of the *Palko* decision applying some of the Bill of Rights to the states, or the *Twining* rule applying none of them, I would choose the *Palko* selective process. But rather than accept either of these choices, I would follow what I believe was the original purpose of the Fourteenth Amendment—to extend to all the people of the nation the complete protection of the Bill of Rights.

Thus, Black's "strict" or "straight" incorporation approach would apply *all* the provisions of the Bill of Rights to the states, tic for tac, no less and no more. In *Adamson* the majority concluded that the right against self-incrimination was not so fundamental to a scheme of ordered liberty as to be incorporated and applied to the states. This decision was overturned in *Malloy v. Hogan* (1964).[15] Some years later Justice Black was asked which of his many dissents that later became the prevailing view was the most important. He answered that it was his dissent in *Adamson*. This was undoubtedly because *Adamson* gave him the opportunity to fully articulate his "straight" incorporation approach.

Black was joined in dissent in *Adamson* by Justices Douglas, Murphy, and Rutledge. Rutledge's separate dissent in *Adamson*, which was joined by Murphy, deserves close scrutiny as a means of distinguishing between the "strict" or "straight" approach to incorporation and the more expansive approach of "incorporation plus." According to the Rutledge–Murphy position, "occasions may arise where a [criminal] proceeding falls so short of conforming to 'fundamental standards' of procedure as to warrant constitutional condemnation in terms of a lack of due process despite the absence of a specific provision in the Bill of Rights." Thus Rutledge and Murphy read the Fourteenth Amendment as absorbing the entire Bill of Rights *plus* unspecified "fundamental rights" that would supplement the Bill of Rights "in order to fill in the chinks."[16] This approach has been labeled the "incorporation plus" position and its distinction from Black's "strict" or "straight" incorporation is evident in Rutledge's dissent in *Wolf v. Colorado* (1949).[17]

In this case the Court ruled that the Fourth Amendment's protection against unreasonable searches and seizures *was* applicable to the states. Black agreed with the majority, however, that this prohibition did *not* carry with it the federal exclusionary rule, which prohibits the use of evidence secured through the illegal search and seizure, since that rule was not an explicit requirement of the Fourth Amendment but simply a federal remedy, "a judicially created rule of evidence which Congress might negate." Rutledge vehemently dissented. He asserted that the federal exclusionary rule was a "fundamental standard of procedure" that must be made applicable to the states because the "Fourth Amendment without the sanction" would be "a dead letter." Twelve years later, in *Mapp v. Ohio* (1961),[18] Rutledge's "incorporation plus" approach was used by the Court to overturn *Wolf* and to apply the exclusionary rule to the states.

In *Griswold v. Connecticut* (1965),[19] a case we examined in a different context in Chapter Seven, the seven-justice majority agreed that a right of personal privacy is implicit in the Constitution, but it could not agree on the specific source of this right. The majority opinion of Justice Douglas, the concurring opinions of Justices Goldberg and Harlan, and the dissenting opinion of Justice Black allow us to observe all three approaches to incorporation in one case. Justice Douglas articulated one version of "incorporation plus" by finding the implicit right to privacy in the "penumbras" or "emanations" from a number of expressed provisions in the Bill of Rights.

> Various guarantees create zones of privacy. The right of association contained in the penumbra of the First Amendment is one. . . . The Third Amendment in its prohibition against the quartering of soldiers "in any house" in time of peace without the consent of the owner is another facet of that privacy. . . . The Fourth and Fifth Amendments . . . [are] described . . . as protection against all governmental invasions "of the sanctity of a man's home and the privacies of life. . . . " The Ninth Amendment provides: "The enumeration of the Constitution of certain rights shall not be construed to deny or disparage others retained by the people. . . . " The present case, then, concerns a relationship lying without the zone of privacy created by several fundamental constitutional guarantees.

Douglas, then, saw the Fourteenth Amendment as incorporating *all* of the Bill of Rights *plus* other fundamental rights, such as the right to privacy, formed by emanations from the Bill of Rights. Douglas's reference to at least five different amendments from which the right to privacy emanates produced the following responses from one critic: "[In *Griswold* Justice Douglas] skipped through the Bill of Rights like a cheerleader— 'Give me a P . . . give me an R . . . an I . . . ,' and so on, and found P-R-I-V-A-C-Y as a derivative or penumbral right."[20] Justice Goldberg, in his concurring opinion, found the right to privacy in the Ninth Amendment. He states at the outset that he did *not* accept the view that due process as used in the Fourteenth Amendment includes *all* the provisions of the Bill of Rights (in this sense, Goldberg's approach is "selective"). But, he wrote,

> I do agree that the concept of liberty protects those personal rights that are fundamental, and is not confined to the specific terms of the Bill of Rights. My conclusion that it embraces the right of marital privacy though that right is not mentioned explicitly in the Constitution is supported . . . by the language and history of the Ninth Amendment. . . . The Ninth Amendment shows a belief of the Constitution's authors that fundamental rights exist that are not expressly enumerated.

Thus, while Goldberg's approach is "selective," he is careful to point out that the liberty protected by the Fourteenth Amendment against state infringement includes rights, such as privacy, that are not mentioned in the Bill of Rights but are deeply rooted in the "traditions and collective conscience of our people." Justice Harlan, always a "selective incorporationist," wrote a concurring opinion in which he made clear his understanding of the Fourteenth Amendment. He opposed "strict" incorporation because that approach would require *all* requirements of the Bill of Rights be *imposed* upon the states. He also opposed that version of "incorporation plus" that found fundamental rights in the penumbra of the Bill of Rights because that approach *restricts* the reach of the Fourteenth Amendment by implying that the only rights protected are those found in the letter or penumbra of the Bill of Rights. In this case Harlan found a right to marital privacy protected against state action, not by the Bill of Rights or radiations from it, but by the due process clause of the Fourteenth Amendment itself, a guarantee of ordered liberty that "stands . . . on its own bottom." Finally, we have Justice Black's dissent. Again, as before, Justice Black reiterates his belief that the Fourteenth Amendment applies *all* the requirements of the Bill of Rights to the states, *but nothing more.* In *Griswold* Black makes clear that which may have been implicit in his *Adamson* dissent. Specifically, while considering himself a champion of civil liberties, Black emphasizes that he is as opposed to using the fundamental rights test to *add* to the protections of the Fourteenth Amendment as he is opposed to it as a means of *selecting out* from protection rights not deemed fundamental. For Black, the fundamental rights test as used by both "selective" and "plus" adherents is hopelessly and inescapably mired in subjectivity.

Black's "strict" incorporation theory has never commanded majority support among the justices, and the Supreme Court has proceeded over the years in a pattern of "selective" incorporation determining case by case which Bill of Rights provisions should be regarded as so fundamental as to be included in the protection of the Fourteenth Amendment's due process clause. The process continues today with each new incorporation, though produced through a "selective" approach, bringing us closer to the triumph of Justice Black's "strict" or "straight" incorporation theory. At this writing, all of the First, Fourth, and Sixth Amendments have been incorporated, parts of the Fifth and Eighth, and none of the Second, Third, or Seventh. Most Supreme Court scholars do not expect that *all* of the Bill of Rights will ever be incorporated. An overview is provided by Figure 8–1.

FIGURE 8–1   The Nationalization of the Bill of Rights

AMENDMENT	RIGHT	INCORPORATION ACTION: CASE AND DATE
I.	Speech Press Assembly Religion	*Gitlow v. New York* (1925) *Near v. Minnesota* (1931) *DeJonge v. Oregon* (1937) *Cantwell v. Connecticut* (1940)
II.	Right to Bear Arms	*Not Incorporated* (Generally, the Supreme Court has upheld reasonable regulations of the right of private citizens to bear arms. Should a tough gun control law be adopted by a state or local government and a challenge to it be made, a test of incorporation might be presented to the Court in the future.)
III.	No quartering of soldiers	*Not Incorporated* (The quartering problem has not recurred since colonial times, and the Third Amendment has thus not figured significantly in our constitutional history.)
IV.	Unreasonable Searches and Seizures The Exclusionary Rule	*Wolf v. Colorado* (1949) *Mapp v. Ohio* (1961)
V.	Just Compensation Self-Incrimination Double Jeopardy Grand Jury Indictment	*Chicago, B&Q RR. Co. v. Chicago* (1897) *Mallory v. Hogan* (1964) *Benton v. Maryland* (1969) *Not Incorporated* (Indeed, the trend in state criminal cases is away from the use of grand juries and toward reliance upon the sworn written accusation of the prosecuting attorney; there is little reason to believe that this trend will be

AMENDMENT	RIGHT	INCORPORATION ACTION: CASE AND DATE
		reversed or that the federal requirement of indictment by a grand jury will be incorporated.)
VI.	Public Trial	*In re Oliver* (1948)
	Right to Counsel	*Gideon v. Wainwright* (1963)
	Confrontation of	
	Witnesses	*Pointer v. Texas* (1965)
	Impartial Trial	*Parker v. Gladden* (1966)
	Speedy Trial	*Klopfer v. North Carolina* (1967)
	Compulsory Process	*Washington v. Texas* (1967)
	Jury Trial	*Duncan v. Louisiana* (1968)
VII.	Right to Jury Trial in Civil Cases	*Not Incorporated* (Indeed, Warren Burger while chief justice conducted a campaign to abolish jury trials in civil cases to save the judicial process time and money, and for other reasons.)
VIII.	Cruel or Unusual Punishment	*Robinson v. California* (1962)
	Excessive fines or bail	*Not Incorporated*

FIGURE 8-1 *(Continued)*

THE DOCTRINE OF PREFERRED FREEDOMS

The concept of preferred freedoms was first stated in Justice Harlan Fiske Stone's famous "Footnote 4" in *U.S. v. Carolene Products Co.* (1938).[21] It is "one of the singularly most important pieces of legal text produced by the Supreme Court in the twentieth century."[22] *Carolene Products* was decided in 1938 and confirmed the decline of "substantive due process" (as described in Chapter Three). The Court upheld a federal law prohibiting the interstate shipment of certain types of skimmed milk, indicating that when laws are challenged as violations of or as interferences with economic rights, states' rights, or the free flow of commerce, the Court will uphold them so long as the regulation in question has a "rational basis." The Court's decision reflected its impending shift away from an emphasis on the protection of economic rights and toward the greater protection of individual rights.[23] In the body of his opinion Justice Stone wrote, "Regulatory legislation affecting ordinary commercial transactions is not to be pronounced unconstitutional unless in the light of the facts . . . it is of such a character as to preclude the assumption that it rests upon some rational basis within the knowledge and experience of the legislators." However, as stated in the famous "Footnote 4," "there may be a narrower scope for the operation of the presumption of constitutionality when legislation appears on its face to be within a specific prohibition of the Constitution, such as those of the first ten Amendments, which are deemed equally specific when held to be embraced within the Fourteenth."

Simply stated, the theory of preferred freedoms holds that some constitutional rights are more important than others and deserve special protection. In practice the theory requires that the usual presumption of the constitutional validity of challenged laws be reversed when the challenged law adversely affects these preferred freedoms, especially First Amendment rights. Having been first stated in 1938 in the *Carolene Products* case, the concept was further developed in *Schneider v. Irvington*[24] in 1940. The actual phrase "preferred position" was first used in *Jones v. Opelika*[25] in 1942. Then in 1945 came *Thomas v. Collins*[26] in which Justice Wiley Rutledge offered "the most clearly, expressly, and extremely stated" argument for the doctrine, forthrightly elaborating on and surpassing Justice Stone's first statement.[27] Rutledge's opinion also became the "high watermark in the use of the clear-and-present danger test," which had gradually become the touchstone of constitutionality in all cases involving freedom of expression.[28] *Thomas v. Collins* involved the validity of a particular application of a Texas statute requiring all persons soliciting members for labor unions to register with the Texas secretary of state in order to receive an organizer's card. To secure the card an organizer had to give his name and affiliation and show his credentials, but no discretion was vested in state officers to withhold the card.[29] The state courts were given power to issue restraining orders or injunctions to enforce the provisions of the act.[30] Additional enforcement proceedings included civil penalties not exceeding $1,000 against the union for violations, and misdemeanor penalties against the union or organizer not to exceed $500 and/or confinement not to exceed 60 days.[31] R. J. Thomas, president of the United Auto Workers, deliberately challenged the law by soliciting members for a union without observing the registration provisions. In an address before an assembly of Houston oil refinery employees, Thomas invited nonunion persons to join the Oil Workers Industrial Union. This was in violation of a restraining order issued only a few hours before the address enjoining Thomas from soliciting unless he registered. Defining the whole speech and assembly as "solicitation," the state court held Thomas in contempt. He appealed to the U.S. Supreme Court, which, by a 5–4 vote, held the law unconstitutional. Rutledge wrote for the majority. His position was that the legislation in question unduly restrained orderly discussion and assembly without the presence of any public danger that would make such restraint necessary. He began by labeling as established doctrine the recently developed tenet that First Amendment freedoms enjoy a preferred position in our constitutional scheme, and then he went on to link this doctrine with the "clear and present danger" test:

> This case confronts us again with the duty our system places on this Court to say where the individual's freedom ends and the State's power begins. Choice on that border, now as always delicate, is perhaps more so where *the usual presumption supporting legislation is balanced by the preferred place given in our scheme to the great, the indispensable freedoms secured by the First Amendment.* That priority gives these liberties a sanctity and a sanction not permitting dubious intrusions. And it is the character of the right, not of the limitation, which determines what standard governs the choice.
>
> For these reasons *any attempt to restrict those liberties must be justified by clear public interest, threatened not doubtfully or remotely, but by clear and present danger.* . . . Only the gravest abuses, endangering paramount interests, give occasion for permissible limitation. . . . Where the line shall be placed in a particular application rests . . . on the concrete clash of particular interests and the community's relative evaluation both of them and of how the one will be affected by the specific restriction, the other by its absence. That judgement in the first instance is for the legislative body. But *in our system where the line can constitutionally be placed presents a question this Court cannot escape answering independently,* whatever the legislative judgement, in light of our constitutional tradition. And the answer, under the tradition, can be affirmative, to support an intrusion upon this domain, only if grave and impending public danger requires this. [Emphasis added.]

The minority argued that there was no more involved here than a paid organizer and a business transaction involving labor unions as business associations. They rejected the preferred freedoms doctrine and would have upheld the law on the so-called rational basis test; that is, when the Court is confronted with a law alleged to infringe basic freedoms, it is limited to judging whether a "reasonable man" could have reached the legislature's conclusion as to the existence of a danger demanding that protective action be taken. Rutledge, however, rejected the argument that First Amendment freedoms do not apply to business and economic activity. The First Amendment, he argued, guards "great secular courses, and small ones." It is "a charter for government not for an institution of learning. . . . 'Free trade in ideas' means free trade in the opportunity to persuade to action, not merely to describe facts." Thus, although a state's power to regulate may in most cases include the power to impose restrictions the legislature has a "rational basis" for adopting, the great First Amendment freedoms "may not be infringed on such slender grounds."

In essence, for roughly the last 50 years the Supreme Court has for the most part followed the twin dictates of *Carolene Products* and *Thomas v. Collins:* (1) The Court has a special role to play as defender of those rights prerequisite to the effective functioning of a democratic political process —the provisions of the Bill of Rights generally, the First Amendment and the right to vote in particular; and (2) when laws allegedly contravene these democratic rights, the usual presumptions of constitutionality must be curtailed or even waived. It is true that some justices such as Felix Frankfurter criticized the preferred freedoms doctrine in the late 1940s, and that with the appointment of four Nixon justices the early 1970s first seemed to signal a new era. As a whole, however, the Supreme Court has continued to give the First Amendment what even the moderately conservative Justice Powell recognized as "a special solicitude."[32] In short, the First Amendment freedoms of speech, press, assembly, and religion have been "first" in three ways: (1) the first listed in the Bill of Rights; (2) the first among the amendments to be fully incorporated and applied to the states; and (3) the first in importance among individual rights, having been granted a preferred position in the scale of constitutional values.[33]

THE NEW RIGHTS: AFFIRMATIVE ACTION AND GENDER EQUALITY

As we learned in Chapters One and Three, the Warren Court (1953–69) is properly regarded as the most civil libertarian, activist Supreme Court in our history to date. In the several decades since, though the Court has cut back significantly on some Warren Court precedents, it has also broken some new ground in issue areas not on the Warren Court's agenda, matters barely touched upon by the Court prior to 1970. Perhaps most notable among such matters are affirmative action and gender equality.

Nearly 100 years ago Justice John Harlan announced in a dissenting opinion that the Constitution is "color-blind." By the 1950s and 1960s, the Supreme Court used this "race-neutral" criterion to reach its many historic decisions outlawing racial discrimination and segregation. But beginning in the 1970s, questions of great historical and legal importance arose: Is it enough merely to abolish legal hurdles and governmental barriers to the progress of minority groups and women? Does past discrimination against blacks and women require an equality-of-results approach? Does true equality of opportunity for minority groups and women require positive action by government and the private sector to bring these groups to an equal starting place in society? Affirmative action programs, whereby minority groups and women are given preferences in college admissions, job training, and hiring and promotion practices are based on the assumption that the answers to these questions are yes. As such, affirmative action programs are created as temporary, "color-conscious" attempts to achieve true equality of opportunity. Inevitably, though, such attempts raise the legal question of whether or not they, like policies and practices that discriminate against minorities and women, are violations of constitutional equality. The Supreme Court first began to address the questions of affirmative action in the 1970s.[34]

The first major decision came in 1978 in the case of *Regents of University of California v. Bakke*. [35] As we learned earlier, the disputed preferential admissions policy involved here was invalidated by a 5–4 majority. But a different 5–4 majority offered guidelines for a permissible preferential admissions process. Although "target quotas" may be unlawful, the Court said, there are circumstances in which race may be taken into consideration in making admission decisions. For example, once a middle group of applicants has been identified as "admissible" (that is, capable of doing the work), race may be used to "tip the balance" in favor of black applicants just as a criterion of geographic distribution might. In his separate opinion in *Bakke,* concurring with the conclusion that race may be considered in admissions processes but dissenting from the invalidation of the program in this case, Justice Thurgood Marshall made the strongest case to date *for* affirmative action.

> In light of the sorry history of discrimination and its devastating impact on the lives of Negroes, bringing the Negro into the mainstream of American life should be a state interest of the highest order. To fail to do so is to ensure that America will forever remain a divided society. . . . While I applaud the judgment of the Court that a university may consider race in its admissions process, it is more than a little ironic that, after several hundred years of class-based discrimination against Negroes, the Court is unwilling to hold that a class-based remedy for that discrimination is permissible. . . . It is because of a legacy of unequal treatment that we now must permit the institutions of this society to give consideration to race in making decisions about who will hold the positions of influence, affluence and prestige in America. . . . We should not let color blindness become myopia.

Within one year after *Bakke* it became clear that not only public but also private affirmative action efforts would be challenged by whites as color-conscious plans working illegally to their detriment. The first major challenge to private, or "voluntary," plans came in 1979 in *United Steel Workers v. Weber*. [36] This case involved an affirmative action plan collectively negotiated by an employer and a union that reserved for black employees 50 percent of the openings in an inplant training program until the percentage of black craft workers in the plant was commensurate with the percentage of blacks in the local labor force. Weber, a white unskilled worker, applied for a lot in this "one-for-one" (one black for one white) program but was insufficiently "senior" to obtain one of the white slots, though he had more seniority than some of the blacks who were awarded slots. Weber challenged the plan on the grounds that it violated Title VII of the Civil Rights Act of 1964, which prohibits employers and labor organizations from discriminating on the basis of race. The Court, however, sustained the plan. Writing for the Court, Justice Brennan said that Congress did not intend to forbid all voluntary race-conscious affirmative action plans when it passed the Civil Rights Act. While the opinion did not specify a line of demarcation between permissible and impermissible plans, it did suggest that the purpose of the Civil Rights Act of 1964 was to help overcome years of racial injustice. And it quoted Senator Hubert Humphrey in debate on the bill in the Senate as saying that the bill is an attempt to do something *for* those people "who have been left out of the American dream for so long." Thus, Brennan concluded, it would be "truly ironic" if that bill were now turned against the very people it was designed to help.

The late Burger Court and early Rehnquist Court of the 1980s produced mixed results in affirmative action cases. In 1984 a court-ordered affirmative action plan for firefighters in the Memphis Fire Department came into direct conflict with a contractually established seniority system when a city budget shortage required a reduction in personnel. The city's "last-hired, first-fired" layoff plan had an adverse proportionate impact on black firefighters. However, the Supreme Court held in *Firefighters v. Stotts*[37] that a bona fide seniority system must be protected in a suit such as this unless it was adopted with discriminatory intent. The practical effect of this decision was that the gains made by blacks in their employment as firefighters under the affirmative action plan were largely undermined.[38] In 1986, in *Wygant v. Jackson Board of Education,*[39] the Court again opposed an affirmative action plan when it ruled against a collective bargaining agreement giving minorities protection from layoffs. However, in the same case the Court said that, generally, if past job discrimination has been demonstrated, a public employer (such as a school board) may attempt to redress its own past discrimination through the use of numerical hiring goals favoring members of minorities. In the same year, in *Local 28 v. EEOC,*[40] the Court upheld a lower court decree requiring a union to eradicate its own "egregious" discrimination by meeting a specific hiring quota of 29.23 percent in an apprenticeship program. And in 1987, in *U.S. v. Paradise,*[41] the Court upheld a lower court's order requiring that a state temporarily use a strict racial quota, one black for one white, in promoting state troopers in order to make up for severe past discrimination against blacks.

In its *first gender-based affirmative action ruling* the Supreme Court sustained in 1987 a government-sponsored affirmative action plan for women. The plan in dispute here was adopted by the Santa Clara County Transportation Agency in 1978 to produce a "statistically measurable yearly improvement in hiring, training, and promotion of . . . women throughout the Agency." When this case arose, however, none of the 238 "skilled worker" positions in the agency were held by women. When a job in the skilled worker job classification opened up, Paul Johnson and Diane Joyce applied for promotion to the position and were both rated "well qualified" based on experience and interview results, although Johnson had scored a few more points on the test given for promotion to the position. The job was awarded to Joyce based on the agency's affirmative action plan, and Johnson brought suit under both Title VII of the Civil Rights Act of 1964 and the equal protection clause of the Constitution, claiming he was a victim of reverse sex discrimination. The Supreme Court, in *Johnson v. Transportation Agency,*[42] ruled in favor of the county's affirmative action plan. The Court's reasoning emphasized the history of past discrimination against women in the skilled worker job classification and the fact that both Joyce and Johnson were well qualified to receive the promotion.

Although an affirmative action case, *Johnson* leads us to a consideration of the second area of "new rights" generated since 1970, namely, rights emerging from gender discrimination cases. The simple fact is that *the first decision of the Supreme Court holding sex discrimination violative of equal protection did not occur until 1971.* One hundred years earlier the Court had upheld a state law denying women the right to practice law. The Court explained: "[T]he natural and proper timidity and delicacy which belongs to the female sex evidently unfits it for many of the occupations of civil life. [The] paramount destiny and mission of women are to fulfill the noble and benign offices of wife and mother."[43] Indeed, as recently as 1961 the Court upheld a state practice of excluding women from jury service unless they made a specific request to serve. The Court explained that women are "still regarded as the center of home and family life."[44] Finally, in 1971, in *Reed v. Reed,*[45] the Court brought the rights of women within the scope of the equal protection clause. This case involved a state law listing 11 classes of persons entitled to administer the estates of a deceased, and in the order of their right to do so. Although the words *father or mother* were listed in the same class, the law went on to provide that whenever two persons were otherwise equally entitled, males were to be preferred to females. Thus, when Richard Reed, son of Cecil and Sally Reed, died and both parents, who were separated, applied to administer his estate, the state courts enforced the law and appointed the father. When the mother's appeal finally reached the Supreme Court, the state's lawyers defended the law's preference for male administrators on the grounds that it reduced the workload and increased the efficiency of the state's probate courts by eliminating one class of contests (that is, the need for hearings on the merits over which applicant was better qualified to serve as the administrator). The Supreme Court unanimously disagreed. Chief Justice Burger wrote that all classifications by gender are not necessarily unconstitutional. To be valid, however, such classifications may not be arbitrary; they must be reasonable and rationally related to a legitimate state objective. The objective here, to reduce the workload of the state's probate courts, is "not without some legitimacy." However,

> to give a mandatory preference to members of either sex over members of the other, merely to accomplish the elimination of hearings on the merits is to make the very kind of arbitrary legislative choice forbidden by the Equal

Protection Clause of the Fourteenth Amendment; and whatever may be said as to the positive values of avoiding intrafamily controversy, the choice in this context may not lawfully be mandated solely on the basis of sex.

Thus for the first time the Supreme Court condemned gender discrimination as a violation of the equal protection clause. However, although unanimous, the decision was not a complete victory for gender rights advocates. The Court had invalidated the discriminatory state law but had done so on the basis that it was potently arbitrary and had no rational relationship to the state objective it sought to advance. Also, the burden of proof had rested on those challenging the law. This is the "traditional" or "rational basis" test frequently used by the Court in equal protection clause cases. In sponsoring the *Reed* case, the American Civil Liberties Union (ACLU) had hoped that the Court would make gender classifications, like racial classifications, "inherently suspect," thus shifting the burden of justification to the government. The distinction between the "rational basis" test and the "suspect classification" test is an extremely important one because under the latter the law in dispute is "presumptively invalid," necessitates "strict judicial scrutiny," and requires the government to bear an extremely heavy burden of justifying the law. *Reed v. Reed* was a major step forward for gender rights advocates, but classifications by gender were *not* made inherently suspect.[46]

Gender rights and the fight over which test to use in gender discrimination cases arose again two years after *Reed* in *Frontiero v. Richardson*.[47] This case involved a federal law permitting males in the armed services an automatic dependency allowance for their wives (for example, housing and medical benefits) but requiring service women to prove that their husbands were in fact dependent on them for at least half their support. The government defended the law as a matter of administrative convenience. It argued that the general purpose of providing benefits to the spouses of military personnel was to attract people into the armed services. Whereas it is "likely" that a spouse *is* dependent when the military person is a male, it is "unlikely" that a spouse is dependent when the military person is a female. Thus, when it is unlikely, the military person must prove actual dependence. And it is not reasonable to require the same proof from male military personnel because the government would then have to assume the huge administrative burden and costs of requiring a million and a half men (at that time) to show actual dependence. The Supreme Court, by an 8–1 vote, ruled that the law violated the equal protection clause, but only a minority was willing to make gender a suspect classification. The *plurality* opinion of *four* justices argued that "classifications based on sex are inherently suspect and must therefore be subject to close judicial scrutiny. . . . Our nation has had a long and unfortunate history of sex discrimination. Traditionally, such discrimination was rationalized by an attitude of 'romantic paternalism' which, in practical effect, put women not on a pedestal but in a cage." The other four justices in the majority, however, voted to overturn the law based on the authority of *Reed;* that is, any law that draws a line between the sexes merely to achieve an administrative convenience violates the equal protection clause. They also said they would reserve for the future any expansion in the *Reed* rationale because ERA (Equal Rights Amendment), which was then pending before the states for ratification, would, if adopted, resolve the question. This is a particularly interesting statement because opponents of the ERA were arguing at the time that the ERA was an unnecessary, even redundant, amendment to a Constitution that already contained an equal protection clause. In any event, the ERA ultimately failed to gain ratification, and in the cases subsequent to *Frontiero* the Court has continued to resist making gender a suspect classification.

Nevertheless, with some exceptions Supreme Court decisions since the early 1980s have continued to expand gender rights. Perhaps the most notable exception is the "all-male draft" case of 1981, *Rostker v. Goldberg*. [48] Here, the Court upheld a Military Selective Service Act provision authorizing a draft "registration of males and not females." The Court reiterated that gender is not a suspect classification but said that gender classifications must be based on a compelling governmental interest. The Court's rationale for upholding the law was severalfold: (1) The law was passed by Congress only after careful consideration and extended debate; (2) the classification is not an "accidental by-product of a traditional way of thinking about women"; (3) the draft registration involved is for "combat ready troops" only, and women are statutorily prohibited from combat (and even the dissenters agreed that excluding women from combat positions does not offend the Constitution); (4) women and men are "simply not similarly situated for purposes of the draft"; and (5) Congress needs broad discretion in military affairs while the Court has little competence in this area. The Court's controversial decision was not a surprise. An invalidation in the face of strong congressional support for the law would have put the Court precariously on an activist limb; and as we learned in previous chapters, the early 1980s were years in which the Court tended to show great deference to the other branches of the federal government. However, as Laurence Tribe has argued, *Rostker* should not be seen only as a typical "military affairs" case in which the Court defers to the other branches on matters of national defense. *Rostker* is, rather,

> yet another instance of courts invoking a legacy of female subordination to men to justify further gender discrimination. By being excluded from the draft and barred from service in many of the military capacities open to men, including combat, women lose major economic opportunities and are

effectively denied equal status as citizens with full civil obligations commensurate with those of male members of society. In return, women are spared exposure to that *bête noir*, the threat of sexual molestation at the hands of the enemy or their own male comrades, thereby perpetuating an image of women less as hardy citizens willing and able to pull their own weight than as vulnerable creatures who must be sequestered at home for their own safety. Asked not what they can do for their country, women are *told* what their countrymen will do for them.[49]

Although no Supreme Court majority has yet concluded that gender-based classifications are inherently suspect and thus uniformly subjected to strict scrutiny, and although cases such as *Rostker* illustrate continuing obstacles to gender equality, recent Court history yields a series of "firsts" in progress toward the protection of women's rights. In *Meritor Savings Bank v. Vinson*[50] in 1986 the Court held unanimously that sexual harassment in the workplace can constitute a violation of Title VII of the Civil Rights Act of 1964. This was the *first* case on sexual harassment ever heard by the Court. The Court ruled, as we learned in Chapter Three, that a supervisor's sexual harassment of an employee that is so "severe or pervasive" as to create "a hostile or abusive work environment" is a violation of federal law. In *Johnson v. Transportation Agency*[51] in 1987 the Court, as we learned earlier in this chapter, issued its *first* gender-based affirmative action ruling when it upheld a Santa Clara County affirmative action plan. Also in the 1980s the Court for the *first* time cast doubt on claims by private clubs that they have a right to discriminate against women by virtue of exclusionary membership rules. First in 1984[52] and again in 1987[53] the Court rejected attempts by all-male clubs to invoke their right of association to shield themselves from pressure to admit women. In the latter case the Court held that Rotary International's policy of excluding women is not protected by the First Amendment right to free association. Rotary International is an association of thousands of local Rotary Clubs. One such club, in Duarte, California, had no desire to exclude women and thus contested the International's right to impose its exclusionary policy on local chapters. The Duarte Rotary Club argued that California's law prohibiting gender discrimination precluded it from engaging in discriminatory membership policies and precluded the International from enforcing its policy on the Duarte chapter. The Supreme Court agreed, saying that the California law did not interfere with freedom of association for the purpose of engaging in political speech or religious activities because the law made no distinction based on the organization's viewpoint and required no club to abandon or alter its activities. Even if this antidiscrimination law works "some slight infringement" on Rotary members' right of expressive association, the Court concluded that infringement is "justified because it serves the state's compelling interest in eliminating discrimination against women."

Finally, the Court was given its *first* opportunity to rule on the thorny questions revolving around "pregnancy leave" laws. In 1987, in *California Federal Savings and Loan Association v. Guerra*,[54] a number of the current dilemmas over what the Constitution and federal law require in terms of gender equality were drawn out.[55] The case involved a California state law requiring employers to grant up to four months of unpaid leave to women disabled by pregnancy and childbirth, even if similar leaves are not granted for other disabilities. The law requires leave only for women who are physically disabled by "pregnancy, childbirth, or related medical conditions"; it further requires that employers reinstate such women to their jobs or to "substantially similar" jobs after their return from pregnancy disability leave. California was one of ten states in 1987 that required employers to provide some kind of special leave and reinstatement benefits to pregnant employees. The outcome of a challenge to the California law was likely, therefore, to be of major policy importance, since a ruling upholding the leave law would likely encourage efforts to pass similar laws in other states.

The challenge to the California law originated when Lillian Garland, a receptionist at a branch office of Cal Fed in Los Angeles, left work to have a baby by Caesarian section. Cal Fed's policy was to grant unpaid leaves of absence for a number of reasons, including pregnancy, but to retain the right to fire an employee who had taken such a leave if no similar positions were available upon the employee's desired return date. Thus, when Garland attempted to return to work she was told her job was filled and no similar jobs were available. Although Garland was offered other jobs, she filed a complaint with a state agency against Cal Fed for violating the state pregnancy leave law. The state charged Cal Fed with a violation of the law. In response, Cal Fed sought a ruling in federal court that the state law was invalid under a 1978 federal law, the Pregnancy Discrimination Act (PDA). The PDA amended Title VII of the Civil Rights Act of 1964 to read that "women affected by pregnancy, childbirth or related medical conditions shall be treated the same for all employment-related purposes" as other employees who are "similar in their ability or inability to work." Cal Fed's position was that the leave law was in conflict with and preempted by the PDA because it treated pregnant women *better* than other disabled employees. The state's position was that the leave law was entirely consistent with the general purpose of the PDA, namely, to provide equal employment opportunities to pregnant women. The Ninth Circuit Court of Appeals in California, agreeing with the state's position, upheld the state law and said that in passing the PDA, Congress intended "to construct a floor beneath which pregnancy disability benefits may not drop—not a ceiling above which they may not rise."

As the case came to the Supreme Court, several outcomes were possible, each supported by *amicus curiae* briefs. *Cal Fed*, supported by the Reagan administration and various employer's groups such as the U.S.

chamber of commerce, argued that the PDA prohibits preferential treatment of pregnant employees and that the California law should be invalidated because, among other reasons, it is based on a "stereotype" that
women "need special protection in order to be brought up to the level of
men" and is thus "destructive to women." The law should not provide
preferential treatment for pregnant women when other temporarily disabled employees, such as men having hernia operations, are not covered.
Those persons and groups taking this position proposed that the California law simply be invalidated, leaving employers free to deny disability
benefits to all employees. California, supported by some civil rights
groups such as Equal Rights Advocates, Inc., argued in favor of the leave
law as written, asserting that preferential treatment for pregnant women
actually grants them equality, given the obstacles women confront on the
job because of their reproductive biology. A more inclusive leave plan for
pregnancy than for other disabilities is permissible because women do
require recognition of the unique condition of pregnancy in order to be
equally able to hold a job. This is one area in which the law can legitimately
consider differences between men and women. In any event, they argued,
the PDA was not intended to prohibit discrimination in favor of pregnant
employees. As California's deputy attorney general put it, the law is
"simply an equilizer" that "corrects for a biological burden that only
women and not men in the workplace face." The National Organization
for Women (NOW) and the American Civil Liberties Union (ACLU),
joined by other groups and individuals, argued, like Cal Fed and the
Reagan administration, that the PDA bars preferential treatment for
pregnant women. Such preferences resemble the protective factory legislation of the early 1900s, reinforce sexist stereotypes, and make employers
reluctant to hire women of child-bearing age. Unlike the remedy proposed
by Cal Fed and the Reagan administration, however, the preferred outcome of these advocates was that the Court strike down the California law
and avoid all preferential policies by requiring employers to extend the
same benefits to all disabled employees.

The Court chose the middle ground. By a vote of 6–3 the Court
upheld the California law. Justice Thurgood Marshall wrote that the PDA
did not preempt California from passing legislation that would give special treatment to pregnant women because the intent of Congress in passing the PDA was to see to it that pregnant women be treated at least as well
as other employees, not to preclude states from providing a more complete
protection. The special leave program "promotes equal employment opportunity," Marshall wrote, because it "allows women, as well as men, to
have families without losing their jobs." Marshall saw no conflict between
the PDA and the California leave law, but he said that "even if we agreed"
that the PDA bars special treatment for pregnant women, "we would
nonetheless reject" the assertion that the PDA and the pregnancy leave law

are incompatible. In explanation, Marshall wrote in an important sentence: "Employers are free to give comparable benefits to other disabled employees, thereby treating 'women affected by pregnancy' no better than 'other persons not so affected but similar in their ability or inability to work.'" Thus, although the Court did not go so far as to urge a gender-neutral parental leave policy or to require employers to extend the same benefits to all disabled employees, it did emphasize that nothing in either the PDA or the California law precluded employers from granting the same disability benefits to all employees.[56]

NOTES

[1] See M. Glenn Abernathy, *Civil Liberties under the Constitution* (Columbia, S.C.: University of South Carolina Press, 1985), pp. 48–49.

[2] *7 Peters* 243 (1833).

[3] *Adamson v. California*, 332 U.S. 46 (1947).

[4] Charles Fairman, "Does the Fourteenth Amendment Incorporate the Bill of Rights? The Original Understanding," 2 *Stanford Law Review* 5 (1949).

[5] Elder Witt, *The Supreme Court and Individual Rights* (Washington, D.C.: Congressional Quarterly, 1988), p. 3.

[6] 211 U.S. 78 (1908).

[7] 262 U.S. 390 (1923).

[8] 268 U.S. 652 (1925).

[9] 283 U.S. 697 (1931).

[10] 299 U.S. 353 (1937).

[11] 310 U.S. 296 (1940).

[12] 302 U.S. 319 (1937).

[13] 395 U.S. 784 (1969).

[14] 332 U.S. 46 (1947).

[15] 378 U.S. 1 (1964).

[16] Landon G. Rockwell, "Justice Rutledge on Civil Liberties," 59 *Yale Law Journal* (1949), p. 30.

[17] 338 U.S. 25 (1949).

[18] 367 U.S. 643 (1961).

[19] 381 U.S. 479 (1965).

[20] James Dixon, "The 'New' Substantive Due Process and the Democratic Ethic: A Prolegomenon," 43 *B.Y.U. Law Review* (1976), p. 84.

[21] 304 U.S. 144 (1938).

[22] John Brigham, *The Cult of the Court* (Philadelphia: Temple University Press, 1987), p. 126.

[23] Witt, *The Supreme Court and Individual Rights*, p. 7.

[24] 308 U.S. 88 (1940).

[25] 316 U.S. 584 (1942).

[26] 323 U.S. 516 (1945).

[27] Henry J. Abraham, *Freedom and the Court* (New York: Oxford University Press, 1977), pp. 19–20n47.

[28] Alpheus T. Mason and William M. Beaney, *American Constitutional Law* (Englewood Cliffs, N.J.: Prentice Hall, 1968), p. 500.

[29] Rockwell, *Justice Rutledge Civil Liberties,* p. 45.

[30] W. Howard Mann, "Justice Rutledge and Civil Liberties," 25 *Indiana Law Review* (1950), p. 538n31.

[31] Ibid.

[32] Alpheus T. Mason, William M. Beaney, and Harold G. Stephenson, *American Constitutional Law* (Englewood Cliffs, N.J.: Prentice Hall, 1983), pp. 319, 498–99.

[33] Witt, *The Supreme Court and Individual Rights,* p. 7.

[34] James A. Curry, Richard B. Riley, and Richard M. Battistoni, *Constitutional Government: The American Experience* (St. Paul: West Publishing Co., 1989), pp. 380–81.

[35] 438 U.S. 265 (1978).

[36] 443 U.S. 193 (1979).

[37] 467 U.S. 561 (1984).

[38] Curry, Riley, and Battistoni, *Constitutional Government,* p. 385.

[39] 476 U.S. 267 (1986).

[40] 478 U.S. 421 (1986).

[41] 480 U.S. 149 (1987).

[42] 480 U.S. 616 (1987). Also see Curry, Riley and Battistoni, *Constitutional Government,* p. 385, from which this account is drawn.

[43] *Bradwell v. Illinois,* 83 U.S. 130 (1873).

[44] *Hoyt v. Florida,* 368 U.S. 57 (1961).

[45] 404 U.S. 71 (1971).

[46] For a concise yet clear analysis of equal protection clause "tests" and their application to gender rights cases, see Richard C. Cortner, *The Supreme Court and Civil Liberties* (Palo Alto, Calif.: Mayfield, 1975), pp. 183–212.

[47] 411 U.S. 677 (1973).

[48] 453 U.S. 57 (1981).

[49] Laurence H. Tribe, *American Constitutional Law* (Mineola, N.Y.: Foundation Press, 1988), pp. 1573–74.

[50] 477 U.S. 57 (1986).

[51] 480 U.S. 616 (1987).

[52] *Roberts v. U.S. Jaycees,* 468 U.S. 609 (1984).

[53] *Board of Directors of Rotary International v. Rotary Clubs of Duarte,* 485 U.S. 537 (1987).

[54] 479 U.S. 272 (1987).

[55] See Curry, Riley, and Battistoni, *Constitutional Government,* p. 393.

[56] This account of the law and politics of the *Cal Fed* case is drawn from ibid., pp. 393, 429n12; Stuart Taylor, Jr., "Court Hears Case on Pregnancy Law," *New York Times* (September 9, 1986); Stuart Taylor, Jr., "Job Rights Backed by Supreme Court in Pregnancy Case," *New York Times* (January 14, 1987); and Susan Lehr, "Equality and Gender Issues," IV *Focus on Law Studies* 1 (Fall 1988), pp. 1, 8–9.

From Burger to
Rehnquist and Beyond
The Supreme Court
Approaches a New Century

When Chief Justice Burger retired in 1986, President Reagan continued his effort to move the Supreme Court further to the ideological right by nominating conservative associate justice William H. Rehnquist for the chief justiceship. To take Rehnquist's seat as associate justice, Reagan nominated a federal appeals court judge of at least equally conservative credentials, Antonin Scalia. Rehnquist, of course, was a well-known figure whose confirmation hearings, when first appointed to the Court in 1971, were heated and difficult. In 1986 his confirmation hearings were again hard and controversial. Questions were raised about positions he had taken earlier in his career on school desegregation issues and other civil rights matters. Even his more distant past as a Republican poll watcher in Arizona became an issue when he was alleged to have harassed black and Hispanic voters. Further, an anti-Semitic restrictive covenant was found in a deed he had to a home in Vermont. As in 1971 Rehnquist survived the challenge, but the confirmation vote of 65 to 33 contained more negative votes than any other successful Senate confirmation of a Supreme Court nominee in the twentieth century. Scalia had a somewhat easier time. A former University of Chicago law professor, Scalia had been appointed by Reagan to the United States Court of Appeals for the District of Columbia in 1982. He was known for his opposition to abortion and affirmative action and for his support of deregulation. But his reputation as a legal scholar served him well. His hearings were brief. He was confirmed in the Senate by a 98–0 vote.[1]

The 1986–87 Supreme Court term, the first for Scalia, and Rehnquist's first as chief justice, came to be Justice Powell's last. His retirement in June 1987 led to perhaps the most acrimonious Supreme Court confirmation hearings in history. To take Powell's seat President Reagan nominated 60-year-old Robert H. Bork. Like Scalia, at the time of his nomination Bork was serving on the D.C. Court of Appeals. Bork was the former Solicitor General who had fired Watergate special prosecutor Archibald Cox in the "Saturday night massacre." He had also established a high profile as both a law professor and a judge with his controversial speeches and writings opposing abortion, privacy rights, and some forms of free speech. Though highly unusual, it is perhaps not surprising that his nomination was followed by nearly four months of contentious hearings. Bork was questioned in far greater detail than is normally the case (his testimony alone lasted five days), and interest-group activity for and against his nomination was unusually high. In the end Bork came across as both competent and ethical (traits normally alleged to be absent when nominees are rejected) but as all too willing to undo established precedents to achieve his vision of the Constitution. Bork was rejected on ideological grounds; simply, he was perceived by both the public and the Senate as outside the mainstream. The vote of 58–42 against confirmation, which finally came on October 23, 1987, was the largest margin of defeat of a Supreme Court nominee in Senate history.[2]

Six days after the Senate rejected Judge Bork, President Reagan nominated 41-year-old federal judge Douglas H. Ginsburg. Although a conservative intellectual, Ginsburg, unlike Bork, was a little-known expert on the technical aspects of regulatory and antitrust law. The Reagan administration therefore thought there was very little for opponents to use against him. However, questions were quickly raised about his lack of experience (less than one year on the D.C. Court of Appeals) and allegations arose concerning his ethical conduct (conflict-of-interest charges regarding his involvement with a cable TV station while working in the Justice Department drafting regulations of the cable TV industry). The nail in Ginsburg's coffin came six days after his nomination with his public admission that he had regularly used marijuana in the 1960s and 1970s. This revelation was, of course, extremely disconcerting to an administration well known for its antidrug campaign and for its law-and-order ideology. Under pressure from the administration and his supporters in the Senate, Ginsburg withdrew his name from nomination just little over a week after he had been nominated.[3]

Again acting quickly, Reagan four days later nominated 51-year-old Anthony M. Kennedy, for 12 years a judge on the United States Court of

Appeals for the Ninth Circuit. Kennedy attempted successfully to appear moderately conservative at his comparatively calm and brief confirmation hearings, which lasted just three days. His record was one of a conservative and restraintist judge; Kennedy, unlike Bork, had not been openly critical of prior Supreme Court decisions. He succeeded in convincing the Senate that irrespective of his own views he would not, as a Supreme Court justice, attempt to undo settled law. He came across as a restrained pragmatist with a respect for precedent. Kennedy was confirmed by a vote of 97–0 on January 19, 1988.[4]

THE EARLY REHNQUIST COURT

However, the potentially more conservative Rehnquist Court was in place by 1989 (see Figure 9–1). The first term of the Rehnquist Court (1986–87) was not, all in all, dramatically different in its basic tone from the 17 terms of the Burger Court. The Court remained "moderately liberal" on the so-called social issues of race and gender discrimination, abortion, and church-state relations, and "conservative" in the areas of criminal justice and civil liberties. Thus, given that social issues were at the core of the Reagan administration's "ideological agenda," the 1986–87 term was in some ways a disappointment to conservatives. Rehnquist's elevation to chief justice and the addition of Scalia had relatively little effect. Indeed, Rehnquist was in dissent almost as frequently in 1986–87 as in other recent terms, and he was joined by Scalia a little less frequently than he had been in previous terms by Burger.[5] As in other recent terms a number of important cases were decided by narrow margins, with Justice Powell playing a pivotal role. More than anyone else, Powell was the spokesperson for a moderate, pragmatic, case-by-case approach. Perhaps more so than in any other recent term, the Court's sharp ideological divide was highly visible, but Powell was normally dead center. Thus, Powell was in the majority in nearly every important case decided by narrow margins. Some went left, some went right, but Powell was pragmatic, not ideological; he went neither left nor right. Powell was in the 5–4 "liberal" majority in the Alabama

FIGURE 9–1   The Court from Burger to Rehnquist

THE BURGER COURT	Burger	Blackmun	Powell	Rehnquist
1986	Stevens	O'Connor	Brennan	Marshall	White
THE REHNQUIST COURT	Rehnquist	Blackmun	Kennedy	Scalia
1989	Stevens	O'Connor	Brennan	Marshall	White

state trooper affirmative action case (*U.S. v. Paradise*) and the Maryland death penalty case (*Booth*), but also in the 5–4 "conservative" majority in the Georgia and Arizona death penalty cases (*McClesky* and *Tison*). In other major decisions Powell joined the "liberal" majority in the creationism case (*Edwards v. Aguillard*), the pregnancy leave case (*Guerra*), and the key affirmative action case (*Johnson*); but he joined the "conservative" majority in the Court's highly controversial endorsement of preventive detention (*Salerno*). In effect, Powell determined whether Chief Justice Rehnquist's conservative wing or Associate Justice Brennan's liberal wing would win in the important and controversial cases. That circumstance perhaps more than any other single factor explains why the debate over Powell's proposed successor (Bork, Ginsburg, Kennedy) was so intense.[6]

Although Powell's successor was likely to be to his right, Powell should not be remembered as a frequent ally of the liberal Brennan wing. In fact, in the 1986–87 term Powell voted with Chief Justice Rehnquist in 71 percent of the 87 cases in which Rehnquist and Brennan were on different sides. Why, then, did the liberals win more sweeping victories in 1986–87 under the new chief justice, Rehnquist, than they were able to win under the less conservative Burger? Supreme Court analyst Stuart Taylor, Jr., has written that this result may have been one of the paradoxical effects of Rehnquist's elevation to the chief justiceship. Burger was known to vote with the majority in some cases when he in fact agreed with the other side in order to preserve his power as chief justice to assign the writing of the opinion. He would then assign the opinion to himself or to someone else who would frame the decision as narrowly as possible. But in 1986–87 Rehnquist did not so compromise his conservative views, with the consequence that Brennan, the Court's most senior associate justice, was able to assign a large number of important opinions. Frequently Brennan would assign them to himself and write in expansive liberal language.[7]

Chief Justice Rehnquist's role in his second term at the helm was played quite differently. As the 1987–88 term opened amid the rancor of the Bork battle in October 1987, a thumbnail sketch of Court voting blocs would suggest a 4–4 tie between the conservative bloc of Rehnquist, O'Connor, Scalia, and White and the liberal bloc of Brennan, Marshall, Blackmun, and Stevens. The judicial philosophy and voting tendencies of Powell's replacement remained unknown. By term's end several patterns were evident. (1) Chief Justice Rehnquist, adapting to his new role, was less consistently conservative as he attempted to "marshal the Court" to speak with a more unified voice. (2) Justice O'Connor continued to vote most regularly with the conservatives, especially with Justice Scalia, her most frequent ally; but in some important cases she appeared ready to assume Justice Powell's more moderate and intermediate position and his role as swing voter. (3) Justice Scalia clearly became the Court's most combative conservative. (4) Justice Kennedy emerged as at least marginally more conservative than Justice Powell, whom he eventually replaced at midterm, tipping the balance in favor of the conservative bloc in a number of important 5–4 decisions.[8] A brief elaboration follows.

Chief Justice Rehnquist, as we learned earlier, joined with the Court's liberals against the Reagan administration in his opinion upholding the independent counsel law (*Morrison*). He also astounded conservatives with his majority opinion in *Pennell v. San Jose*,[9] upholding the constitutionality of a local rent control law against the claims of landlords that rent control laws are a form of taking of private property without just compensation. Rehnquist's broadly worded opinion frustrated property rights advocates who had hoped that at least some types of rent control would be invalidated. Scalia, joined by O'Connor, sharply dissented. For a unanimous Court, Rehnquist shocked his conservative supporters off the Court with his opinion holding that the Rev. Jerry Falwell could not collect damages for emotional distress imposed on him by a parody in Larry Flynt's *Hustler* magazine that portrayed Falwell as an incestuous drunk. This opinion, in *Hustler v. Falwell*,[10] was particularly notable because Rehnquist appeared to be setting aside his prior more restrictive views on freedom of expression in order to convey the notion that the Court's precedents in protecting the freedom to engage in offensive attacks on public figures are settled and stable. Rehnquist also rejected the administration's position in his opinion for a 6–2 majority holding that the courts may review for any violations of constitutional rights the Central Intelligence Agency's (CIA's) dismissal of an employee after the employee's disclosure that he was a homosexual (*Webster v. Doe*).[11] The employee had claimed there was no legal basis for his dismissal because the CIA director had no reason to believe he was a national security risk. Again Scalia and O'Connor dissented. Rehnquist's more moderate stance in the 1987–88 term was construed by some Court-watchers, such as the conservative Heritage Foundation's Bruce Fein, as a tactical maneuver to control opinion-assignment and thus the content of majority opinions. Rehnquist might also compromise his own jurisprudential views while stretching to write opinions the liberals could more easily join. But other Supreme Court experts such as Harvard's Laurence Tribe rejected the notion that Rehnquist was guided by the manipulative motive of voting with the majority only to retain the opinion-assignment power. The alternative explanation was that by his second term Rehnquist had grown more comfortably into the job of chief justice and desired to play the role of coalition builder and consensus maker. This role, driven by the desire to guide the evolution of decisions, to seek the stability of settled principles, and to enhance the general stature of the Court, necessarily led Rehnquist to shoulder the burden of "massing the Court" even if that meant he must occasionally set aside or compromise his personal preferences.[12]

Justice Scalia dissented bitingly in the independent counsel case, the CIA dismissal case, and the rent control case. In the latter Scalia endorsed a broad theory of constitutional property rights, writing acerbically that the law in effect established a "welfare program privately funded by those landlords who happen to have 'hardship tenants.'" Although Justice O'Connor joined Scalia in the rent control and CIA cases, she carved out a more Powell-like intermediate stance in a 5–3 decision prohibiting the death penalty for killers who were 15 years old or younger when they committed their offenses.[13] O'Connor said that while the death penalty for those under 16 is unconstitutional under current state laws (37 states had death penalty laws at the time this case was decided, and many of them specified no minimum age for capital punishment), states might, if they chose, enact new laws specifying that persons under 16 could be executed. This was a middle-ground position between that of Brennan, Marshall, Blackmun, and Stevens, who would have prohibited the execution of juveniles altogether, and that of Rehnquist, Scalia, and White, who claimed the Constitution sets no such age limits for executions.[14]

Justice Kennedy joined the Court in February 1988. By term's end he had not yet been tested on the highly charged issues of abortion and affirmative action. However, indications were that he would help to mold a more conservative majority. He did vote in twenty-nine of the cases in which Rehnquist and Brennan were on opposite sides, supporting Rehnquist in 62 percent of these. And in the eight cases out of thirteen decided 5–4 in which the other eight justices split along liberal-conservative lines, Kennedy cemented the conservative majority in seven.[15] Most notable among these was his crucial fifth vote in the *Patterson* case (discussed in detail at the end of Chapter Four) to reconsider in 1988–89 the landmark 1976 civil rights ruling in *Runyon v. McCrary.*

THE COURT IN CONFLICT

As we approach this book's conclusion, it is perhaps helpful to look back before attempting to look forward. As we learned in Chapter One, President Nixon made the Supreme Court a political issue in the presidential election of 1968. He pledged to appoint, if elected, "strict constructionists," not "superlegislators," to the Court and promised to "strengthen the peace forces against the criminal forces" in American society. Before leaving office in 1974 Nixon managed to appoint a new chief justice and three associate justices, and his four appointees had, by the mid-1970s, made a difference, especially in rendering increasingly conservative decisions in the areas of criminal justice, the censorship of obscenity, reapportionment, and race discrimination. But, as we learned in Chapters One and Three, Nixon's Burger Court was not consistently conservative during its first decade (1969–79). Its abortion and busing decisions were particularly offensive to conservatives who argued, as we learned in Chapter Six, that the Court had become "permanently activist" and that "corrective action" had to be taken. The question was, What type of corrective action? If discriminating presidential appointments alone had not been fully successful in moving the Court to the right, what else could be done?

Supreme Court history suggests a number of options at least hypothetically open to the "Court-curbers" of the late 1970s and early 1980s. First, the Court's power might be reduced by the direct action of requiring the votes of at least six justices to invalidate legislation. When the conservative Court of the early twentieth century invalidated progressive legislation of that era (for example, child labor laws, minimum wage and maximum hour laws), statutes were introduced by progressives and liberals in Congress to do exactly that. Second, if the Court's critics truly believed, as the neoconservatives of the late 1970s and early 1980s apparently did, that the Court's decisions ran clearly contrary to the popular will or at least to majority preferences, they could introduce constitutional amendments mandating the popular election and recall of Supreme Court justices, or even all federal judges. Again such amendments were supported by some mentors of Congress in the early twentieth century during the progressive era. Third, if the critics thought that Supreme Court justices were out of step with their counterparts in state supreme courts who would be more likely to read the will of the people and more likely to protect states' rights, they could prepare the creation of a new high court made up of the chief justices of all of the states to review and possibly overturn Supreme Court decisions. Exactly such a "Court of the Union" was proposed in the 1960s by conservative critics of the Court's "one man, one vote" reapportionment decisions. Of course, the most straightforward approach, and a fourth possibility, would be to introduce constitutional amendments directly overturning Supreme Court decisions that the critics oppose (for example, amendments banning abortion or school busing). In fact, the Eleventh, Fourteenth, and Sixteenth Amendments were added to the Constitution for the express purpose of annulling unpopular Supreme Court decisions. Of course, this is a time-consuming, cumbersome, and difficult process requiring support from two-thirds of the members of both the House and the Senate and ratification by three-quarters of the states. Thus, the Court-curbers of the 1970s and 1980s adopted a simpler, though dubious, approach.[16]

They seized upon the so-called exceptions and regulations clause of Article III of the Constitution to develop a tactic that if successful would deny the Supreme Court jurisdiction to review cases such as those dealing with abortion and busing. Specifically, the Constitution grants the Supreme Court appellate jurisdiction over all cases arising under the Constitution but "with such exceptions and under such regulations as the Congress shall make." As we learned in Chapter Seven, the exact meaning of this clause has long been a matter of intense debate. While it is true that the Court acquiesced in Congress's withdrawal of its jurisdiction to review the validity of the Reconstruction Acts in 1869, most legal experts say that that precedent would not stand more than 100 years later. In any event, the more recent Court-curbers saw in the exceptions and regulations clause a political strategy whereby the Court could be divested of jurisdiction to hear certain classes of cases (for example, on abortion and busing), thus enabling the Court-curbers to get their way while tactically bypassing the cumbersome amendment process. Their strategy was simple: "Since the popular support to override Court decisions by amending the Constitution is difficult to garner, why not accomplish the same result with a simple statute restricting the power of the courts to consider the constitutional principles they dislike?"[17] Thus, in the fall of 1981 there were more than 30 bills pending in Congress that proposed to reduce sharply the power of the Supreme Court and other federal courts by divesting them of jurisdiction over various matters, and many of their supporters openly admitted their tactic was to achieve their policy goals while bypassing the amendment process.[18]

Most legal experts condemned this approach to curbing the Court's power. They argued, among other things, that the intent of the framers in drafting the exceptions and regulations clause was to allow Congress to regulate the Court's docket or workload with reasonable, procedural, housekeeping measures, not to give Congress substantive control over the legal and constitutional issues the Court could hear and decide. They also argued that Congress cannot interfere with the Court's "essential functions," which include the monitoring of state court decisions that deny claims made under federal law (for example, a state court decision sustaining a state anti-abortion law against the claim that the state law violates a federal constitutional right to privacy).[19] The ABA denounced the Court-curbers' proposals as a threat to the fundamental system of checks and balances, and Harvard's Laurence Tribe labeled one of the bills "too palpably unconstitutional to permit reasonable persons to argue the contrary."[20] If any of these divestiture bills had become law, the Supreme Court would have had to acquiesce in the restrictions or invalidate the law. If the Court were to invalidate the law, then Congress would have to acquiesce in the Court's decision or move to restrict the Court's power through the more difficult but also more appropriate process of constitutional amendment.[21] As it turned out, none of these measures became law, and attempts from off-the-court to influence its policy direction returned to the more conventional tactics of appointment politics.

Thus, the Supreme Court again became a political issue in the presidential election of 1980, with conservative candidate Ronald Reagan promising to make the reversal of the Court's "liberal" decisions a high priority. As president, Reagan's first step in that direction was the appointment of Sandra Day O'Connor to replace the retiring Potter Stewart in

1981. Also, the Reagan administration's Justice Department became increasingly bold during Reagan's first term in its efforts to induce the Court to accept a more conservative version of American constitutional law. As the presidential election of 1984 approached, the Court became increasingly polarized ideologically and closely divided in its votes. In the 1981–82, 1982–83, and 1983–84 terms a relatively large number of cases were decided by one vote (33, 32, and 29 respectively), and the prospect of major changes in the Court's voting balance loomed large. During the campaign of 1984 the Court's three most liberal members, Brennan, Marshall, and Blackmun, were 78, 76, and 75 years old respectively; the chief justice, Mr. Burger, was 77, as was the Court's key centrist and swing voter, Mr. Powell. It is not surprising, then, that the Democratic candidate in 1984, Walter Mondale, attempted to make Supreme Court appointments a major issue in his challenge to unseat Ronald Reagan. There is little evidence, however, that many voters were affected by Mondale's plea, and in any event, Reagan won reelection. In his second term President Reagan continued his effort to move the Court to the right, appointing Rehnquist to the chief justiceship and Antonin Scalia to replace Rehnquist in 1986. Although Scalia was to be somewhat more conservative than Burger, the net effect of his appointment on the Court's ideological center of gravity in 1986–87 and 1987–88 was slight. Thus, as we have seen, the departure of Powell in 1987 led to one of the more ferocious confirmation fights in history. Powell's voting record overall had been conservative, but he had cast some key swing votes with the liberal Brennan bloc. Thus, Reagan's final appointment of Anthony Kennedy to succeed Powell (Kennedy took his Supreme Court seat in February 1988) was the departing president's last chance to cement a conservative Court majority.

As Reagan left office in January 1989 the Supreme Court was a more conservative body than the one he inherited at the start of his first term in January 1981. But the Court had not yet moved the country, completely at least, to the right. The Court's 1988 decision upholding the independent counsel law against Reagan administration wishes appeared to be a coda to the administration's eight-year effort to fundamentally redirect the Supreme Court, an effort ultimately frustrated by the longevity of the liberal justices and the will of the Senate. Conservative policy goals in the areas of abortion, affirmative action, and church–state relations had largely eluded the Reagan administration.[22] In part this failure is attributable to the three departed justices whom Reagan replaced (Stewart, Burger, and Powell), all of whom were moderately conservative, each replaced by only slightly more conservative justices. At the same time, the Court's three most liberal members (Brennan, Marshall, and Blackmun) remained. Of course, by the time the presidential election of 1988 rolled around, Brennan, Marshall, and Blackmun were 82, 80, and 79 years old respectively, and one would suppose that the prospective departure and subsequent replacement of any one of them could make a large difference in the Court's voting alignments. The Court was at the tipping point, and if history were to have been our guide, we would have expected Supreme Court appointment politics to be yet again a lively issue in the presidential election.

Justice Blackmun in several speeches attempted to get the ball rolling. He expressed concern about the "shift in emphasis" produced by Reagan's conservative appointees. The prospect of his own departure and that of his liberal colleagues caused him to worry aloud about even more dramatic changes after the election. "The Court could become very conservative, well into the 21st century if the election goes the wrong way," he said. He categorized himself as a "member of the center of the Court" and said that in recent terms the Court's center had "bled a lot." He concluded, "It needs more troops; where it's going to get them I don't know." Why did a sitting justice speak out? Perhaps to warn the Democratic-controlled Senate to be careful not to confirm yet another conservative nominee. Perhaps to prompt the presidential nominees, George Bush and Michael Dukakis, to address more openly the subject of what they would do with the Court if elected.[23] Ironically, although the stakes were perhaps higher in 1988 than in either 1984 or 1980, neither presidential candidate wanted to make the Supreme Court an issue. Dukakis was apparently too worried about "winning back the Reagan Democrats" to push social issues, while Bush, remembering Bork's bitter defeat in the Senate, apparently saw Supreme Court appointment politics as too "two-edged" to take a strong stand. There was, however, little doubt that the Court's long-term future would be in the next president's hands. If Dukakis were to win, he could replace the aging liberals with like-minded justices and possibly replace the conservative Justice White, then 71 years old and rumored to be ready for retirement. The result at minimum would be the maintenance of a moderately conservative and divided Court or possibly a moderate shift to the left. If Bush were to win, however, the conservative and relatively young bloc of Rehnquist, O'Connor, Scalia, and Kennedy (then 64, 58, 52, and 52 respectively) could get its own new troops producing a dominant conservative coalition.[24] In fact, of course, Bush won the election. The long-term impact is yet to be felt.

THE COURT AT THE CROSSROADS

As the Supreme Court entered its third century in 1989, predictions of how a Bush presidency would affect its future were rather consistent in anticipating a more conservative trend. Patrick McQuigan, head of the conservative Center for Law and Democracy, said that whereas Reagan's appointments had produced a "moderate shift to the right," Bush's victory would produce a "dramatic shift." John Powell, the ACLU legal director, said that Bush's victory "could set us back judicially more than 40 years." Herman Schwartz, constitutional law expert at American University, said that liberals "can kiss the Court goodbye." Bruce Fein suggested that the Court was already moving to the right and would continue to; much would depend on who leaves and who replaces them. "There's an institutional restraint on doing too many 5–4 reversals. . . . They will do some, but there is a kind of quota on the number." However, if the liberals are replaced, "we will have a reversal of the Warren Court." A minority viewpoint was expressed by Burt Neuborne, a former ACLU legal director and then a New York University law professor. He argued that the likelihood of "a rightist revolution on the Court . . . [is] exaggerated. Bush will appoint Justices who are not ideologues but out of the good, gray middle."[25]

In 1988–89, the term during which George Bush was inaugurated, the Court turned to the right without the help of any appointees by the new president. Indeed, some saw the 1988–89 term as a "watershed in the Court's modern history," a term during which, at least on the important issues of abortion, race and gender discrimination, and the death penalty, "a conservative majority, for the first time in a generation, was in a position to control the outcome."[26] In the area of abortion the Court decided in *Webster v. Reproductive Health Services*[27] to allow sharp new restrictions (for example, states may prohibit the use of public hospitals for performing abortions not necessary to save a woman's life and may prohibit the use of tax money for "encouraging or counseling" women to have abortions). In the area of race and gender discrimination the Court ruled in *Wards Cove Packing v. Atonio*[28] that employees, not employers, have the burden of proving whether a job requirement that screens out minorities and women is a "business necessity." (Prior to this ruling the Court had allowed employees to demonstrate with statistical evidence that an employer's policies had the practical effect of discriminating against broad groups of workers. Under the new ruling the employees must also prove that the employer's policies cannot be justified as necessary for the employer's business.) In the area of the death penalty, the Court ruled that states may execute murderers who are mentally retarded (*Penry v. Lynaugh*[29]) and murderers who are as young as 16 when they commit their crimes (*Stanford v. Kentucky*[30]). All these decisions were reached by 5–4 votes won by the conservative bloc of Rehnquist, White, O'Connor, Scalia, and Kennedy. Other indications of a conservative trend can be found in such cases as the two decisions allowing mandatory drug testing. Regulations were upheld requiring drug tests for railroad workers after accidents (*Skinner v. Railway Labor Executives*[31]) and for Customs Service employees in some job categories (*National Treasury Employees v. Von Raab*[32]).

Apart from the decisions reached in 1988–89, there were yet other indicators that this was a "watershed" term. First, Chief Justice Rehnquist finally emerged as the molder and leader of the conservative bloc.

Previously, the consensus was that Rehnquist had been outmaneuvered by Brennan, the superior strategist and tactician of intra-Court politics in his first year as chief justice (1986–87), and that he had appeared to be a somewhat more effective leader during his second year (1987–88), but only because he had moderated his conservative views in order to assign and shape the majority opinion in many cases. In 1988–89, however, Rehnquist led the way, and the two key areas in which the conservative justices had made little progress previously, abortion and civil rights, were exceptions no more.[33] Second, the 1988–89 term was characterized not only by extreme ideological polarization, in which the liberal bloc voted together in 22 of the 31 cases decided by 5–4 votes, but also by a conservative dominance in the close cases, in which the liberal bloc won only 3 of these 22 5–4 decisions.[34] Third, Justice O'Connor did not fully take Justice Powell's place as the Court's moderate "swing" voter but voted rather consistently with the conservatives. She did vote with the liberals in 2 of the 3 5–4 votes they won. And she did, by most accounts, prevent the Court from directly overturning *Roe v. Wade* in the abortion case. For the most part, however, O'Connor voted as a solid member of the conservative bloc. Fourth, and perhaps most importantly, Justice Kennedy made the difference. In *all* 31 cases decided 5–4, Rehnquist and Brennan were on opposite sides bidding for the votes of the justices in between. Kennedy voted with Rehnquist in all but 2 of the 31 cases. Indeed, some have observed that no other single appointment had produced such a pronounced shift in the Court's direction since President Kennedy appointed Arthur Goldberg to the Court in 1962. The addition of Goldberg in 1962 produced the working liberal majority now known as the Warren Court. Duke law professor Walter Dellinger observes that "that liberal majority remained dominant or nearly so for the next two decades, and the new conservative majority is likely to remain dominant for at least that long."[35]

There is little doubt that the Supreme Court of the 1990s is a Court in transition, and it will have on its docket cases and issues almost perfectly designed as measures of the Reagan legacy and as tests of the Bush impact. There will be civil rights cases raising the important question of whether laws favoring minorities are just as suspect as laws favoring majority whites. There will be cases offering the Court the opportunity to refine further its position on abortion and the death penalty. There will be some old issues revisited, such as separation of powers, and there will be some new issues opened up, such as drug and AIDS testing. Even if the older, liberal justices say they were "appointed for life" and deliver on their promise to "serve out their terms," the new conservative activists may come close to molding and holding a majority. Future vacancies and appointments may make a difference. But the new appointees, like a few of their predecessors, may begin their service on one side of the ideological spectrum and end up on the other.[36]

Thus it is, as always, difficult to predict future lines of doctrinal development. Nonetheless, the lessons of history do permit us to generalize about the role of the Supreme Court, whether a current majority of its members are liberal or conservative. As we have learned, the Supreme Court's judicial activists can be either liberal or conservative. The Court that invalidated early New Deal legislation was conservative. The activist Warren Court was liberal. The Court's "new" conservative activists can be just as creative as their liberal counterparts in reaching their policy goals. Those goals appear to include the expansion of constitutionally protected property rights, the reduction of governmental regulation, the restriction or elimination of abortion rights, and the invalidation of federal and state affirmative action programs. Further, the new conservatives use the same tactics as their liberal activist colleagues. They overrule the Court's own precedents, they overturn legislative policies with judicially created rules, and they pronounce broad policy preferences on issues not technically raised by the cases. Of course, the current conservative activists might contend that their approach is one of judicial "reactivism"—an approach designed to undo what the liberal activists have already done. But the serious student of the Supreme Court should not assign normative judgments to the roles justices play, though values are obviously present in the substance of the cases themselves. The simple point is that most of our justices have been, irrespective of what they may have publicly proclaimed, outcome-oriented activists. The new conservative reactivists are no more or less principled than their liberal activist counterparts. Activism is not so much an analytical tool by which scholars study the Court as it is "an imprecation hurled at the ins by the outs," irrespective of who is in and who is out.[37]

The United States Supreme Court works within an administrative apparatus and a political environment that encourage and facilitate judicial activism—both liberal and conservative. That activism inevitably invites criticism—both academic and popular. Nevertheless, the Court is the final arbiter of what the United States Constitution means. To paraphrase one of our justices, the Court is not final because it is infallible; but it is infallible because it is final. That is a constitutional reality. It is sometimes difficult for both academics and citizens to accept that reality, especially when the Court's final word clashes with their own policy preferences. But the Court will continue to render decisions and opinions that transcend the immediate results of their particular cases to pronounce and protect the fundamental principles of American democracy. Debates about the Court's proper role in that democracy are normally healthy and probably inevitable. It is perhaps the case that the Court has performed better than it has been given credit for by either its academic or its popular critics. If not, the last best hope for a better Court lies not in scholarly prescriptions but in the pleas of the people themselves. Some scholars may think that the people are insufficiently informed about both law and politics to play such a role, but as

Jefferson said, if we think the people "not enlightened enough to exercise their control with a wholesome discretion, the remedy is not to take it from them, but to inform their discretion."[38] This book has attempted to provide exactly that kind of information.

NOTES

[1] Congressional Quarterly, *Current American Government: Fall 1988 Guide* (Washington, D.C.: Congressional Quarterly, 1988), pp. 120, 124.

[2] James A. Curry, Richard B. Riley, and Richard M. Battistoni, *Constitutional Government: The American Experience* (St. Paul: West Publishing Co., 1989), pp. 106–107; Louis Fisher, *Constitutional Dialogues* (Princeton, N.J.: Princeton University Press, 1988), pp. 139–40. For a detailed account see Ethan Bronner, *Battle for Justice: How the Bork Nomination Shook America* (New York: W.W. Norton, 1989).

[3] Curry, Riley, and Battistoni, *Constitutional Government*, pp. 106–107; Fisher, *Constitutional Dialogues*, pp. 140–41; and Steven V. Roberts, "Ginsburg Withdraws Name as Supreme Court Nominee, Citing Marijuana 'Clamor,'" *New York Times* (November 8, 1987).

[4] Congressional Quarterly, *Current American Government*, pp. 114, 117, 124–25; Robert Reinhold, "Restrained Pragmatist: Anthony M. Kennedy," *New York Times* (November 12, 1987).

[5] Stuart Taylor, Jr., "Powell's Pivotal Votes Marked '87 Court Term," *New York Times* (June 27, 1987).

[6] Ibid.

[7] Ibid.

[8] Anthony Lewis, "The Chief Justice," *New York Times* (March 1, 1988); Stuart Taylor, Jr., "High Court Rulings Hint Move to Right," *New York Times* (July 3, 1988).

[9] 485 U.S. 1 (1988).

[10] 485 U.S. 46 (1988).

[11] 485 U.S. 210 (1988).

[12] See Stuart Taylor, Jr., "A Pair of Rehnquist Opinions Set Legal Experts Buzzing," *New York Times* (February 28, 1988).

[13] *Thompson v. Oklahoma*, 485 U.S. 375 (1988).

[14] See "Ban on Executing Juveniles Weighed," *New York Times* (July 1, 1988).

[15] See "Kennedy Casts Key Votes in 7 Conservative Rulings," *New York Times* (July 3, 1988).

[16] Irving R. Kaufman, "Congress v. The Court," *New York Times Magazine* (September 20, 1981), pp. 44, 48, 54, 56, 96, 98, 100, 102, 104.

[17] Ibid., p. 56.

[18] Ibid.

[19] Lawrence Sager, "The Shortcut to Outlaw Abortion," *New York Review of Books* (June 25, 1981), p. 41.

[20] Kaufman, "Congress v. The Court," p. 48.

[21] Ibid.

[22] See Linda Greenhouse, "Fetters on the Executive: By Finding No Threat in Prosecutor Law, the Court Rejects a Constitutional Vision," *New York Times* (June 30, 1988).

[23] This account of Blackmun's role is described in David M. O'Brien and Ronald Collins, "The Wisdom of Judicial Lockjaw," *New York Times* (September 29, 1988).

[24] See Al Kamen, "A Chance to Shape High Court," *Washington Post* (September 11, 1988).

[25] Ibid.

[26] Linda Greenhouse, "The Year the Court Turned to the Right," *New York Times* (July 7, 1989).

[27] ——— U.S. ——— (1989).

[28] ——— U.S. ——— (1989).

[29] ——— U.S. ——— (1989).

[30] ——— U.S. ——— (1989).

[31] ——— U.S. ——— (1989).

[32] ——— U.S. ——— (1989).

[33] Richard Carelli, "Rehnquist Court Establishes Its Conservative Credentials," *Columbus Dispatch* (July 6, 1989); R. Chris Burnett, "Conservatives Take Command of Court," *Columbus Dispatch* (July 9, 1989).

[34] Greenhouse, "The Year the Court Turned to the Right."

[35] Quoted in ibid.

[36] See Stuart Taylor, Jr., "Waiting to Hear the Court's Ninth Voice," *New York Times* (June 12, 1988); Stuart Taylor, Jr., "Re: Shaping the Court," *New York Times* (July 1, 1988); and Linda Greenhouse, "New Court Term May Show Extent of Reagan's Influence," *New York Times* (October 12, 1988).

[37] Stuart Taylor, Jr., "The 'Judicial Activists' Are Always on the Other Side," *New York Times* (July 3, 1988).

[38] Thomas Jefferson, letter to William Charles Jarvis (September 28, 1820).

Index